MEMOIRS

OF

THE JACOBITES

OF 1715 AND 1745.

BY MRS. THOMSON,

AUTHOR OF

"MEMOIRS OF THE COURT OF HENRY THE EIGHTH, "
"MEMOIRS OF SARAH, DUCHESS OF MARLBOROUGH, " ETC.

VOLUME I.

1845.

Memoirs of the Jacobites of 1715 and 1745 - Volume I

Mrs. Thomson

DODO PRESS

PREFACE.

In completing two volumes of a work which has been for some years in contemplation, it may be remarked that it is the only collective Biography of the Jacobites that has yet been given to the Public. Meagre accounts, scattered anecdotes, and fragments of memoir, have hitherto rather tantalized than satisfied those who have been interested in the events of 1715 and 1745. The works of Home, of Mr. Chambers, and the collections of Bishop Forbes, all excellent, are necessarily too much mingled up with the current of public affairs to comprise any considerable portion of biographical detail. Certain lives of some of the sufferers in the cause of the Stuarts, printed soon after the contests in behalf of those Princes, are little more than narratives of their trials and executions; they were intended merely as ephemeral productions to gratify a curious public, and merit no long existence. It would have been, indeed, for many years, scarcely prudent, and certainly not expedient, to proffer any information concerning the objects of royal indignation, except that which the newspapers afforded: nor was it perfectly safe, for a considerable time after the turbulent times in which the sufferers lived, to palliate their offences, or to express any deep concern for their fate. That there was much to be admired in those whose memories were thus, in some measure, consigned to oblivion, except in the hearts of their descendants; much which deserved to be explained in their motives; much which claimed to be upheld in their self-sacrifices, the following pages will show. Whatever leaning the Author may have had to the unfortunate cause of the Stuarts, it has not, however, been her intention only to pourtray the bright ornaments of the party. She has endeavoured to show that it was composed, as well as most other political combinations, of materials differing in value—some pure, some base, some noble, some mean and vacillating.

As far as human weakness and prejudice can permit, the Author has aimed at a strict scrutiny of conduct and motives. In the colouring given to these, she has conscientiously sought to be impartial: for the facts stated, she has given the authorities.

It now remains for the Author publicly to acknowledge the resources from which she has derived some materials which have never before been given to the Public, and for which she has to thank, in several instances, not only the kindness of friends, but the liberality of strangers.

A very interesting collection of letters, many of them written in the Earl of Mar's own hand, and others dictated by him, is interwoven with the biography of that nobleman. These letters were written, in fact, for the information of the whole body of Jacobites, to whom they were transmitted through the agent of that party, Captain Henry Straiton, residing in Edinburgh. They form almost a diary of Lord Mar's proceedings at Perth. They are continued up to within a few hours of the evacuation of that city by the Jacobite army. For these curious and characteristic letters, pourtraying as they do, in lively colours, the difficulties of the General in his council and his camp, she is indebted to the friendship and mediation of the Honourable Lord Cockburn, and to the liberality of James Gibson Craig, Esq.

To the Right Honourable the Earl of Newburgh, the descendant and representative of the Radcliffe family, her sincere and respectful acknowledgments are due for his Lordship's readily imparting to her several interesting particulars of the Earl of Derwentwater and his family. She owes a similar debt of gratitude to the Viscount Strathallan, for his Lordship's communication to her respecting the House of Drummond. To the Honourable Mrs. Bellamy, the descendant of Viscount Kenmure, she has also to offer similar acknowledgments, for information respecting her unfortunate ancestor; and for an original letter of his Lordship; and she must also beg to express her obligations to William Constable Maxwell, Esq., and to Mrs. Constable Maxwell, of Terregles, the descendants of the Earl of Nithisdale, for their courteous and prompt assistance. To James Craik, Esq., of Arbigland, Dumfriesshire, she is indebted for a correspondence which continues, as it were, an account of that family during the later part of the year 1745. To Sir Fitzroy Grafton Maclean, Bart., she owes the account of his clan and family, which has been printed for private circulation. She is also grateful to a descendant of the family of Lochiel, Miss Mary Anne Cameron, for some interesting particulars of the burning of Achnacarry, the seat of her ancestors.

In some of these instances the information derived has not been considerable, owing to the total wreck of fortune, the destruction of houses, and the loss of papers, which followed the ruthless steps of the conquering army of the Duke of Cumberland. Most of the hereditary memorials of those Highland families who engaged in both rebellions, perished; and their representatives are strangely destitute of letters, papers, and memorials of every kind. The practice of burying family archives and deeds which prevailed during the troubles, was adopted but with partial advantage, by those who anticipated the worst result of the contest.

In recalling with pleasure the number of those to whom the Author owes sincere gratitude for kindness and aid in her undertaking, the name of Charles Kirkpatrick Sharpe, Esq. renews the remembrance of that store of antiquarian information from which others, far more worthy to enjoy it than herself, have owed obligations. The Author has also most gratefully to acknowledge the very kind and valuable assistance of Archibald Macdonald, Esq., of the Register Office, Edinburgh, to whom she is indebted for several original letters; and of Robert Chambers, Esq., to whose liberality she is indebted for several of her manuscript sources, as well as some valuable advice on the subject of her work. To Dr. Irvine, Librarian of the Advocate's Library, Edinburgh, the Author offers, with the most lively pleasure, her sincere acknowledgments for a ready and persevering assistance in aid of her undertaking. Again, she begs to repeat her sense of deep obligation to Mr. Keats, of the British Museum, the literary pilot of many years' historical research.

LONDON,
October 27, 1845.

INTRODUCTION.

The history of the Jacobites properly begins with the brave and conscientious men who followed James the Second to France, or fought and bled for him in the United Kingdom. Of the few nobles whom that Monarch had distinguished by his friendship when Duke of York, or graced with his favours when King, three only in Scotland remained attached openly to his interests: these were the Duke of Gordon, the Lord Balcarras, and Claverhouse of Dundee, who may be regarded as the parents of the Jacobite party in Scotland. "The other nobles of the late King's party, " remarks a great historian, [1] "waited for events, in hopes and in fears, from the Old Government and the New, intriguing with both, and depended upon by neither. "

Upon the death of Dundee, a troop of officers who had fought under the standard of that great General, and who had imbibed his lofty opinions and learned to imitate his dauntless valour, capitulated, and were suffered to leave the country and retire to France. Their number amounted to a hundred and fifty: they were all of honourable birth, and glorying in their political principles. At first these exiles were pensioned by the French Government, but, upon the close of the civil war, those pensions ceased. Finding themselves a burden upon King James, they formed themselves into a body-guard, which was afterwards incorporated with the French army. It may fairly be presumed that this remnant of Dundee's army, four of whom only returned to Scotland, were instrumental during their abode in France in maintaining a communication between the Court of St. Germains and their disheartened countrymen who had remained in their Highland homes. Abroad, they supported their military character as soldiers who had fought under Dundee: they were always the foremost in the battle and the last to retreat, and were distinguished by a superiority in order and discipline, no less than by their energy and courage.

There can be no doubt but that the majority of the great landholders in England, as well as the Highland chiefs, continued, through the reign of William and Mary, disposed to high Tory views; and that had not the popular cry of the Church being in danger aided the designs of the Whigs, the Highflyers, or rigid Tories, would not have remained in quiescence during that critical period, which resembled the settling of a rushing current of waters into a frothing and bubbling pool, rather than the calm tenour of a gently-flowing stream. Throughout the distractions of his reign, it was the wise policy of William the Third to balance parties; to bestow great posts upon moderate men; to employ alternately persons of different opinions, and by frequent changes in his Ministry, to conciliate the good-will of both factions; —and this was all that that able Monarch could effect, until time should extinguish political animosity.

Queen Mary, educated in Tory principles, and taught by her maternal uncle, the Earl of Rochester, to consider every opposition to the Sovereign's will as rebellion, was scarcely regarded in the light of an enemy to the doctrine of passive obedience and non-resistance, notwithstanding her unfilial conduct; [2] and it is remarkable that, during her life, great favour was shown at Court to the Highland partisans of James the Second; distinctions were as much avoided as it was possible; and the personal prepossessions of the Queen were supposed to be on the side of the High Church Tories.

During the reign of Anne, notwithstanding the coalition of Godolphin, Marlborough, and other leaders of the moderate Tories with the Whigs, and the reputation and glory which their combined abilities and characters obtained, a conviction was still prevalent that the heart of the Queen was disposed to the restoration of the ancient race, and that her days would not close before a design to secure the succession to her nephew would be matured, and the Act of Succession, which was chiefly the offspring of Whig policy, should be set aside. There was, doubtless, not only in the mind of Anne, but in that of her sagacious predecessor, an apprehension that after the death of the last of their dynasty, the succession would again be fiercely disputed. Impressed with this conviction, it was a favourite scheme of William to invite the child, who afterwards, under the name of the Chevalier St. George, was the hero, in dumb show, it must be acknowledged, of the Insurrection of 1715, to receive his education in England under his kingly care; to be bred up a Protestant; and to make that education the earnest of his future succession. The proposal was rejected by James the Second, to the great prejudice of his son's interests, and to the misfortune, it may be presumed, of the British nation. For one can scarcely suppose a more perfect combination of all the qualities calculated to form a popular Monarch, in this country, than the natural abilities of the Stuart race, perfected under the able guidance of so reflective a ruler—so accomplished a general—so consummate a statesman, as William. The education which that Monarch had planned for the young Duke of Gloucester shows how enlarged and practical were his views of the acquirements necessary for a Sovereign: it presents a scheme of tuition which, if it may be deemed not wholly adapted to the present day, was on the most comprehensive and liberal scale. But James, acting, at all events, with the consistency of a sincere believer, returned, as Dalrymple expresses it, "slowly and sadly to bury the remembrance of his greatness in the convent of La Trappe; " and all future attempts on the part of his posterity to recover the throne of their ancestors were frustrated by the hollowness of French professions of friendship.

The tranquil demeanour of the Jacobite party during the reign of Anne may seem surprising, when we consider the avowed favour and protection which were held out by Louis the Fourteenth to the royal exiles of St. Germain. During the lifetime of James, who considered that he had exchanged the hope of an earthly for that of a heavenly Crown, there was little to wonder at in this inactivity and apparent resignation. Had it not been for the influence of an enthusiastic, high-minded, and fascinating woman, the very mention of the cause would probably have died away in the priest-thronged saloons of St. Germains. To Mary of Modena the credit is due—if credit on such account is to be assigned—for maintaining in the friends of her consort, for instilling in the breast of her son, a desire of restoration; —that word, in fact, might be found, to speak metaphorically, written in her heart. To her personal qualities, to her still youthful attractions, to her pure mind, and blameless career of conjugal duty—to the noble, maternal ambition which no worthy judge of human motives could refuse a tribute of pity and admiration—to her disregard of low and unworthy instruments to advance her means, as in the case of Lovat, even the warmest partisans of the Revolution were forced to do justice. The disinterested and sagacious Godolphin is said to have done more: he is supposed to have cherished such a respectful enthusiasm for the young mother who thus supported the claims of her son, as might have become the chivalric Surrey. Whatever were the fact, during the existence of Anne, the payment of a dowry to Mary of Modena, the favourable understanding between her son, as he grew up to man's estate, and the English Court, the small reward offered for his apprehension, the conniving at the daily enlistment of men in his service, and the indulgence shown to those who openly spoke and preached against the Revolution, were certain indications and ample proofs that had the Queen's life been prolonged, some effectual steps would have been taken to efface from her memory the recollection of her early failure of duty to King James, and to satisfy the reproaches of her narrow, though conscientious mind. That such was the fact, the declaration or manifesto of the Chevalier, dated from Plombières, August 2, 1714, and printed in French, English, and Latin, attests; and the assertion was confirmed by a letter from the Duke of Lorrain to the English Government. This favourable disposition on the part of Anne proves that she gave no credence to the report of the supposititious birth of the Prince; although, in her youthful days, and when irritated against her step-mother, she had entered into the Court gossip on that subject, with all the eagerness of a weak and credulous mind.

Nourished in secret by these hopes, the Jacobites in England constituted a far more important party than our historians are generally willing to allow. The famous work entitled, "English Advice to the Freeholders of Great Britain, " supposed to be written by Bishop Atterbury, was extensively circulated throughout the country: it tended to promote an opposition cry of "the Church in danger! " by insinuating that the Whigs projected the abolition of Episcopacy. It was received with great enthusiasm; and was responded to with fervour by the University of Oxford, which was inflamed with a zeal for the restoration of the Stuarts; and which displayed much of the same ardour, and held forth the same arguments that had stimulated that seat of learning in the days of Charles the First. To these sentiments, the foreign birth, the foreign language, and, above all, the foreign principles of the King added considerable disgust: nor can it be a matter of surprise that such should be the case. It appears, nevertheless, extraordinary that the opposition to so strange an engrafting of a foreign ruler should not have been received with greater public manifestations of dislike than the unorganized turbulence of Oxford under-graduates, or the ephemeral fury of a London populace.

In Scotland a very different state of public feeling prevailed. In England men of commerce were swayed in their political opinions by the good of trade, which nothing was so likely to injure as a disputed succession. The country gentlemen were, more or less, under the influence of party pamphlets, and were liable to have their political prejudices smoothed down by collision with their neighbours. Excepting in the northern counties, the dread of Popery prevailed also universally. The remembrance of the bigotry and tyranny of James the Second had not faded away from the remembrance of those whose fathers or grandfathers could remember its details. In the Highlands of Scotland the memory of that Monarch was, on the other hand, worshipped as a friend of that noble country, as the Stuart peculiarly their own, as the royal exile, whose health and return, under various disguises, they had pledged annually at their hunting-matches, and to whose youthful son they transferred an allegiance which they held sacred as their religion.

Nor had James the Second earned the devotion of the Highland chieftains without some degree of merit on his own part. The most incapable and unworthy of rulers, he had yet some fine and popular qualities as a man; he was not devoid of a considerable share of ability although it was misapplied. His letters to his son, his account of his own life, show that one who could act most erroneously and criminally, did, nevertheless, often think and feel rightly. His obstinate adherence to his own faith may be lamented by politicians; it may be sneered at by the worldly; but it must be approved by all who are themselves staunch supporters of that mode of faith which they conscientiously adopt. In private society James had the power of attaching his dependents; and perhaps from a deeper source than that which gave attraction to the conversation of his good-natured, dissolute brother. His melancholy and touching reply to Sir Charles Littleton, who expressed to him his shame that his son was with the Prince of Orange: —"Alas! Sir Charles! why ashamed? Are not my daughters with him? " was an instance of that readiness and delicacy which are qualities peculiarly appropriate to royalty. His exclamation at the battle of La Hogue, when he beheld the English sailors scrambling up the sides of the French ships from their boats—"None but my brave English could do this! " was one trait of a character neither devoid of sensibility, nor destitute of certain emotions which appear incompatible with the royal patron of Judge Jeffries, and with the enemy of Monmouth.

During his residence, when Duke of York, at Holyrood, accompanied by Anne Hyde, when Duchess of York, James became extremely popular in Edinburgh; in the Highlands his hold of the affections of the chieftains had a deeper origin. The oppressor of the English had endeavoured to become the emancipator of the chieftains. The rigour of the feudal system, which was carried to its utmost extent in the Highlands, although softened by the patriarchal character of the chiefs, was revolting to the chieftains or landholders under the yoke of some feudal nobleman or chief; and they became ambitious of becoming direct holders from the Crown. It was a scheme of James the Second to abolish this system of infeudation, by buying up the superiorities, —a plan, the completion of which was attempted by William the Third, but defeated by the avarice and dishonesty of those who managed the transaction. The chieftains, however, never forgot the obligation which they owed to James: [3] they refused all offers of emolument or promotion from his successor; and they adhered to the exiled King with a loyalty which was never shaken, and which broke forth conspicuously in the Insurrection of 1715. "The Highlanders, " says Dalrymple, "carried in their bosoms the high point of honour without its follies. "

Without entering into the various reasons which strengthened this sentiment of gratitude and allegiance; without commenting upon the partly patriarchal nature of the clan system, and the firm compact which was cemented between every member of that family by a common relationship of blood; it is sufficient to remark, that to a people so retired, in many parts insulated, in all, apart from daily intelligence, far away from communication with any whose free disquisitions might possibly stake their opinions, it was not surprising that the loyalty to James should continue unalloyed during two successive reigns. It burned, indeed, with a steady though covered flame. The Insurrection of 1715, which seems, in the pages of history, to break forth unexpectedly, was long in being organized. From Anne's first Session of Parliament until the completion of the Union, Scotland was in a state of ferment, and violent party divisions racked civil society. In 1707, the famous Colonel Hooke was sent to the northern parts of Scotland from France, to sound the nobility and chieftains with respect to their sentiments, to ascertain the amount of their forces, and to inquire what quantity of ammunition and other warlike stores should be necessary to be sent from France. A full account of affairs was compiled, and was signed by fifteen noblemen and gentlemen, amongst whom the Duke of Athole, who aspired, according to Lockhart, to be another General Monk, was foremost in promoting the restoration of the youthful son of James the Second. This mission was followed by the unsuccessful attempt at invasion on the part of James, in 1708; when, according to some representations, there was a far more reasonable prospect of success than at any later period. The nobility and gentry were, at that time, well prepared to receive the royal adventurer; the regular army was wholly unfit, either in numbers or ammunition, to oppose the forces which they would have raised. The very Guards, it is supposed, would have done duty on the person of James Stuart the night that he landed. The equivalent money sent to Scotland to reward the promoters of the

Union, was still in the country, and a considerable part of it was in the Castle of Edinburgh; and a Dutch fleet had recently run aground on the coast of Angus, and had left there a vast quantity of powder, shot, and cannon, and a large sum of money, which might have been secured. England was, at this time, distracted with jealousies and factions; and although the great Marlborough was then in the vigour of his youth, ready to defend his country, as well as to extend her dominions, there were suspicions that the General was not wholly adverse to the claims of James Stuart. [4]

How far these expectations might have been realised, it is difficult to say. The French newspapers had proclaimed the preparations for invasion, and Louis the Fourteenth had taken leave of James, wishing him a prosperous voyage, and expressing, as the highest compliment, "the hope that he should never see him again, " when a slight, accidental indisposition disturbed the whole arrangement. The royal youth was taken ill with the measles; upon which the French troops which had embarked at Dunkirk disembarked. A fatal delay was occasioned; and the French fleet, after an ineffectual voyage, went "sneakingly home, " "doing, " as one of the most active Jacobites remarks, "much harm to the King, his country, and themselves. "

Such was the fate of the attempt, in 1708, to place James Stuart on the throne of his ancestors; and it will readily be believed that the ill-starred endeavour did not add to the probable success of any future enterprise. Scarcely had the accession of George the First, an event which a certain historian denominates "a surprising turn of Providence, " taken place, than the removal of Lord Bolingbroke from office announced to the Tory party that they had lost their best friend at Court. Upon this intelligence reaching the Highlands, many of the Jacobites took up arms; but this hasty demonstration of good will to their cause was instantly suppressed. The Chevalier was, nevertheless, proclaimed King in the night time, and three noblemen, the Duke of Gordon, the Marquis of Huntley, and Lord Drummond, were kept prisoners in their own houses. In the middle of November, the Chevalier's Declaration, asserting his right and title to the Crown of England, was sent by a French mail to many persons of rank in this country. For some months the country was in a state of ferment, such as, perhaps, had never been witnessed since the days of the Great Rebellion. The Jacobites were centered in Oxford, but Bristol was also another of their strongholds; the course of justice was impeded there by riots; and every effort was made, both there and elsewhere, to influence the elections, which were carried on with a degree of venom and fury, exasperated by the cry of "the Church in danger! "

In February, 1715, the Duke of Argyle, Commander-in-Chief of his Majesty's forces in Scotland, received information that a vessel containing arms and ammunition had landed in the Isle of Sky, and that five strangers had disembarked there, and had instantly dispersed themselves throughout the country. This was the first positive indication of the combination, which already comprised most of the ancient and respected names in Scotland. This confederacy, as it may be called, had existed ever since the peace of Utrecht, under the form of the Jacobite Association. In 1710, the formation of the October Club had shewed plainly the bias of the country gentlemen, who, according to a judge of men's motives who was rarely satisfied, "did adhere firmly to their principles and engagements, acting the part of honest countrymen and dutiful subjects. "[5]

About the month of May, the report of James Stuart's intended invasion of Scotland, and particulars of the preparations made for it in England, Scotland, and France, became public. Measures were, of course, instantly taken to guard the coasts of England and Scotland, and to augment land forces. The Habeas Corpus Act was suspended in England, and in Scotland. An Act, passed in 1701, for preventing wrong imprisonments, and against undue delay in trials, was also suspended from the twenty-third of July, 1715, until the twenty-fourth of the ensuing January. A fleet, under the command of Sir George Byng, was ordered to cruise in the Downs; and the most active and vigilant measures were taken in order to put the nation into a position of defence. The former intended invasion of 1708 was not forgotten, and it acted like a warning voice to the English Ministry. A Whig Association was framed among persons of rank and influence; and in Edinburgh a body of volunteers was formed, who might daily be seen exercising in the Great Hall of the College.

Meantime the Jacobites were increasing in strength. During the last six years collections had been made in the continental nations, purporting to be for a "gentleman in distress, " and the amount was said to have exceeded twelve millions. [6] Of this sum, one hundred thousand pounds was entrusted to the Earl of Mar.

The whole scheme of the insurrection was matured, and the Chevalier had been proclaimed King in different towns in Scotland, when the death of Louis the Fourteenth cast such a damp over the spirits of the party, that there ensued a consultation as to the expediency of their separating and returning to their homes. In this emergency, unhappily for the brave and ardent men whom he had assembled at Braemar, the influence of the Earl of Mar, and the arguments which his sanguine spirit suggested, prevailed; and the assembled chiefs parted, only to meet again at their appointed places of rendezvous.

The scheme of the Insurrection of 1715 embraced three different movements. In the north, the Earl of Mar was to possess himself of all the rich coasts of Fife, and also to maintain, in the name of James the Third, the northern counties, which, with few exceptions, were soon under the control of the insurgents. An attempt was made upon the southern parts of Scotland, by sending Brigadier Mackintosh, with a strong detachment of men, to cross the Firth of Forth, and to land in the Lothians, there expecting to be joined by friends on the borders and from England. In the west, a rising of the south-country Scots, under the command of Lord Kenmure, was projected; whilst in Northumberland the English Jacobites, headed by Mr. Forster, with a commission of General from Lord Mar, and aided by the Earl of Derwentwater, was to give the signal and incentive to the adherents of James in the sister Kingdom, as well as to co-operate with the Scottish forces under the commands of Brigadier Mackintosh and Viscount Kenmure. An attack upon Edinburgh was also concerted.

Such is the outline of a plan of an insurrection to the effect of which the Earl of Mar declared the Jacobites had been looking for six and twenty years. How immature it was in its conception—how deficient in energy and union was its execution—how unworthy was its chief instrument—how fatal to the good and great were its results—and, by a singular fortune, how those who least merited their safety escaped, whilst the gallant and honest champions of the cause suffered, will be fully detailed in the following pages. Let it be remembered that the task of compiling these Memoirs has been undertaken with no party spirit, nor with any wish to detract from the deep obligations which we owe to those who preserved us from inroads on our constitution, and oppression in our religious opinions. It has been, however, begun with a sincere wish to do justice to the disinterested and the good; and, as the task has proceeded, and increased information on the subject has been gained, it has been continued with a conviction that, whatever may be the nature or merits of the abstract principles on which it was undertaken, the Insurrection of 1715 forms an episode in the history of our country as creditable to many of the ill-fated actors in its tragic scenes, as any that have been detailed in the pages of that history.

LONDON,
October 28, 1845.

FOOTNOTES:

[1] Dalrymple.

[2] Rapin. Dissertation on the Origin and Government of England, vol. xiv. p. 423.

[3] See Introduction to the Memoirs of Cameron of Lochiel, p. 22.

[4] Lockhart, vol. i. p. 239.

[5] Lockhart, vol. i. p. 324.

[6] Reay, p. 187.

CONTENTS TO THE FIRST VOLUME.

JOHN ERSKINE, EARL OF MAR.

JOHN ERSKINE,
EARL OF MAR

"The title of Mar, " observes Lord Hailes, "is one of the Earldoms whose origin is lost in its antiquity. " It existed before our records, and before the era of general history: hence, the Earls of Mar claimed always to be called first in the Scottish Parliament in the roll of Earls, as having no rival in the antiquity of their honours.

From the time of Malcolm Canmore, in the year 1065, until the fourteenth century, the family of De Mar enjoyed this Earldom; but on the death of Thomas, the thirteenth Earl of Mar, in 1377, the direct male line of this race ended. The Earldom then devolved upon the female representatives of the house of De Mar; and thence, as in most similar instances in Scotland, it became the subject of contention, fraud, and violence.

Isabel, Countess of Mar and Garioch, the last of the De Mar family, was won in marriage by a singular and determined species of courtship, formerly common in Scotland; the influence of terror. The heiress of the castle of Kildrummie, and a widow, her first husband, Sir Malcolm Drummond, having died in 1403, her wealth and rank attracted the regards of Alexander Stewart, the natural son of Robert Earl of Buchan, of royal blood. Without waiting for the ordinary mode of persuasion to establish an interest in his favour, this wild, rapacious man appeared in the Highlands at the head of a band of plunderers, and planting himself before the castle of Kildrummie, stormed it, and effected a marriage between himself and the Countess of Mar. Alexander Stewart, in cooler moments, however, perceived the danger of this bold measure, and resolved to establish his right to the Countess and to her estates by another process. One morning, during the month of September 1404, he presented himself at the Castle gate of Kildrummie, and formally surrendered to the Countess the castle, its furniture, and the title-deeds kept within its chests; thus returning them to her to do with them as she pleased. The Countess, on the other hand, holding the keys in her hand, and declaring herself to be of "mature advice, " chose the said Alexander for her husband, and gave him the castle, the Earldom of Mar, with all the other family estates in her possession. She afterwards conferred these gifts by a charter, signed and sealed in the open fields, in the presence of the Bishop of Ross, and of her whole tenantry, in order to show that these acts were produced by no unlawful coercion on the part of her husband. The said honours and estates were also to descend to any children born in that marriage. Some of her kindred listened resentfully to the account of these proceedings of Isabel of Mar.

The next heir to the Earldom, after the death of Isabel, was Janet, grand-daughter of Gratney, eleventh Earl of Mar. This lady had married Sir Thomas Erskine, the proprietor of the Barony of Erskine, on the Clyde, the property of the family during many ages; and she expected, on the death of the Countess of Mar, to succeed to the honours which had descended to her by the female line. By a series of unjust and rapacious acts on the part of the Crown, not only did Robert, Lord Erskine, her son, fail in securing his rights, but her descendants had the vexation of seeing their just honours and rights revert to the King, James the Third, who bestowed them first upon his brother, the accomplished and unfortunate John Earl of Mar, who was bled to death in one of the houses of the Canongate, in Edinburgh; and afterwards, upon Cochrane, the favourite of James the Third. The Earldom of Mar was then conferred on Alexander Stewart, the third son of King James; and after his death, upon James Stewart, Prior of St. Andrews, who had a charter from his sister, Queen Mary, entitling him to enjoy the long contested honour. But he soon relinquished the title, to assume that of Moray, which had also been bestowed upon him by the Queen: and in 1565 Mary repaired the injustice committed by her predecessors, and restored John Lord Erskine to the Earldom of Mar.

The house of Erskine, on whom these honours now descended, has the same traditional origin as that of most of the other Scottish families of note. In the days of Malcolm the Second, a Scottish man having killed with his own hand Enrique, a Danish general, presented the head of the enemy to his Sovereign, and, holding in his hand the bloody dagger with which the deed had been performed, exclaimed, in Gaelic, "Eris Skyne, " alluding to the head and the dagger; upon which the surname of Erskine was imposed on him. The armorial bearing of a hand holding a dagger, was added as a further distinction, together with the motto, *Je pense plus,* in allusion to the declaration of the chieftain that he intended to perform even greater actions than that which procured him the name which has since been so celebrated in Scottish history. The crest and motto are still borne by the family.

This anecdote has, however, been rejected for the more probable conjecture that the family of Erskine derived its appellation from the estate of Erskine on the Clyde: [7] yet it is not impossible but that tradition may, in most cases, have a deeper source than we are willing to allow to it. "There are few points in ancient history, " observes a modern writer, "on which more judgment is required than in the amount of weight due to *tradition*. In general it will be found that the tradition subsisting in the families themselves has a true basis to rest upon, however much it may be overloaded with collateral matter which obscures it. "[8]

But that which ennobled most truly the first Earl of Mar, of the house of Erskine, was his own probity, loyalty, and patriotism. Destined originally to the church, John, properly sixth Earl of Mar, carried into public life those virtues which would have adorned the career of a private individual. In the melancholy interest of Queen Mary's eventful life, it is consolatory to reflect on the integrity and moderation of this exemplary nobleman. Too good and too sensitive for his times, he died of a broken heart, the result of that inward and incurable sorrow which the generous and the honest experience, when their hopes and designs are baffled by the selfish policy of their own party. "He was, perhaps, " says Robertson, "the only person in the kingdom who could have enjoyed the office of Regent without envy, and have left it without loss of reputation. "[9]

From the restoration of John Earl of Mar to his family honours, until the reign of Charles the First, the prosperity of this loyal and favoured family increased, interrupted indeed by some vicissitudes of fortune, but by no serious reverses, until that period which, during the commotions of the Great Rebellion, reduced many of our proudest nobility to comparative poverty.

Among other important trusts enjoyed by the family of Erskine, the government of the Castle of Edinburgh, and the custody of the principal forts in the kingdom, attested the confidence of their Sovereigns. To these was added by Mary Queen of Scots, the command of the Castle of Stirling, and the still more important charge of her infant son. To these marks of confidence numerous grants of lands and high appointments succeeded, —obligations which were repaid with a fidelity which impoverished the family of Erskine; and which produced, towards the close of the seventeenth century, a marked decline in their fortunes, and decay of their local influence.

John, ninth Earl of Mar, the grandfather of the Jacobite Earl, suffered severely for his loyalty in joining the association at Cumbernauld, in favour of Charles the First. He afterwards raised forces at Brae-Mar for the King's service, for which he was heavily fined by the Parliament, and his estates were sequestrated. During all this season of adversity he lived in a cottage at the gate of his house at Alloa, until the Restoration relieved him from the sequestration.

His son Charles, who raised the first regiment of Scottish Fusileers, and was constituted their Colonel, began life as a determined

Royalist; but disapproving of the measures of James the Second, he had prepared to go abroad when the Prince of Orange landed in England. He appears afterwards to have pursued somewhat of the same wavering course as that of which his son has been accused, and, joining the disaffected party against William, he was arrested, but afterwards released. The heavy incumbrances upon his estates, contracted during the civil wars, were such as to oblige him to sell a great portion of his lands, and to part with the ancient Barony of Erskine, the first possession of the family. This necessity may almost be considered as an ill omen for the future welfare of a family; which never seems to be so utterly brought low by fortune, as when compelled to consign to strangers that from which the first sense of importance and stability has been derived.

Under these circumstances, certainly not favourable to independence of character, John, eleventh Earl of Mar of the name of Erskine, and afterwards Lieutenant-general to the Chevalier St. George, was born at Alloa, in Clackmannan, where his father resided. He was a younger son of a numerous family, five brothers, older than himself, having died in infancy. His mother, the Lady Mary Maule, eldest daughter of George Earl of Panmure, gave birth to eight sons, and a daughter. Of the sons, the Earl of Mar and his brothers, James Erskine of the Grange, afterwards the husband of the famous and unfortunate Lady Grange; and Henry, killed at the battle of Almanza in 1707, alone attained the age of manhood. The only sister of Lord Mar, Lady Jean, was married to Sir Hugh Paterson of Bannockburn, in Stirlingshire.

The Earl of Mar succeeded to the possession and management of estates, heavily encumbered, in 1696. [10] His qualities of mind and person, at this early period of his life, were not eminently pleasing. His countenance, though strongly marked, had none of the attributes of intellectual strength. In person he is said to have been deformed, although his portrait by Kneller was skilfully contrived to hide that defect; his complexion was fair: he was short in stature. In his early youth the Earl is declared by historians who were adverse to the Stuarts, to have been initiated into every species of licentious dissipation, by Neville Payne: and the young nobleman is characterized as "the scandal of his name. "[11] Although his ancestors had been devotedly attached to the interests of the exiled family, yet, it was to be shewn how far Mar preferred those interests to his own, or upon what principles he eventually adopted the cause of hereditary monarchy, which had already brought so much inconvenience, and so many losses to his father and grandfather.

The first political prepossessions of the young Earl must certainly have been those of the Cavaliers; such was the name by which the party continued to be called who still desired the restoration of James the Second, and fervidly believed in the fruition of their hopes. His father had indeed, to use the words of Lockhart of Carnwath, "embarked with the Revolution; " but had given tokens of his deep contrition for that act, so inconsistent with his hereditary allegiance. But the unformed opinions of the young are far more easily swayed by events which are passing before their eyes than by the cool reasonings of the closet; and the inclinations of the Earl of Mar's childhood were likely soon to be effaced by the state of public affairs. The later occurrences of the reign of William the Third were calculated not only to repress the spirit of Jacobitism, but to shame even the most enthusiastic of its partisans out of a scheme which the sagacity of William had defeated, and which his wisdom had taught him to forgive. It was in the year 1696, just as the Earl of Mar succeeded to his title, that the projected invasion of the kingdom, and the scheme of assassinating the King, were defeated: —that William, hastening to the House of Commons, gave to the nation an account of the whole conspiracy. The House of Commons, without rising from their seats, then "declared that William was their rightful king, and that they would defend him with their lives. " It was at this important æra that James the Second, after long waiting at Calais, and casting thence many a wishful look towards England, returned to St. Germains, "to thank God that he had lost his country, because it had saved his soul. "[12] The hopes of the Cavaliers were thus wholly extinguished: and to these circumstances were the first observations of the youthful Earl of Mar doubtless directed.

His guardians, seemingly desirous of retrieving the affairs of the family, had endeavoured to imbue his mind with Revolution principles; [13] and the famous association which acknowledged the title of William to the throne of England, framed about this time, was signed by many who became in after life the friends of the Earl of Mar. This was precisely the period when that political profligacy, too justly charged upon the leading men in this country, and which induced them, under the impression that the exiled family would be eventually restored, to correspond with the Court of St. Germains, was tranquillized, although not eradicated by the great policy and forbearance of William. [14] That single reply of William's to

Charnock, who had trafficked between France and England with these negotiations, and who offered to disclose to the King the names of those who had employed him; —these few words, "I do not wish to hear them, "[15] did more to soothe discontents, and to repress the violence of faction, than the subsequent executions in the reign of George the First.

The Earl of Mar, left as he was at the early age of fourteen to his own guidance, very soon displayed a remarkable prudence in his pecuniary affairs, and a desire to repair by good management the fortunes of his family, —a point which he accomplished, to a certain extent. His dawning character shewed him to be shrewd and wary, but possessing no extended views, and disposed to rest his hopes of elevation and distinction upon petty intrigues, rather than to look upon probity and exertion as the true basis of greatness. His great talent consisted in the management of his designs, "in which, " remarks one who knew him well, "it was hard to find him out when he desired to be incognito; and thus he shewed himself to be a man of good sense, but bad morals. "[16]

On the 8th of September, 1696, the Earl of Mar took his seat in the Scottish Parliament, protesting, as his forefathers had done, against any Scottish Earl being called before him in the Roll. He became a frequent, but indifferent speaker in Parliament; but his continual activity, and the address which he soon acquired as the fruit of experience, together with the position which he held, as one generally understood to be well affected to the new order of things, yet of sufficient importance to be gained over to the other side, soon made him an object for party spirit to assail.

During the reign of William, the Earl of Mar continued constant to the side to which he had declared himself to belong. His pecuniary embarrassments, acting upon a restless, ambitious temper, rendered it difficult to a man weak in principle to retain independence of character: and it must be avowed, that there are few temptations to depart from the road of integrity more urgent than the desire to raise an ancient name to its original splendour. No encumbrances are so likely to drag their victim away from integrity as those by which rank is clogged with poverty.

In April, 1697, Lord Mar was chosen a privy councillor; and shortly afterwards invested with the Order of the Thistle; and the command of a company of foot bestowed upon him. On the death of William his fortune was rather improved than deteriorated, although he continued to attach himself to the Revolution Party, who, it was generally understood, were very far from being acceptable to the Queen. "At her accession, " declares a Jacobite writer, "the Presbyterians looked upon themselves as undone; despair appeared in their countenances, which were more upon the melancholic and dejected than usual. " The management of Scottish affairs was, nevertheless, entirely in the hands of the advocates of the Revolution; and one of their greatest supporters, the Duke of Queensbury, was appointed High Commissioner of the Scottish Parliament, notwithstanding the representations of some of the most powerful nobility in Scotland.

To the party of this celebrated politician the Earl of Mar attached himself, with a tenacity for which those who recollected the hereditary politics of the Erskine family, could find no motives but self-interest. James, Duke of Queensbury, was, it is true, the son of one of the most active partisans of the Stuart family, to whom the house of Queensbury owed both its ducal rank and princely fortune. Possessed of good abilities, but devoid of application, and with the disadvantage to a public man of being of an easy, indolent temper, this celebrated promoter of the union between Scotland and England, had acquired, by courtesy, and by a long administration of affairs, a singular influence over his countrymen. His character has been written with a pen that could scarcely find sufficient invectives for those politicians who, in the opinion of the writer, were the ruin of their country. The Duke of Queensbury falls under the heaviest censures. "To outward appearance, " says Lockhart, "he was of a gentle and good disposition, but inwardly a very devil, standing at nothing to advance his own interest and designs. Though his hypocrisy and dissimulation served him very much, yet he became so well known, that no man, except such as were his nearest friends, and *socii criminis*, gave him any trust; and so little regard had he to his promises and vows, that it was observed and notorious, that if he was at any pains to convince you of his friendship, and by swearing and imprecating curses on himself and family to assure you of his sincerity, then, to be sure, he was doing you underhand all the mischief in his power. "[17]

These characteristics must be viewed as proceeding from the pen of a partisan; nor can we wonder at the contrariety of opinion which prevails respecting any public man who proposes a great and startling measure. Honours, places, and a pension were showered down upon this most fortunate of ministers; and his career is remarkable as having been cheered by the favour of four sovereigns of very different tempers. In his early youth, after his return from his travels, the Duke of Queensbury was appointed a Privy Councillor of Scotland by Charles the Second. He held the same post under James the Second, but resigned it in 1688. The reserved and doubting William of Orange placed him near his person, making him a Lord of the Bedchamber, and captain of his Dutch guard; eventually he became Lord High Treasurer of Scotland, and—to abridge a list of numerous employments and honours—Lord High Commissioner of Scotland. So far had Queensbury's fortunes begun with the Stuarts and continued under the House of Orange. It appeared unlikely that the successor of William—she who in her first speech announced that her heart was "wholly English, " to mark the distinction between herself and the foreigner who had sat on the throne before her, —would adopt as her own representative in Scotland the favourite of William; yet she continued Queensbury in that high station which it was believed none could fill so adequately in the disturbed and refractory kingdom of Scotland. [18]

During the early years of Queen Anne's reign, and in the season of his own comparative prosperity, the young Earl of Mar entered into his first marriage, at Twickenham, with Lady Margaret Hay, daughter of John Earl of Kinnoul. The wife whom he thus selected was the daughter of a house originally adverse to the principles of the Revolution. William Earl of Kinnoul, in the time of James the Second, had remained at St. Germains with that monarch. But the same change which had manifested the political course of Lord Mar, had been apparent in the father of Lady Margaret Hay. The Earl of Kinnoul was afterwards one of the Commissioners for the Union, and supported that treaty in Parliament; yet, when the Rebellion of 1715 commenced, this nobleman was one of the suspected persons who were summoned to surrender themselves, and was committed a prisoner to Edinburgh Castle. His daughter, the Countess of Mar, was happily spared from witnessing the turmoils of that period. Married in her seventeenth year, she lived only four years with a husband whose character was but partially developed, when, in 1707, she died at the age of twenty-one, having given birth to two sons. She was buried at the family seat at Alloa Castle, an ancient fortress, built in the year 1300, one turret of which still remaining rises ninety feet from the ground. Seven years intervened before Lord Mar supplied the place of his lost wife by another union.

His days were, indeed, consumed in public affairs, varied by the improvement of his Scottish estates, embellishing the tower of Alloa by laying out beautiful gardens in that wilderness style of planting which the Earl first introduced into Scotland. [19] He had the reward of seeing his efforts succeed, the gardens of Alloa being much eulogized and visited. This was by no means Lord Mar's only recreation; architecture was his delight, and he introduced into London the celebrated Gibbs, who, out of gratitude, eventually bequeathed a large portion of his fortune to the children of the Earl. [20] It is refreshing to view this busy and versatile politician in this light before we plunge into the depths of those intricate politics which form the principal features of his life.

It was during the year 1703 that a political association or club was framed consisting of the chief nobility and gentlemen of fortune and afterwards known by the name of the *Squadrone Volante*. They acquired distinguished popularity and influence by the patriotic character of the measures which they introduced into the Scottish Parliament; and by their professions of being free from any court interest, they gained the confidence of the country. They were firm friends of the Revolution party, great sticklers to the Protestant succession, forming a *separate band* distinct from the Whigs, yet opposed to the Cavaliers, or, as they were afterwards called, Jacobites. The power of the Squadrone was, in a great measure, the result of those jarring counsels in the Scottish Parliament, which only coalesced upon one theme, —independence of England—interference of "foreign" or English counsels, as they were termed. This combination was headed by the Duke of Montrose, the Marquis of Tweedale, and several other Scottish noblemen, to whom adhered thirty commoners. [21]

During the existence of this association, the celebrated "Queensbury affair, " as it was usually called, involved the temporary disgrace of the Duke of Queensbury, and first brought to view those convenient doctrines of expediency which afterwards formed so marked a feature in the character of Lord Mar.

The "sham plot, " as it is called by Jacobite writers, was a supposed intended invasion of Great Britain, disclosed to the Duke of Queensbury by Simon Fraser of Beaufort, afterwards Lord Lovat; whose very name seems to have suggested to his contemporaries, as it has since done to posterity, the combination of all that is subtle, treacherous, and base, with all that is dangerous, desperate, and remorseless in conduct.

This tool of the court of St. Germains came over from France, in company with John Murray, who was sent to watch his proceedings, and also to aid his object in procuring the promises of the most distinguished Highland chieftains to the furtherance of the projected invasion of England. The assistance of Captain Murray was conjoined on this occasion, the fidelity of that gentleman having been ascertained by the court of St. Germains; whilst there existed not a human being who did not instinctively distrust Beaufort: to Mary of Modena, who far more ardently desired the restoration of the Stuarts than her consort James, he was peculiarly obnoxious.

The exiled Queen's fears proved well founded, for no sooner had Beaufort landed in England, than he formed the scheme of converting this secret enterprise into a means of obtaining reward and protection from the Duke of Argyle, whose mediation with the Duke of Queensbury he required for private reasons; he therefore notified his arrival to Argyle, who had been his early and hereditary friend, offering at the same time to make great disclosures, if he had previous assurances of remuneration.

Such is the account of most impartial writers, and more especially of those who lean to the Whig party: but, by the Jacobites, the very existence of a conspiracy to invade England at this time was denied, and the whole affair was declared to be a scheme of the Duke of Queensbury's to undermine the reputation of the Cavaliers, and "to find a pretence to vent his wrath, and execute his malice against those who thwarted his arbitrary designs, " for the completion of a treaty of union between Scotland and England, which had been in contemplation ever since the days of William the Third. [22]

After much deliberation the Duke of Queensbury was induced to have several communications with Fraser of Beaufort, and to listen to the information which he gave, all of which the Duke transmitted to Queen Anne, although he concealed the name of his informant. In consequence of Fraser's disclosures, several persons coming from France to England were apprehended on suspicion of being engaged in the Pretender's service, and an universal alarm was spread, as well as a distrust of the motives and proceedings of Queensbury, who thus acted upon the intelligence of an avowed spy, and noted outlaw, like Fraser. A temporary loss of Queensbury's political sway in Scotland was the result, and a consequent increase of power to the Squadrone Volante.

It was at this juncture that the Earl of Mar came forward as the advocate of the Duke of Queensbury's measures, and the opponent of the Squadrone Volante, who had now completely fixed upon themselves that name, from their pretending to act by themselves, and to cast the balance of contending parties in Parliament. The opposition of Lord Mar to the Squadrone was peculiarly acceptable to the Tories, or Cavaliers, who had recently applied to that faction to assist them in the defence of their country against the Union, but who had been greeted with an indignant and resolute refusal.

The Earl of Mar therefore appeared as the champion of the Cavaliers, and for the first time won their confidence and approbation. "He headed, " writes the bitter and yet truthful Lockhart, "such of the Duke of Queensbury's friends as opposed the Marquis of Tweedale and his party's designs; and that with such art and dissimulation, that he gained the favour of all the Tories, and was by them esteemed an honest man, and well inclined to the royal family. Certain it is, he vowed and protested as much many a time; but no sooner was the Marquis of Tweedale and his party dispossessed, than he returned as a dog to the vomit, and promoted all the court of England's measures with the greatest zeal imaginable. "[23] The three parties in the Scottish Parliament, according to the same authority, consisted of the Cavaliers, —that remnant of the Jacobite party which remained vigorous, more especially in the Highlands, since the days of Dundee, —of the Squadrone, "or *outer* court party, " and of the present court party, consisting of true blue Presbyterians and Revolutioners. [24] With the interests of the latter party the Earl of Mar was undoubtedly engaged.

Scotland was at this time, and continued for several years, racked with dissensions regarding the Treaty of Union. No one can form an adequate idea of the heartburnings, feuds, parties, and tumults, by which that great measure was preceded, and followed, without looking into the contemporary writers, whose aim it ever is to heighten the picture of passing events; whereas the calm historian subdues it into one general effect of keeping.

The Earl of Mar took a prominent part in seconding the treaty; no man's commencement of a career could be more opposed to its termination than that of this politician of easy virtue. The Duke of

Queensbury was for some time so hated in Scotland as scarcely to venture to appear there, but contented himself with sending the Duke of Argyle as commissioner, and "using him as the monkey did the cat in pulling out the hot roasted chesnut. " But when he was, after an interval, reinstated in power, Lord Mar was again his devoted ally. The influence of the Duke over every mind with which he came into collision was, indeed, almost irresistible. "I cannot but wonder, " remarks the indignant Lockhart, "at the influence he had over all men of sense, quality, and estate; men that had, at least many of them, no dependance on him, yet were so deluded as to serve his ambitious designs, contrary to the acknowledged dictates of their own conscience. "[25]

In 1706, in the beginning of the session of Parliament, the Earl of Mar presented the draught of an Act for appointing Commissioners, to treat of an Union of the two kingdoms of Scotland and England. Thus was he the instrument of first presenting to the Scotch that measure so revolting to their prejudices, so singularly distasteful to a proud and independent people. It is impossible to judge how far Lord Mar was convinced of the expediency of the Treaty, or whether he was, in secret, one of those who feigned an affection for the measure, whilst, in their hearts, they wished for the preponderance of the votes against it. The Treaty of Union was espoused by those in whose opinions Lord Mar had been nurtured, —and originally, according to De Foe, it had been mooted by William the Third, who declared that this Island would never be easy without an union. "I have done all I can in that affair, " he once observed; "but I do not see a temper in either nation that looks like it: it may be done, but not yet. "[26]

The Treaty, retarded by many interests, clashing between nations, but, more especially, by the burning recollections of massacred countrymen in the blood-stained valley of Glencoe, was now brought into discussion just when the Earl of Mar was at that age when a thirst for gain, or an ambition to rise is unquenched, in general, by disappointment. Differing in one respect from many Cavaliers, in being of a family strictly Protestant, Lord Mar had not the inducement which operated upon the Catholics, in their undiminished, ardent desire to restore the young Prince of Wales to the throne. Differing, again, in another respect from many of the Jacobites, Lord Mar had not the tie of a personal knowledge of the exiled King to fix his fidelity; or, what was considered far more likely to have sealed his, or any adherent allegiance, he had enjoyed no opportunities of cultivating the favour of the enthusiastic, bigoted, and yet intelligent Mary of Modena, whose exertions for her family kept alive the spirit of Jacobitism during the decline of her royal devotee and the childhood of her son. Lord Mar seems to have been reared entirely in Scotland, and he might perhaps come under the description given by the eloquent Lord Belhaven of a Whig in Scotland: —"A true, blue Presbyterian, who, without considering time or power, will venture all for the Kirk, but something less for the State; "[27] but that his subsequent conduct contradicts this supposition.

The Treaty struggled on through a powerful and memorable opposition. It is a curious instance of Scottish pride, that one of the objections made to the Commissioners appointed to treat of the Union, was, that there were six or eight newly-raised families amongst them, and but few of the great and ancient names of Hamilton, Graham, Murray, Erskine, and many others. [28] Never was there so much domestic misery and humiliation, abroad, for poor Scotland, as during the progress of this Treaty. The fame of Marlborough, and the fortunes of Godolphin, were now at their zenith; they were considered as the great arbiters of Scottish affairs, —the Queen being only applied to for the sake of form. These two great statesmen treated the Scottish noblemen to whom the Cavaliers entrusted the success of their representations, with a lofty insolence, which galled the proud Highlanders, and went to their very hearts.

"I myself, " writes the author of Memoirs of Scotland, "out of curiosity, went sometimes to their levées, where I saw the Commissioners, the Duke of Queensbury, the Chancellor, the Secretary, Lord Mar, and other great men of Scotland, hang on near an hour; and when admitted, treated with no more civility than one gentleman pays another's valet-de-chambre; and for which the Scots have none to blame but themselves, for had they valued themselves as they ought to have done, and not so meanly and sneakingly prostituted their honour and country to the will and pleasure of the English Ministry, they would never have presumed to usurp such a dominion over Scotland, as openly and avowedly to consult upon and determine in Scots' affairs. "[29]

At home, the spirit of party ran to an extent which cannot be called insane, because the interests at stake were those dearest to a high-spirited people. "Factions, " exclaimed Lord Belhaven, "in Parliament, are now become independent, and have got footing in councils, in parliaments, in treaties, in armies, in incorporations, in families, among kindred; yea, man and wife are not free from them. "[30] "Hannibal, my Lord, " he cried, in one of what Lockhart calls his long premeditated harangues, "Hannibal is at our gates; Hannibal is come the length of this table; he is at the foot of this throne: he will demolish the throne; if we take not notice, he will seize upon these regalia; he'll take them as our *spolia opima,* and whip us out of this House, never to return again. "

In order to understand the effect of the Act of Union upon the hopes of the Jacobite party, it is necessary to take into consideration the following facts. The Act of the English Parliament, by which the Crown had been settled on Queen Mary and her sister, extended only to the Princess Anne and her issue. After the death of the Duke of Gloucester, and about the end of the reign of William the Third, another settlement was made, by which the Crown was settled on the House of Hanover; but no similar Act was passed in Scotland. And at the beginning of Queen Anne's reign, and until after the Union, the Scottish Parliament were legally possessed of a power to introduce again the exiled family into Great Britain. [31]

During the course of the negotiations for the Treaty of Union, the Earl of Mar formed an alliance with the celebrated Duke of Hamilton. In the consideration of public affairs at this period, it may not appear a digression to give some insight into the character of one who headed the chief party in the Scottish Parliament, and with whom the Earl of Mar was, at this period of his life, in frequent intercourse.

James Duke of Hamilton was at this period nearly fifty years of age. His youth had been passed in the gay court of Charles the Second, as one of the Gentlemen of the Bedchamber of that monarch, —an office which he only relinquished to become Ambassador Extraordinary to France, where he remained long enough to serve in two campaigns under Louis the Fourteenth. Upon the death of Charles the Second, Louis recommended the young nobleman, then termed Earl of Arran, strongly and essentially to James the Second, who made him Master of his Wardrobe, and appointed him to other offices.

Under these circumstances it is not surprising that in the honest and warm feelings of the Duke of Hamilton, affection for the Stuarts should form a principal feature. He had the courage to adhere firmly to James the Second, amid the general obloquy, and to accompany the monarch on his abdication to his embarkation at Rochester. "I can distinguish, " he said, at a meeting of the Scottish nobility in London, over which his father, the Duke of Hamilton presided, "between the King's popery and his person. I dislike the one, but have sworn to do allegiance to the other, which makes it impossible to withhold that which I cannot forbear believing is the King my master's right: for his present absence in France can no more affect my duty, than his longer absence from us has done all this while. "

Notwithstanding these professions, upon the unfortunate conclusion of the affair of Darien, the Earl of Arran, after twice encountering imprisonment upon account of the Stuarts, esteemed it his duty to his country to take the oaths to King William, in order to qualify himself to sit in Parliament.

The character of the Duke of Hamilton presents a favourable specimen of the well-principled and well-intentioned Scotchman, with the acknowledged virtues and obvious defects of the national character. He was disinterested in great matters, refusing many opportunities of worldly advantage, and bearing for the first eight years of his public career, a retirement which is always more galling to an ambitious temper than actual danger; yet, it was supposed, and not without reason, that, whilst his heart was with the Cavaliers, or country party, the considerations of his great estate in England occasioned a lukewarmness in his political conduct, and broke down his opposition to the Union. Wary and cautious, he could thus sacrifice his present hopes of a distinction which his talents would have readily attained, to his adherence to a lost cause; but his resolution failed when the sacrifice of what many might deem inferior interests, was required.

The Duke soon formed a considerable party in the Parliament; and his empire over the affections of his countrymen grew daily. To those to whom he confided, the Duke was gracious and unbending; but a suspicion of an insult recalled the native haughtiness attributable to his house. [32] "Frank, honest, and good-natured, " as he was esteemed by Swift, and displaying on his dark, coarse countenance, the characteristics of good sense and energy, the Duke was a bitter and vindictive foe[33]—characteristics of his age, and of a nation undoubtedly prone to wreak a singular and remorseless revenge on all who offend the hereditary pride, or militate against the prejudices of its people.

Endowed with these qualities, the whole career of James Duke of Hamilton was a struggle between his love for his country, and his consideration for what he esteemed its truest interests, and his desire to support the claims of the royal family of Stuart. His political career has been criticised by writers of every faction; but it must be judged of as having taken place in times of peculiar difficulty, and a due credit should be given to the motives of one who displayed, during the greater portion of his life, forbearance and consistency. "Had not his loyalty been so unalterable, " writes Lockhart, "and that he would never engage in King William's and his Government's service, and his love to his country induced him to oppose that King and England's injustice and encroachments on it, no doubt he had made as great a figure in the world as any other whatsoever, and that either in a civil or military capacity. "[34] "The Duke of Hamilton's love for his country, " observes a contemptuous, anonymous assailant, "made him leave London, and follow King James, who had enslaved it. His love to his country had engaged him in several plots to restore that prince, and with him, tyranny and idolatry, poverty and slavery. "[35] Upon the odious principle of always seeking out for the lowest and the most selfish motive that can actuate the conduct of men, —a principle which is thought by weak and bad minds to display knowledge of the world, but which, in fact, more often betrays ignorance, —another part of his conduct was misjudged. The reluctance of the Duke of Hamilton, in 1704, to nominate a successor to the throne of England, before framing the treaty touching "the Commerce of Scotland and other Concerns, " was ascribed by many to the remote hope of succeeding to the Crown, since, in case of the exclusion of the Princess Sophia and her descendants, his family was the next in succession, of the Protestant Faith. Such was one of the reasons assigned for the wise endeavour which this nobleman exerted to prevent an invasion of the kingdom by James Stuart during the reign of Anne, and such the motive adduced for his advice to the Chevalier to maintain terms of amity with his royal sister. It was the cause calumniously assigned of his supposed decline in attachment to the exiled family. [36]

But, notwithstanding the inference thus deduced, the Duke of Hamilton continued to enjoy, in no ordinary degree, popular applause and the favour of Queen Anne, until his tragical death in 1712 occurring just before the Rebellion of 1715, spared him the perplexity of deciding on which side he should embark in that perilous and ill-omened insurrection.

This celebrated statesman, —one who never entered into a new measure, nor formed a project, ("though in doing thereof, " says Lockhart, "he was too cautious") that he did not prosecute his designs with a courage that nothing could daunt, —now determined to win over the Earl of Mar from the Duke of Queensbury. The Duke of Hamilton was the more induced to the attempt, from the frequent protestations made by the Earl of Mar of his love for the exiled family; and he applied himself to the task of gaining this now important ally with all the skill which experience and shrewdness could supply. Hamilton was considered invincible in such undertakings, and was master of a penetration which no one could withstand. "Never was, " writes Lockhart, "a man so qualified to be the head of a party as himself; for he could, with the greatest dexterity, apply himself to, and sift through, the inclinations of different parties, and so cunningly manage them, that he gained some of all to his. " But the Duke met in Lord Mar with one equally skilled in diving into motives, and in bending the will of others to his own projects. In the encounter of these two minds, the Duke is said to have been worsted and disarmed; and the Earl of Mar, by his insinuations, is suspected to have materially influenced the conduct of that great leader of party. "I have good reason to suppose, " says Lockhart, "that his Grace's appearing with less zeal and forwardness in this ensuing than in former Parliaments, is attributable to some agreement passed between them two. "[37]

For the effect of his newly-acquired influence over the Duke of Hamilton, and for his other services in promoting the Union, the Earl of Mar was amply rewarded. During the Parliament of 1705, he was constituted one of the Commissioners of that Treaty, his name being third on the list. In 1706, he was appointed one of the Secretaries of State for Scotland; and afterwards, upon the loss of that office, in consequence of the Union between the two countries, he was compensated by being made Keeper of the Signet, with the addition of a pension. [38] Those who were the promoters of the Treaty must have required some consolation for the general opprobrium into which the measure brought the Commissioners. The indignant populace converted the name of "Treaters" into Traitors: the Parliament Close resounded with "very free language, " denouncing the "Traitors. " That picturesque enclosure, since destroyed by fire, was crowded by a vehement multitude, who rushed into the outer Parliament House to denounce the Duke of Queensbury and his party, and to cheer the Duke of Hamilton, whom they followed to his residence in Holyrood House, exhorting him to stand by his country, and assuring him of support. The tumults were, indeed, soon quelled by military force; but the deliberations of Parliament were carried on at the risk of summary vengeance upon the "Traitors: " and the eloquence of members was uttered between walls which were guarded, during the whole session, by all the military force that Edinburgh could command. The Duke of Queensbury was obliged to walk "as if he had been led to the gallows, "[39] through two lanes of musqueteers, from the Parliament House to the Cross, where his coach stood; no coaches, nor any person who was not a member, being allowed to enter the Parliament Close towards evening: and he was conveyed in his carriage to the Abbey, surrounded both by horse and foot guards.

On the 1st of May, 1707, the Articles of Union were ratified by the Parliament of England. That day has been set down by the opponents of the measure as one never to be forgotten by Scotland, —the loss of their independence and sovereignty. Superstition marked every stage of the measure as happening upon some date adverse to the Stuarts. On the fourth of November the first Article of the Union was approved; on a fourth of November was William of Orange born. On the eighth of January the Peerage was renounced; on an eighth of January was the warrant for the Murder at Glencoe signed. The ratification of the Article of Union was on the sixteenth of January. On a sixteenth of January was the sentence of Charles the First pronounced. The dissolution of the Scottish Parliament took place upon the twenty-fifth of March, according to the Old Style, New Year's Day: that concession might therefore be esteemed a New-year's Gift to the English.

Finally, —The Equivalent, or Compensation Money, that is, "the price of Scotland, " came to Edinburgh on the fifth of August, the day on which the Earl of Gowrie designed to murder James the Sixth. [40]

The discontents and tumults which attended the progress of the Union ran throughout the whole country, and pervaded all ranks of people. Yet it is remarkable, that the nobility of Scotland should have been the first to fail in their opposition to the measure; and that the middle ranks, together with the lowest of the people, should have been foremost to withstand what they considered as insulting to the independence of their country. The very name and antiquity of their kingdom was dear to them, although there remained, after the removal of James the First into England, little more than "a vain shadow of a name, a yoke of slavery, and image of a kingdom. "[41] It was in vain that the Duke of Hamilton had called, in the beginning of the debates on this measure, upon the families of "Bruce, Campbell, Douglas, " not to desert their country: the opposition to the Union was bought over, with many exceptions, with a price; — twenty thousand pounds being sent over to the Lords Commissioners to employ in this manner, twelve thousand pounds of which were, however, returned to the English Treasury, there being no more who would accept the bribe. The Earl of Mar and the Earl of Seafield had privately secured their own reward, having bargained "for greater matters than could be agreed upon while the kingdom of Scotland stood in safety. "[42]

Amidst the resentment of the Scotch for their insulted dignity, it is amusing to find that this Union of the two countries could be deemed derogatory to English dignity; yet Dean Swift, among others, considered it in that light. "Swift's hatred to the Scottish nation, " observes Sir Walter Scott, "led him to look upon that Union with great resentment, as a measure degrading to England. The Scottish themselves hardly detested the idea more than he did; and that is saying as much as possible. "[43]

Swift vented his wrath in the verses beginning with these lines:

"The Queen has lately lost a part
Of her entirely-English heart,[44]
For want of which, by way of botch,
She piec'd it up again with Scotch.
Blest Revolution! which creates
Divided hearts, united states!
See how the double nation lies
Like a rich coat with skirts of frize:
As if a man in making posies,
Should bundle thistles up with roses!"

That the conduct of Lord Mar throughout this Treaty was regarded with avowed suspicion, the following anecdote tends to confirm: Lord Godolphin, at that time First Lord of the Treasury, wishing to tamper with one of a combination against the Queensbury faction, sent to offer that individual a place if he would discover to him how the combination was formed, and in what manner it might be broken. But the gentleman whose fidelity he thus assailed, was true to his engagements; and returned an indignant answer, desiring the

Lord Treasurer's agent "not to think that he was treating with such men as Mar and Seafield. "[45]

At this time the Earl of Mar was said to be in the full enjoyment of Lord Godolphin's confidence, and to have been one of those whom the treasurer consulted, in settling the government of Scotland. The rumour was not conducive to his comfort or well-being in his native country; and the Earl appears to have passed much more time in intrigues in London than among the gardens of Alloa.

It was not long before the effects of the general discontent were manifested in the desire of the majority of the Scottish nation to restore the descendant of their ancient kings to the throne, and even the Cameronians and Presbyterians were willing to pass over the objection of his being a Papist. "God may convert the Prince, " they said, "or he may have Protestant children, but the Union never can be good. "[46] The middle orders openly expressed their anxiety to welcome a Prince to their shores, whom they regarded as a deliverer: the nobility and gentry, though more cautious, yet were equally desirous to see the honour of their nation, in their own sense of it, restored. Episcopalians, Cavaliers, and Revolutionists, were unanimous, or, to use the Scots' proverb, "were all one man's bairns. " This state of public feeling was soon communicated to St. Germains, and Colonel Hooke, famous for his negotiations, was, according to the writer of the Memoirs, "pitched upon by the French King, and palmed upon the court of St. Germains, and dispatched to sound the intentions of the principal Scottish nobility. " This agent arrived in Scotland in the month of March, 1707. The paper containing assurances of aid to James Stuart was signed by sixteen noblemen and gentlemen; but the Earl of Mar was, at that time, engaged in a very different undertaking, and was in close amity with Sunderland, Godolphin, and the heads of the Whig party.

The spring of 1708 discovered the designs of Louis, and the news of great preparations at Dunkirk spread consternation in England. At this juncture, the first in which the son of James the Second was called upon to play a part in that drama of which he was the ill-starred hero, the usual fate of his race befel him. He came to Dunkirk hastily, and in private, intending to pass over alone to the Firth of Forth. He was attacked by the measles; at a still more critical moment of his melancholy life, he was the victim of ague: both of them ignoble diseases, which seem to have little concern with the affairs of royalty. The delay of the Prince's illness, although shortened by the peremptory commands of the French King to proceed, was fatal, for the English fleet had time to make preparations. A storm drove the French fleet northwards; in the tempest the unfortunate adventurer passed the Firth of Forth and Aberdeen; and although the fleet retraced its course to the Isle of May, it was only to flee back to France, daunted as the French admirals were by the proximity of Sir George Byng and the English fleet, who chased the enemy along the coasts of Fife and Angus. It was shortly after this event that the Pretender, upon whose head a price of a hundred thousand pounds was set by the English Government, first assumed the title of Chevalier of St. George, in order to spare himself the expense of field equipage in the campaign in Flanders.

The conduct of the Earl of Mar, in relation to conspiracy, has been alluded to rather than declared by historians. He is supposed not to have been, in secret, unfavourable to the undertaking. He was, nevertheless, active in giving to the Earl of Sunderland the names of the disaffected with whom he was generally supposed to be too well acquainted. Many of those who were suspected were brought to London, and were in some instances committed to prison, in others confined to their own houses. On this occasion the advice of the great Marlborough was followed, and the guilty were not proceeded against with more severity than was necessary for the Queen's safety. The same generous policy was in after times remembered, in mournful contrast with a very different spirit.

It was the ill-fortune of Mar to give satisfaction to none of those who had looked on the course of public affairs during the recent transactions; nor was it ever his good fortune to inspire confidence in his motives. Some notion may be formed of the thraldom of party in Scotland by the following anecdote: —

In 1711-12 the Queen conferred upon the Duke of Hamilton a patent for an English dukedom; but this, according to a vote of the House of Lords, did not entitle him to sit as a British Peer. Indignant at being thought incapable of receiving a grace which the King might confer on the meanest commoner, the Scotch Peers took the first opportunity of walking out of the House in a body, and refusing to vote or sit in that House. In addition to the affront implied by their incapacity of becoming British Peers, it was more than hinted that it would not be advisable for the independence of the House if the

King could confer the privileges of British Peers upon a set of nobles whose poverty rendered them dependent on the Crown.

Just when this offensive vote of the House was the theme of general conversation, Dean Swift encountered the Earl of Mar at Lord Masham's. "I was arguing with him, (Lord Mar), " he writes, "about the stubbornness and folly of his countrymen; they are so angry about the affair of the Duke of Hamilton, whom the Queen has made a Duke of England, and the Lords will not admit him. He swears he would vote for us, but dare not, because all Scotland would detest him if he did; he should never be chosen again, nor be able to live there. "[47]

The Earl of Mar continued to be one of the Representative Peers for Scotland, having been chosen in 1707, and rechosen at the general elections in 1708, 1710, and 1713. [48]

Upon the death of the Duke of Queensbury in 1711, the office of Secretary of State for Scotland became vacant, and the Duke of Hamilton and the Earl of Mar were rival expectants for the high and important post. Government hesitated for some time before filling up the post, being disposed rather to abolish it than to offend any party by its disposal, and deeming it as an useless expense to the Government; nor was it filled up for a considerable time.

The tragical death of one who, with some failings, deserved the affection and respect of his country, procured eventually to the Earl of Mar the chief management of public affairs in Scotland. Whilst on the eve of embarking as Ambassador Extraordinary to France, upon the conclusion of the peace of Utrecht, the Duke of Hamilton fell in a duel with his brother-in-law, Lord Mohun, —a man whose course of life had been stained with blood, but whose crimes had met with a singular impunity.

The character of Lord Mohun seems rather to have belonged to the reign of Charles the Second, than to the sober period of William and Anne. The representative of a very ancient family, he had the misfortune of coming to his title when young, while his estate was impoverished. "His quality introduced him into the best company, " says a contemporary writer, "but his wants very often led him into bad. " He ran a course of notorious and low dissipation, and was twice tried for murder before he was twenty. His first offence was the cruel and almost unprovoked murder of William Mountford, an accomplished actor, whom Mohun stabbed whilst off his guard. The second was the death of Mr. Charles Coote. For these crimes Lord Mohun had been tried by his peers, and, strange to say, acquitted. On his last acquittal he spoke gracefully before the Peers, expressing great contrition for the disgrace which he had brought upon his order, and promising to efface it by a better course of life. For some time this able but depraved nobleman kept to his resolution, and studied the constitution of his country. [49] He became a bold and eloquent speaker in the House on the side of the Whigs; and he had attained a considerable popularity, when the affair with the Duke of Hamilton finished his career before the age of thirty. [50]

A family dispute, exasperated by the different sides taken by these two noblemen in Parliament, was the cause of an event which deprived the Jacobite party of one of their most valuable and most moderate leaders; for had the counsels of the Duke of Hamilton prevailed, the Chevalier would never have undertaken the futile invasion of 1708, nor perhaps have engaged in the succeeding attempt in 1715. Upon the fortunes of the Earl of Mar, the death of the Duke so far operated that it was not until all fear of offending the powerful and popular Hamilton was ended by his tragical death, that the appointment of Secretary was conferred upon his rival. The Whigs were calumniously suspected of having had some unfair share in the death of the Duke, —an event which took place in the following manner.

Certain offensive words spoken by Lord Mohun in the chambers of a Master in Chancery, and addressed to the Duke of Hamilton, brought a long-standing enmity into open hostility. On the part of Lord Mohun, General Macartney was sent to convey a challenge to the Duke, and the place of meeting, time, and other preliminaries were settled by Macartney and the Duke over a bottle of claret, at the Rose Tavern, in Covent Garden. The hour of eight on the following day was fixed for the encounter, and on the fatal morning the Duke drove to the lodgings of his friend, Colonel Hamilton, who acted as his second, in Charing Cross, and hurried him away. It was afterwards deposed, that on setting out, the Colonel, in his haste, forgot his sword; upon which the Duke stopped the carriage, and taking his keys from his pocket, desired his servant to go to a certain closet in his house, and to bring his mourning-sword, which was accordingly done. This was regarded as a fatal omen in those days, in which, as Addison describes, a belief in such indications existed.

The Duke then drove on to that part of Hyde Park leading to Kensington, opposite the Lodge, and getting out, walked to and fro upon the grass between the two ponds. Lord Mohun, in the mean time, set out from Long Acre with his friend, General Macartney, who seems to have been a worthy second of the titled bravo.

Lord Mohun having taken the precaution of ordering some burnt wine to be prepared for him upon his return from the rencounter, proceeded to the place of appointment, where the Duke awaited him. "I must ask your Lordship, " said Lord Mohun, "one favour, which is, that these gentlemen may have nothing to do with our quarrel. " "My Lord, " answered the Duke, "I leave them to themselves. " The parties then threw off their cloaks, and all engaged; the seconds, it appears, fighting with as much fury as their principals. The park-keepers coming up, found Colonel Hamilton and General Macartney struggling together; the General holding the Colonel's sword in his left hand, the Colonel pulling at the blade of the General's sword. One of the keepers went up to the principals; he found Lord Mohun in a position between sitting and lying, bending towards the Duke, who was on his knees, leaning almost across Lord Mohun, both holding each other's sword fast, both striving and struggling with the fury of remorseless hatred. This awful scene was soon closed for ever, as far as Mohun was concerned. He expired shortly afterwards, having received four wounds, each of which was likely to be mortal. The Duke was raised and supported by Colonel Hamilton and one of the keepers; but after walking about thirty yards, exclaimed that "he could walk no farther, " sank down upon the grass, and expired. His lifeless remains, mangled with wounds which showed the relentless fury of the encounter, were conveyed to St. James's Square, the same morning, while the Duchess was still asleep. [51]

Lord Mohun, meanwhile, was carried, by order of General Macartney, to the hackney-coach in which he had arrived, and his body conveyed to his house in Marlborough Street, where, it was afterwards reported, that being flung upon the best bed, his Lady, one of the nieces of Charles Gerrard, Earl of Macclesfield, expressed great anger at the soiling of her new coverlid, on which the bleeding corpse was deposited. [52]

General Macartney escaped. It appeared on oath that he had made a thrust at the Duke, as he was struggling with Mohun; and it being generally believed that it was by that wound that the Duke died, an address was presented to her Majesty by the Scottish Peers, begging that she would write to all the kings and states in alliance with her, not to shelter Macartney from justice. [53]

A deep and general grief was shown for the death of the Duke of Hamilton. In Scotland mourning was worn, and the churches were hung with black. It was in vain that the Duchess offered a reward of three hundred pounds for the apprehension of Macartney; the murderer had fled beyond seas.

The Cavaliers lost, in Hamilton, an ornament to their party, from the strict honour and fidelity of his known character. But the crisis which the unfortunate Duke had in vain endeavoured to avert was now at hand, and the death of Queen Anne brought with it all those consequences which a long series of cabals, during the later disturbed years of the Queen's existence, had been gradually ripening into importance.

The Earl of Mar had openly espoused the High-church party in the case of Sacheverel; and he had on that account, as well as from the doubt generally entertained of his fidelity, little reason to expect from the House of Hanover a continuance in office. No sooner had the Queen expired, than those whom Lord Mar had long, in secret, been regarding with interest, expressed openly their disappointment at the result of the last reign.

"The accession of George the First, " remarks Dr. Coxe, "was a new era in the history of that Government which was established at the Revolution. Under William and Anne the Stuart family can scarcely be considered as absolutely excluded from the throne; for all parties, except the extreme Whigs, looked forward to the possibility of the Stuarts returning to the throne. But, in fact, the Revolution was not completed till the actual establishment of the Brunswick line, which cut off all hopes of a return without a new revolution. "[54]

When the news of Queen Anne's dangerous condition reached the Chevalier de St. George, he was at Luneville; but he repaired instantly to Barleduc, where he held a council. As he entered the council-chamber, he was heard to exclaim, "If that Princess dies, I am lost. "[55] There was no doubt that a correspondence with the exiled family had been carried on with great alacrity, during the last few years of Queen Anne's reign, with the cognizance of the Sovereign; [56] and that large sums were spent by Mary of Modena, and by her son, in procuring intelligence of all that was going on in the English Court.

Immediately after the Queen's death, Atterbury, Bishop of Rochester, proposed to Lord Bolingbroke to proclaim James at Charing Cross, and offered, himself, to head the procession in lawn sleeves. But Bolingbroke shrank from the enterprise; and, with an exclamation of passion, Atterbury exclaimed, —"There is the best cause in Europe lost for want of spirit. " The boldness of the proposition, and the ardent temper from which it originated, recall, with regret, the remembrance of one who, as Lord Hailes in his notes on Atterbury's Correspondence has remarked, was "incapable of dark conspiracies. "[57]

The Chevalier was then residing at Barleduc, with a suite of sixty persons; some of whom boasted of having taken part in the conspiracies against William the Third, and were proud of having compassed the death of that Sovereign. From time to time, Englishmen of distinction travelled from Paris to Barleduc, under pretext of seeing the country, but in fact to proffer a secret allegiance to the Prince. The individual to whom these attentions were addressed, is described by an anonymous emissary of the English Court, as leading a regular life, —hunting when the weather permitted, and hearing mass every day with great precision and devotion. "Il est fort maigre, " adds the same writer, "assez grand; son teint est brun, son humeur et sa personne ne sont pas désagréables. " In another place, it is added, "Il paroit manquer de jugement et de résolution: " an opinion, unhappily, too correct. [58] On the question being put by Bolingbroke to the Duke of Berwick, whether the Prince was a bigot, the answer was in the negative. "Then, " said Bolingbroke, "we shall have no objection to place him on the throne. " This anecdote, which was told by the Chevalier himself to Brigadier Nugent, probably gave countenance to the rumour spread in England, that James was likely to renounce the Catholic faith, and conform to the English Church. [59]

The Earl of Mar and his brother, Lord Grange, were now the two most considerable men in Scotland. Lord Grange had been made Lord of Session in 1707, and afterwards Lord Justice Clerk, during the three last years of Queen Anne's reign. His character presents traits even more repulsive and more dangerous than the time-serving and duplicity of the Earl of Mar. Lord Grange was one of those men whom the honest adherents to either party would, doubtless, gladly have turned over to the other side. His abilities, if we judge of the high appointments which he held, must have been eminent; but he was devoid of all principle, and was capable, if the melancholy and extraordinary history of his unhappy wife be true, of the darkest schemes.

It would be difficult to reconcile, in any other man, the discrepancy of Lord Grange's real opinions and of his subsequent efforts to restore the House of Stuart; but, in a brother of the Earl of Mar, the difficulty ceases, and all hopes of consistency, or rather of its origin, sincerity, vanish. Lord Grange is declared to have been a "true blue republican, and, if he had any religion, at bottom a Presbyterian; " yet he was deeply involved in transactions with the Chevalier and his friends. [60]

Lord Grange was united to a lady violent in temper, of a dauntless spirit, and a determined Hanoverian. Their marriage had been enforced by the laws of honour, and was ill-omened from the first; therefore, where respect has ceased, affection soon languishes and expires. The daughter of Cheisly of Dalry, a man of uncontrolled passions, who shot Sir George Lockhart, one of the Lords of Session, for having decided a law-suit against him, Mrs. Erskine of Grange, commonly called Lady Grange, inherited the determined will of her father. It was said that she had compelled Lord Grange to do her justice by marrying her, and "had desired him to remember, by way of threat, that she was Cheisly's daughter. " For this menace she suffered in a way which could only be effected in a country like Scotland at that period, and among a people held in the thraldom of the clans. Her singular history belongs to a later period in the annals of those events in which so much domestic happiness was blasted, never to be recovered. [61]

With his brother, Lord Mar was in constant correspondence, during his own residence in London; and although Lord Grange was skilful enough to conceal his machinations, and to retain his seat on the bench as a Scottish judge, there is very little reason to doubt his secret co-operation in the subsequent movements of the Earl.

Acting as if "he thought that all things were governed by fate or fortune, "[62] George the First remained a long time to settle his own affairs in Hanover, before coming to England. This delay was employed by the Earl of Mar, in an endeavour to extenuate the tenor of his political conduct of late years in the eyes of the Sovereign, and in placing before the King the merit of his services and his claims to favour. The letter which he addressed to George the First, when in Holland, was printed by Tonson, during the year 1715, with prefatory remarks by Sir Richard Steele, whose comments upon this production of a man who, scarcely a year after it was written, set up the standard of the Pretender at Braemar, are expressed in these terms:

"It gives me a lively sense of the hardships of civil war, wherein all the sacred and most intimate obligations between man and man are to be torn asunder, when I cannot, without pain, represent to myself the behaviour of Lord Mar, with whom I had not even the honour of any further commerce than the pleasure of passing some agreeable hours in his company: I say, when even such little incidents make it irksome to be in a state of war with those with whom we have lived in any degree of familiarity, how terrible must the image be of rending the ties of blood, the sanctity of affinity and intermarriage, and the bringing men who, perhaps in a few months before, were to each other the dearest of all mankind, to meet on terms of giving death to each other at the same time that they had rather embrace! " Thus premising, and declaring that he could with difficulty efface from his mind all remains of good will and pity to Lord Mar, Sir Richard Steele subjoins a document, fatal to the reputation of Lord Mar—the following letter, which Lord Mar addressed to the King, in explanation of his conduct.

LORD MAR TO THE KING.

"Sir,

"Having the happiness to be your Majesty's subject, and also the honour of being of your servants, as one of your Secretaries of State, I beg leave by this to kiss your Majesty's hand, and congratulate your happy accession to the Throne; which I should have done myself the honour of doing sooner, had I not hoped to have had the honour of doing it personally ere now. I am afraid I may have had the misfortune to be misrepresented to your Majesty, and my reason for thinking so is, because I was the only one of the late Queen's servants whom your Ministers here did not visit, which I mentioned to Mr. Harley and the Earl of Clarendon, when they went from hence to wait on your Majesty; and your Ministers carrying so to me was the occasion of my receiving such orders as deprived me of the honour and satisfaction of waiting on them and being known to them. I suppose I had been misrepresented to them by some here upon account of party, or to ingratiate themselves by aspersing others, as one party here too often occasion; but I hope your Majesty will be so just as not to give credit to such misrepresentations.

"The part I acted in bringing about and making of the Union when the succession to the Crown was settled for Scotland on your Majesty's family, when I had the honour to serve as Secretary of State for that kingdom, doth, I hope, put my sincerity and faithfulness to your Majesty out of dispute. My family had had the honour for a great tract of years to be faithful servants to the Crown, and have had the care of the King's children (when King of Scotland) entrusted to them. A predecessor of mine was honoured with the care of your Majesty's grandmother, when young; and she was pleased afterwards to express some concern for our family, in letters I now have under her own hand.

"I have had the honour to serve her late Majesty in one capacity or other ever since her accession to the Crown. I was happy in a good mistress, and she was pleased to have some confidence in me and regard for my services. And since your Majesty's happy accession to the Crown, I hope you will find that I have not been wanting in my duty in being instrumental in keeping things quiet and peaceable in the country to which I belong and have some interest in.

"Your Majesty shall ever find me as faithful and dutiful a subject and servant as ever any of my family have been to the Crown, or as I have been to my late mistress the Queen. And I beg your Majesty may be so good not to believe any misrepresentations of me, which nothing but party hatred and my zeal for the interest of the Crown doth occasion; and I hope I may presume to lay claim to your royal favour or protection. As your accession to the Crown hath been quiet and peaceable, may your Majesty's reign be long and prosperous; and that your people may soon have the happiness and satisfaction of your presence amongst them, is the earnest and fervent wish of him who is, with the humblest duty and respect, Sir, your Majesty's most faithful, most dutiful and most obedient subject and servant,

MAR. "

"Whitehall, August thirtieth, 1714, o. s."

This disgraceful letter was ineffectual. The Monarch, "whose views and affections were, according to Lord Chesterfield, singly confined to the narrow compass of his Electorate, " and for "whom England was too big, " acted with a promptness and decision which gave no time for the workings of faction. An immediate change of ministry was announced by Kryenberg, the Hanoverian resident, at the first Privy Council; and among other changes, Lord Townshend was appointed in the place of Lord Bolingbroke. Well might Bolingbroke exclaim, "The grief of my soul is this; I see plainly that the Tory party is gone. "[63]

For many months Lord Mar continued to maintain such a demeanour as might blind those of the opposite party to his real intentions. It seems, indeed, certain that at first he hoped to ensure a continuance in office by exerting his influence in Scotland to procure the good conduct of the clans: he was successful in obtaining even from some of those Highland chieftains who were afterwards the most deeply implicated in the Rebellion, an address declaring that they were "ready to concur with his Lordship in faithfully serving King George. " "Your Lordship, " states that memorial, "has an estate and interest in the Highlands, and is so well known to bear good will to your neighbours, that in order to prevent any ill impression which malicious and designing people may at this juncture labour to give of us, we must beg leave to address your Lordship, and entreat you to assure the Government, in our names, and in that of the rest of our clans, who, by distance of the place, could not be present at the signing of our letter, of our loyalty to his sacred Majesty, King George. "[64] This address was signed by Maclean of that Ilk, Macdonald of Glengary, Mackenzie of Fraserdale, Cameron of Lochiel, and by several other chiefs of clans, who afterwards fought under the banners of the Earl of Mar. It furnishes a proof of the great influence which the Earl possessed in his own country, but he had not the courage to present it to the King. His Majesty, on the contrary, on hearing of this address was highly offended, believing that it had been drawn up at St. Germains in order to insult him, and his refusal to receive it was accompanied by an order to Lord Mar to give up the seals.

The Earl lingered, nevertheless, for some time in London, where he had now some attractions which to a less ambitious mind might have operated in favour of prudence. In the preceding year, July, 1714, he had married, at Acton in Middlesex, the Lady Frances Pierrepoint, the second daughter of Evelyn, first Duke of Kingston, and the sister of Lady Mary Wortley. The Countess of Mar was, at the time of her marriage, thirty-three years of age, being born in

1681. She does not appear to have been endowed with the rare qualities of her sister's mind; but that she was attached to her husband, her long exile from England on his account, sufficiently proves. Her married life was embittered by his career, and her latter days darkened by the direst of all maladies, mental aberration.

It is singular that so recently before his final effort, Lord Mar should have connected himself with a Whig family. The Marquis of Dorchester, who was created, by George the First, Duke of Kingston, was a member of the Kit Cat Club, and received early proofs of the good will of the Hanoverian Sovereign. It is true that Lady Mary Wortley augured ill of the match between her sister and Lord Mar, detesting as she did the Jacobite party, and believing that her sister was "drawn in by the persuasion of an officious female friend, " Lord Mar's relation. But there is no reason to conclude that the Duke of Kingston in any way objected to a match apparently so dissonant with his political bias. [65]

Whilst Lord Mar remained near the court, the discoveries made by the Earl of Stair in France, communicated the first surmise of an intended invasion of England. Several seizures of suspected people warned one who was deep in the intrigues of St. Germain, not long to delay the open prosecution of his schemes. The melancholy instance of Mr. Harvey, who was apprehended while he was hawking at Combe, in Surrey, alarmed the Jacobite party. Mr. Harvey being shown a paper written in his own hand, convicting him of guilt, stabbed himself, but not fatally, with a pruning-knife which he had used in his garden. Upon some hope of his confessing being hinted, it was answered that his Majesty and the Council knew more of it than he did. The celebrated John Anstis, the heraldic writer, was also apprehended, and warrants were issued for the seizure of other suspected persons.

Notwithstanding his strong family interest, the Earl of Mar could scarcely consider himself secure under the present state both of the country and the metropolis. The events of the last year had succeeded each other with an appalling rapidity. The flight of Bolingbroke had scarcely ceased to be the theme of comment, before the general elections excited all the ill blood and fanaticism which such struggles at any critical era of our history have always produced. Riots, which have been hastily touched upon in the histories of the period, but which the minute descriptions of memoirs of that period show to have been attended with an unusual display of violence and brutality on both sides, broke out upon every anniversary which could recall the Stuarts to recollection. On St. George's day, in compliment to the Chevalier, who, according to an observer of those eventful days, "had assumed the name of that far-famed Cappadocian Knight, though every one knew he has nothing of the valour, courage, and other bright qualities of the saint, " a tumult was raised in London, and among other outrages, passengers through the streets of the City were beaten if they would not cry "God bless the late Queen and the High Church! " Sacheverel and Bolingbroke were pledged in bumpers by a mob, who burnt, at the same time, King William in effigy. [66] A similar contagion spread throughout the country; Oxford took the lead in acts of destruction; her streets were filled with parties of Whigs and Tories, both of them infuriated, until their mad rage vented itself in acts of murder, under the pretence, on the one hand, of a dread of popery, on the other, on a similar plea of religious zeal. A Presbyterian meetinghouse was pulled down, and cries of "An Ormond! " "A Bolingbroke! " "Down with the Roundheads! " "No Hanover! " "A new Restoration! " accompanied the conflagration. On the same day similar exclamations were again heard in the streets of London; and all windows not illuminated were broken to pieces. The tenth of June, the anniversary of the Chevalier's birthday, was the signal for a still more decisive manifestation. On that day three Scottish magistrates went boldly to the Cross at Dundee, and there drank the Pretender's health, by the name of King James the Eighth, for which they were immediately apprehended and tried.

The impeachment of Lord Oxford still further exasperated the country, which rang with the cry, "No George, but a Stuart. " The peaceable accession of the first monarch of the Brunswick line has been greatly insisted upon by historians; but that stillness was ominous; it was the stillness of the air before a storm; and was only indicative of irresolution, not of a diminished dislike to the sway of a foreigner.

It is supposed that an intercepted letter which the Duke de Berwick, the half-brother of the Chevalier, addressed to a person of distinction in England, first gave the intelligence of an intended invasion. [67] The burden of that letter was to encourage the riots and tumults, and to keep up the spirits of the people with a promise of prompt assistance. The impeachment of Viscount Bolingbroke and of the Duke of Ormond followed shortly afterwards; and although these noblemen provided for their own safety by flight, they were degraded as outlaws, and in the order in Council were styled, according to the usual form of law, "James Butler, yeoman, " and "Henry Bolingbroke, labourer, " and the arms of Ormond were taken from Windsor Chapel, and torn in pieces by the Earl Marshal.

The English fleet, under the command of Sir George Byng, was stationed in the Downs, in case of a surprise. Portsmouth was put in a state of defence; and, during the month of July, the inhabitants of London beheld once more a sight such as had never been witnessed by its citizens since the days of the Great Rebellion. In Hyde Park the troops of the household were encamped, according to the arrangements of General Cadogan, who had marked out a camp. The forces were commanded by the Duke of Argyle. In Westminster the Earl of Clare reviewed the militia, and the trained bands were directed to be in readiness for orders. At the same time fourteen colonels of the Guards, and other inferior officers were cashiered by the King's orders, on suspicion of being in James Stuart's interest; so deep a root had this cause, which many have pretended to treat as a visionary scheme of self-interest, taken in the affections even of the British army.

A proclamation ordering all Papists and reputed Papists to depart from the cities of London and Westminster, was the next act of the Government. All persons of the Roman Catholic persuasion were to be disarmed and their horses sold; a declaration against transubstantiation was to be administered to them, and the oath of abjuration to non-jurors. [68] After such mandates, it seems idle to talk of the tyranny of Henry the Eighth.

There is no doubt but that the greatest alarm and consternation reigned at St. James's. The stocks fell, but owing to the vigilance of the Ministry, information was obtained of the whole scheme of the invasion, in a manner which to this day has never been satisfactorily explained.

The Earl of Mar must have trembled, as he still lingered in the metropolis. It is probable that he waited there in order to receive those contributions from abroad which were necessary to carry on his plans. He was provided at last with no less a sum than a hundred thousand pounds; and also furnished with a commission dated the seventh of September, 1715 appointing him Lieutenant General and Commander in Chief of the forces raised for the Chevalier in Scotland. [69] Large sums were already collected from Switzerland,

Italy, Germany, and France, to the amount, it has been stated, of twelve millions. It has been well remarked by Sir Walter Scott, in his notes on the Master of Sinclair's MS., that "when the Stuarts had the means, they wanted a leader (as in 1715); when (as in 1745) they had a leader, they wanted the means. "

With the eye of suspicion fixed upon him, his plans matured, his friends in the north prepared, the Earl of Mar had the hardihood, under such circumstances, to appear at the court of King George. A few weeks before the Habeas Corpus Act had been suspended; but the Earl trusted either to good fortune, or to his own well-known arts of insinuation. He braved all possibility of detection, and determined to carry on the game of deep dissimulation to the last moment.

On the first of August, 1715, the Earl of Mar attended the levee of King George. One can easily suppose how cold, if not disdainful, must have been his reception; but it is not easy to divine with what secret emotions, the subject on the eve of an insurrection could have offered his obeisance to the Monarch. Grave in expression, with a heavy German countenance, hating all show, and husbanding his time, so as to avoid all needless conversation; without an idea of cultivating the fine arts, of encouraging literature, or of even learning to speak English, George the First must have presented to his English subjects the reverse of all that is attractive. A decided respectability of character might have redeemed the ungainly picture; but, although esteemed a man of honour, and evincing liberal and even benevolent tendencies, the Monarch displayed not only an unblushing and scandalous profligacy, but a love for coarse and unworthy society. His court is said to have been modelled upon that of Louis the Fifteenth; but it was modelled upon the grossest and lowest principles only, and had none of the elegance even of that wretched King's depraved circles; and public decency was as much outraged by the three yachts which were prepared to carry over King George's mistresses and their suite, [70] when he visited Hanover, as by the empire of Madame de Pompadour. It must, independent of every other consideration, have been galling to Englishmen to behold, seated on their throne, a German, fifty-four years of age, who from that very circumstance, was little likely ever to boast, like Queen Anne, "of an English heart. " "A hard fate, " observes a writer of great impartiality, "that the enthronement of a stranger should have been the only means to secure our liberties and laws! "[71]

A week after he had been received at the levee of King George, the Earl embarked at Gravesend in a collier, attended by two servants, and accompanied by General Hamilton and Captain Hay. They were all disguised, and escaping detection, arrived on the third day afterwards at Newcastle. It has been even said, that in order the better to conceal his rank, the Earl of Mar wrought for his passage. [72] From Newcastle Lord Mar proceeded northward in another vessel; and landing at Elie, in Fifeshire, went first to Crief, where he remained a few days. He then proceeded to Dupplin, in the county of Perth, the seat of his brother-in-law, the Earl of Kinnoul, and thence, on the eighteenth of August, crossing the river Perth, he proceeded to his own Castle of Kildrummie, in the Braes of Mar. He was accompanied by forty horse.

On the day after the arrival of the Earl at Kildrummie, he despatched letters to the principal Jacobites, inviting them to attend a grand hunting-match in Braemar on the twenty-seventh of August. This summons was couched in this form, for fear of a more explicit declaration being intercepted, revealing the design; but the great chiefs who were thus collected together were aware that "hunting" was but the watchword.

A gallant band of high-spirited chieftains answered the call. It is consolatory to turn to those who, unaffected by the intrigues of a Court, came heartily, and with a disinterested love, to the cause of which the Earl of Mar was the unworthy leader.

First in rank, was the Marquis of Huntly, eldest son of George, the first Duke of Gordon, and of that daring Duchess of Gordon, a daughter of the house of Howard, who, in 1711, had presented to the Dean and Faculty of Advocates in Edinburgh a silver medal, with the head of the Chevalier on one side, and on the other the British Islands, with the word "Reddite. " The learned body to whom the Duchess had proposed this dangerous gift, at first hesitated to receive it: after a debate, however, among their members, it was agreed that the donation should be accepted, and a vote was passed to return thanks to the Duchess. The Advocates then waited in a body upon the Duchess, and expressed their hopes that her Grace would soon have occasion to present the Faculty with a second medal on the *Restoration*. [73] The Duke of Gordon, notwithstanding his having been brought up a Roman Catholic, was neutral in the troubles of the Rebellion of 1715, but his son took a force of three thousand men into the field, —the clan siding with the young

Marquis rather than with their chief. The Marquis of Huntly was, probably for that reason, spared in the subsequent proceedings against the Jacobites, his participation in their schemes being punished only by a brief imprisonment.

William Marquis of Tullibardine, one of the most constant friends to the House of Stuart, the Earl of Nithisdale, and the Earl Marischal, also appeared at the time appointed. It was the fortune of the Marquis of Tullibardine, like that of the Marquis of Huntly, afterwards to appear in the field unsanctioned by his father, the Duke of Athol, who either was, or appeared to be, in favour of Government, whilst his son headed the clan to the number of six thousand. Lord Nairn, the younger brother of the Marquis, also joined in the undertaking. Of these distinguished Jacobites, separate lives will hereafter be given in this work: it therefore becomes unnecessary any further to expatiate upon them here. Of some, whose biography does not present features sufficiently marked to constitute a distinct narrative, some traits may here be given.

Charles Earl of Traquair, who hastened to Braemar, was one of those Scottish nobles who claimed kindred with royalty. He was descended from Sir James Stewart, commonly called the Black Knight of Lorn, and from Jane, daughter of John Earl of Somerset, and widow of King James the First. One of Lord Traquair's ancestors, the first Earl, had levied a regiment of horse, in order to release Charles the First from his imprisonment in the Isle of Wight; but, marching at the head of it at the battle of Preston, he and his son, Lord Seatoun, were taken prisoners and conveyed to Warwick Castle, where they languished four years in imprisonment, with the knowledge that their estates had been sequestered.

Connected with the family of Seatoun, on his mother's side, the Earl of Traquair had married the sister of Lord Nithisdale, being thus nearly related to two of those chiefs who gladly obeyed the summons of Lord Mar to the hunting-field. The Earl of Traquair appears to have escaped all the penalties which followed the Rebellion of 1715, perhaps because he does not appear to have taken any of his tenantry into the field.

Less prudent, or less fortunate, William Mackenzie, Earl of Seaforth, joined the standard of James Stuart with a body of three thousand men. He was attainted when the struggle was over, and his estates, both in Scotland and England, forfeited. He escaped to the

Continent; but, in 1719, again landed with the Spaniards at Kintail; and was wounded at the battle of Glenshiels, but being carried off by his followers, again fled to the Continent, with the Marquis of Tullibardine and the Earl Marischal. Lord Seaforth was one of those to whom the royal mercy was shown. George the First reversed his attainder, and George the Second granted him arrears of the feu duties due to the Crown out of the forfeited estates. The title has been eventually restored.

James Livingstone, Earl of Linlithgow, was amongst the many who experienced less clemency than the Earl of Traquair. He had been chosen one of the sixteen representative peers of Scotland, on the death of the Duke of Hamilton; and enjoyed the possession of considerable family estates, which were eventually forfeited to the Crown. He led a band of three hundred clansmen to the field.

Perhaps one of the most sturdy adherents of the Chevalier St. George was James Maule, fourth Earl of Panmure. In his youth this nobleman had served as a volunteer at the siege of Luxembourg, where he had signalized his courage. In 1686, he succeeded his brother, and added to the honours of a peerage those of a character already established for bravery. To these distinctions was added that of being a Privy Councillor to James the Second; but he was removed upon his opposing the abrogation of the penal laws against Popery. Whilst thus protesting against what might then be deemed objectionable innovations, Lord Panmure was a firm adherent of James, and vigorously supported his interests in the convention of estates in 1689.

The accession of William and Mary drove this true Jacobite from the Scottish Parliament. He never appeared in that assembly after that event, having refused to take the oaths. Of course he disapproved of the Union; and the next step which he took was to join the standard of the Chevalier.

After that decisive proceeding, the course of this unfortunate nobleman's life was one of misfortune, in which his high spirit was sustained by a constancy of no ordinary character. At the battle of Sherriff Muir, the brave Panmure was taken prisoner, but was rescued by his brother Harry, who, like himself, had engaged in the rebellion. Panmure escaped to France: he was attainted of high treason, —his estates, which amounted to 3456*l.* per annum, and were the largest of the confiscated properties, were forfeited, as well as his hereditary honours. Twice were offers made to him by the English Government to restore his rank and possessions, if he would take the oath of allegiance to the House of Hanover; but Panmure refused the proffered boon, and preferred sharing the fortunes of him whom he looked upon as his legitimate Prince. When he joined the Jacobites at Braemar, Lord Panmure was no longer a young, rash man: he was in the sixty-fifth year of his age. His wife, the daughter of William Duke of Hamilton, was, after his attainder, provided for by act of Parliament in the same manner as if she had been a widow. His brother, Harry Maule, of Kellie, a man of considerable accomplishments, was so fortunate as to be enabled to return to his native country, and died in Edinburgh in 1734. But Lord Panmure, like most of the other brave and honest men who preferred their allegiance to their interest, finished his days in exile, and died at Paris, in 1723. [74]

Kenneth Lord Duffus was another of those noblemen who had already established a character for personal bravery. He was a person of great skill in maritime affairs, and was promoted by Queen Anne to the command of the Advice ship of war, with which, in 1711, this gallant Highlander engaged eight French privateers, and after a desperate resistance of some hours, he was taken prisoner, after receiving five balls in his body.

He was, however, released in time to engage in the Rebellion of 1715; and though it does not appear that he took any followers to fight beneath the Chevalier's standard, he was included in the Act of Attainder. The intelligence was communicated to Lord Duffus when he was in Sweden. He resolved immediately to surrender himself to the British Government, and declared his intention to the British Minister at Stockholm, who notified it to Lord Townshend, Secretary of State. Notwithstanding this manly determination, Lord Duffus was arrested on his way to England, at Hamburgh, and was detained there until the time specified for surrendering had expired. He thence proceeded to London, where he was confined more than a year in the Tower, but released in 1717, without being brought to trial. Lord Duffus died, according to some accounts, in the Russian service; to others, in that of France. He married a Swedish lady, and attained to the rank of Admiral. [75]

Such were some of those Jacobite chieftains whose history has sunk into obscurity, partly from the difficulty of obtaining information concerning their career, after the contest was at an end. Amongst those who met Lord Mar in the hunting-field, but who afterwards became neutral, [76] although most of his clan joined in the Rebellion, was the Earl of Errol, one of a family whose fame for valour was dated from the time of the Danish invasion. The origin of the House of Errol is curious, and marks the simplicity of the times. An aged countryman, named Hay, and his sons, had arrested the progress of the ruthless conquerors in a defile near Lanearty in Perthshire. The old man was rewarded by Kenneth the Third with as much land in the Carse of Gowrie as a falcon from a man's hand flew over until she lighted. The bird flew over a space of six miles, which was thence called Errol, and which is still in possession of the family; and the old man and his sons were raised from the rank of plebeians by the assignment of a coat of arms, on which were three escutcheons, gules, to denote that the father and the two sons had been the shields of Scotland. The family grew in wealth and estimation, and the office of Hereditary High Constable of Scotland was added to their other honours.

The Countess of Errol, the mother of the High Constable, and sister of the Earl of Perth, had already taken a decided part in the affairs of the Jacobite party. When Colonel Hooke had been sent over in 1707 to Scotland, she had met him at the sea-coast, and had there placed in the hands of that emissary several letters from her son, expressing his earnest intention to support the cause of the Chevalier. The Earl of Errol had also received Hooke at his castle, and had entertained him there several days, and employed that time in initiating Hooke into the various characteristics and views of the Jacobite nobility in Scotland. He was thus deeply pledged to aid the undertaking at that time (the year 1707); and in a letter to the Chevalier, the Earl expressed his hopes that he might have the happiness of seeing his Majesty, "a happiness for which, " he adds, "we have long sighed, to be delivered from oppression. " The Countess of Errol also addressed a letter to the mother of James Stuart, as the Queen of England, declaring that the delays which the Scotch had suffered had not "diminished their zeal, although they had prolonged their miseries and misfortunes. "[77] Whether, upon the rising in 1715, the views of Lord Errol were altered, or that female influence had been lessened by some circumstance, does not exactly appear. He kept himself neutral in the subsequent outbreak, notwithstanding his appearance at Braemar, and although his clan were for the most part against the Government. [78] The Earl of Errol died, unmarried, in 1717: his adherence to his Jacobite principles were not, therefore, put to the test in 1745.

To these noblemen were united Seaton, Viscount of Kingston, whose estates were forfeited to the Crown; Livingstone Viscount of Kilsyth, one of the representative peers, who died an exile at Rome in 1733; Lord Balfour of Burleigh; Lord Ogilvy, afterwards Earl of Airly, and Forbes, Lord Pitsligo. This last-mentioned nobleman was a man of a grave and prudent character, whose example drew many of his neighbours to embark in an enterprise in which so discreet a person risked his honours and estate. He was the author of essays, moral and philosophical; and either from respect to his merits, or from some less worthy cause, his defection in 1715 passed with impunity. But, in 1745, the aged nobleman again appeared in the field, infirm as he was: and one of the most pleasing traits in Charles Edward's noble, yet faulty character was his walking at the head of his forces, having given up his carriage for the use of this tried adherent of his father. Attainder and forfeiture followed this last attempt, but the sentence was reversed by the Court of Session, from a misnomer in the attainder; and the venerable Lord Forbes, surviving many who had set out on the same course with him, had the comfort of breathing his last in his native country. He died at Auchiries in Aberdeenshire, in 1762. [79]

Several of these noblemen had been long contemplating the possibility of James's return to Scotland. Like the Earl of Errol, they had been dissatisfied with the prudence of the Duke of Hamilton, whose policy it had been to postpone the risk of a precarious undertaking, and whose foresight was acknowledged when it was too late. Lord John Drummond, Lord Kilsyth, and Lord Linlithgow, had been all deeply concerned in the schemes and speculations which had been formed in 1707, on the subject of the Restoration; but the zeal of Lord Kilsyth had been doubted, from his intimacy with the Duke of Hamilton, who was then objectionable to the violent Jacobite leaders. [80]

These chieftains were not unworthy to come into the same field with Tullibardine, Nithisdale, Marischal, and their brave associates. A still nobler band of associates was formed in the different members of the house of Drummond, a family who could boast of being derived from "the ancient nobility of the kingdom of Hungary: " and from the daughters of whose house Charles the Second was lineally descended in the ninth and sixth degree. Well may it be called "the splendid family of Drummond, " even if we regard only its proud antiquity, or the singular "faithfulness of the family, or the accomplishments and virtues which characterised many of its members. " Nothing can be finer than the manner in which the claims of birth are placed before us, in the address of William Drummond of Hawthornden to "John Earle of Perthe, " in his manuscript "Historie of the Familie of Perthe: "

"Though, as Glaucus sayes to Diomed (in Homer),

'Like the race of leaves
The race of man is, that deserves no question: nor receaves
His being any other breath; the wind in autumn strowes
The earth with old leaves; then the spring the woods with new
endowes,'

"yet I have ever thought the knowledge of kindred and genealogies of the ancient families of a country a matter so far from contempt, that it deserveth highest praise. Herein consisteth a part of the knowledge of a man's own selfe. It is a great spurr to vertue to look back on the worth of our line. In this is the memory of the dead preserved with the living, being more firm and honourable than any epitaph. The living know that band which tyeth them to others. By this man is distinguished from the reasonless creatures, and the noble of men from the base sort. For it often falleth out (though we cannot tell how) for the most part, that generositie followeth good birth and parentage. "[81] The two members of the Drummond family who attended Lord Mar in his famous hunting-field were James Earl of Perth, and William Drummond, Viscount Strathallan.

The Earls of Southesk and Carnwath, the Viscounts Kenmure and Stormont, and the Lord Rollo, complete the list of Scottish peers who were present on this memorable occasion. But perhaps the more remarkable feature of the hunting-match was the arrival of twenty-six gentlemen of influence in the Highlands, men of sway and importance, of which it is impossible, without a knowledge of Highland manners, to form an adequate notion. The constitution of the clans is thus pourtrayed by one who knew it well.

"In every narrow vale where a blue stream bent its narrow course, some hunter of superior prowess, or some herdsman whom wealth had led to wealth and power to power, was the founder of a little community who ever after looked up to the head of the family as their leader and their chief. Those chains of mountains which formed the boundings of their separate districts had then their ascents covered with forests, which were the scene of their hunting-excursions: when their eagerness in pursuit of game led them to penetrate into the districts claimed by the chief of the neighbouring valleys, a rash encounter was the usual consequence, which laid the foundation of future hostilities. "[82]

These petty wars gave room for a display of valour in the chiefs, and led to a mutual dependence from the followers. Alliances offensive and defensive were formed among the clans, and intermarriages were contracted between the confederated clans, who governed their followers by a kind of polity not ill regulated. The chief had the power of life and death over his large family, but it was a power seldom used. A chieftain might be cruel to his enemies, but never to his friends. Nor were those paternal rulers by any means so despotic as they have been represented to be; of all monarchs their power was the most limited, being allowed to take no step without permission of their friends, or the elders of their tribe, including the most distant branches of their family. The kind and conciliatory system adopted towards their clansmen accounts for the warm attachment and fidelity displayed towards their chiefs; and these sentiments were heightened to enthusiasm by the songs and traditions of the bards, in which the exploits of their heroes were perpetuated. Still there is nothing, as it has been justly said, so remarkable in the political history of any country, as the succession of the Highland chiefs, and the long and uninterrupted sway which they held over their followers. [83] The system of clanship gives all the romantic interest which the Rebellions of 1715 and 1745 inspire; —it perfects a picture which would only otherwise be a factious contention for power; it was annihilated only after the last of the Stuarts had fled for ever from the mountains of Scotland.

It was at the head of the clans that the Earl of Mar frequently placed himself, at the battle of Sherriff Muir: he now welcomed their chieftains to the field. Among these were General Hamilton, General Gordon, Glengary, Campbell of Glendarvel, and the lairds of Auchterhouse and Aldebar.

So great an assembly of those whom the Chevalier afterwards not inaptly termed "little kings, " was by no means unusual at that period. It was the custom among the lords and chieftains in the Highlands to invite their neighbours and vassals to a general rendezvous to chase the deer upon the mountains, and after the diversion was over, to entertain the persons of note in the castle hall.

This expedient would, therefore, have excited but little attention, had it not been for several years the practice of the Jacobites to hold these hunting-parties annually, in order to maintain the spirit of the association, which had been carried on since the peace of Utrecht.

The halls of Kildrummie received the noblemen and chieftains that day beneath its roof, and the Earl of Mar addressed his guests in a long, premeditated harangue. He is described as having little pretension to eloquence; but his hearers were probably not very fastidious judges, and from the influence which the Earl acquired over those whom he led on to the contest, it may be inferred that he understood well how to address himself to the passions of a Highland audience.

At first the Earl was heard with distrust, —at least if we may credit the account of one on whom, perhaps, too great a reliance has been placed. [84]

"It is true, that at first, " says Mr. Patten, "he gained little or no credit among them, they suspecting some piece of policy in him to ensnare them; but some were weak enough to suck in the poison, and particularly some of those who were with him at his house, called Brae-Mar. These, listening to him, embraced his project, and, as is reported, engaged by oath to stand by him and one another, and to bring over their friends and dependants to do the like. "[85]

The Earl began his harangue by expressing a deep regret for having promoted the Union, which had delivered his countrymen into the hands of the English, whose power to enslave them was far too great, and whose intentions to do so still further were manifest from the proceedings of the Elector of Hanover ever since he ascended the throne. That Prince regarded, according to Lord Mar, neither the welfare of his people, nor their religion, but solely left the management of affairs to a set of men who made encroachments in Church and State. Many persons, he said, were now resolved to consult their own safety, and determined to defend their liberties and properties, and to establish on the throne of these realms the Chevalier St. George, who had the only undoubted right to the Crown, who would hear their grievances, and redress their wrongs. He then incited his hearers to take arms for the Chevalier, under the title of King James the Seventh; and told them, that for his part, he was determined to set up his standard and to summon all the fencible men of his own tenants, and with them to hazard his life in the cause. To this declaration he added the assurance, that a general rising in England and assistance from France would aid their undertaking; that thousands were in league and covenant with him to establish the Chevalier and depose King George.

To these inducements were added others. Letters from the Chevalier were read to the assembly, promising to come over in person; with assurances that ships, arms, and ammunition would be dispatched to their aid. [86]

The proposals of Lord Mar were unfolded with such address, and his popularity was at that time so great, that one might have supposed an immediate assent to his schemes would have followed. On the contrary some degree of persuasion was required: the Highlanders are slow to promise, but sure to fulfil. The very chieftains who hung back from a too ready consent, never deserted the cause which they once undertook. The universal fidelity to the part which they espoused was violated in no instance during the first Rebellion.

At length the assembled chiefs swore an oath to stand by the Earl of Mar, and to bring their friends and dependants to do the same. However, no second meeting was at that time determined upon: every man went back to his own estate, to take measures for appearing in arms after again hearing from the Earl of Mar, who remained among his own people with few attendants. But the Jacobites were not idle during that interval. They employed themselves in collecting their servants and kindred, but with the utmost secrecy, until everything was ready to break out. Nor were they long kept in suspense. On the third of September, another meeting at Abbone, in Aberdeenshire, was held, and there the Earl directed his adherents to collect their men without loss of time. He returned to Braemar, and continued for several days gathering the people together, until they amounted, according to Reay, to two thousand horse; although some have said that there were only sixty followers at that time assembled. [87]

On the sixth of September, the standard of the Pretender was set up at Braemar, by the Earl of Mar, in the presence of the assembled forces. The superstitious Highlanders remarked with dismay, that, as the standard was erected, the ball on the top of it fell off; and they regarded this accident as an ill omen. "The event, " says a quaint Scottish writer, "has proven that it was no less. "[88]

This grave accordance in the verification of the omen, was a feature of the times and country. "When a clan went upon any expedition, " observes Dr. Brown in his valuable work upon the Highlands, "they were much addicted to omens. If they met an armed man they believed that good was portended. If they observed a deer, fox, hare, or any four-footed beast of game, and did not succeed in killing it, they prognosticated evil. If a woman, barefooted, crossed the road before them, they seized her, and drew blood from her forehead. " This mixture of fear of visionary evils, and courage in opposing real ones, of credulity and distrust, strength and weakness, presents a singular view of the Highland character. It had, however, in many respects, no inconsiderable influence upon the contests of 1715 and 1745.

From Braemar the Earl proceeded to Kirk Michael, a small town, where he proclaimed the Chevalier, and set up his standard. He then marched to Moulin in Perthshire, where he rested some time, collecting his forces.

It is a remarkable fact, that up to this period the Earl of Mar was acting without a commission from the Chevalier. The disposition which is too predominant in society, and which leads men always to add the bitterness of invective to the mortification of failure, has attributed to the Earl of Mar, relatively to this commission, a line of conduct from which it is agreeable to be able to clear his memory. It was not very long after the meeting in Braemar, that Lord Mar discovered that there was what he called "a devil" in his camp, in the person of the Master of Sinclair, whose manuscript strictures upon the unfortunate and incompetent leader of the Jacobites have contributed to blacken his memory.

According to the Master of Sinclair, the Earl of Mar produced at the meeting a forged commission; but this statement is not only contradicted by Lord Mar's own account, but completely invalidated by the fact that the commission is in existence, among various other curious documents and letters, many of which place the character of Lord Mar in a much fairer light than that in which it has hitherto been viewed. The Earl of Mar, in a justification of his conduct, printed at Paris, and added to Patten's History of the Rebellion, gives the following account of the affair:

"It was near a month after the Earl of Mar[89] set up the Standard before he could produce a commission, and it is no small proof of the people's zeal for their country that so great a number followed his advice and obeyed his orders before he could produce one. It must, though, be owned, and it is the less to be wondered at, that his authority being thus precarious, some were not so punctual in joining him, and others performed not so effectually the service they were sent upon, which, had they done, not only Scotland, but even part of England, had been reduced to the Chevalier's obedience, before the Government had been in a condition to make head against us. "[90]

The commission was, however, at that time written, although it had not been sent over to Scotland. It is dated the seventh of September, 1715, and is superscribed James R. [91] The Earl of Mar was doubtless aware that such an instrument was in preparation.

When the Earl had first arrived in Scotland, he found, as he himself alleges, the people far more eager to take arms than his instructions allowed him to permit; but before actual steps were commenced, that ardour was cooled by two circumstances: first, by the Chevalier's not landing in England, as the Jacobites had confidently hoped; and, secondly, by the Duke of Berwick's not coming to Scotland. [92] The vigorous measures adopted by Government made, therefore, a far greater impression on the public mind than could have been expected had the Earl of Mar been boldly seconded by him who was most of all interested in the event of the contest. The Lord Advocate summoned all the principal Jacobites to appear at Edinburgh within specified periods, in order to give bail to Government for their allegiance. "Many, " says Lord Mar, "seemed inclined to comply. " Yet the number of those who did comply with the summons was inconsiderable; the rest, including the most honoured names in Scotland, rushed into the insurrection. The different heads of noble houses dispersed, and each in the district in which he had most power, and in the principal towns proclaimed the Chevalier King. The Fiery Cross was sent throughout the country, with blood at one end, and fire at the other; and it was afterwards asserted by some of the rebels who were tried at Liverpool, that they were forced into the service of the Chevalier, the person who bore that cross assuring them that, unless they hastened to Mar's camp, they were to perish by blood and fire. [93]

Intelligence of the death of Louis the Fourteenth, which had happened during the preceding August, reached Scotland at this time, and cast an universal gloom over his party. It was even disputed whether the Jacobite leaders should not disperse until news of the Chevalier's landing should reassure them, or the certainty of a rising in England should give vigour to their proceedings. At this critical moment Lord Mar published a declaration which has been printed in most of the histories of the period, exhorting all those who were well-affected to the good cause to put themselves under arms, and summoning his confederates to the Tower of Braemar, on the eleventh of September, promising them, in the name of the King, their pay from the moment of setting out.

"Now is the time, " said the Earl, "for all good men to show their zeal for his Majesty's service, whose cause is so deeply concerned, and the relief of our native country from oppression and a foreign yoke too heavy for us and our posterity to bear.

"In so honourable, good, and just a cause, " he added, "we cannot doubt of the assistance, direction, and blessing of Almighty God, who has so often rescued the royal family of Stuart, and our country from sinking under oppression.

"Your punctual observance of these orders is expected, for the doing of all which, this shall be to you, and all you employ in the execution of them, a sufficient warrant. "

In a very different tone was a letter, written the same night by the Earl to his baillie of Kildrummie: from this epistle, so characteristic of the politic Earl of Mar, it was manifest that his own followers were more tardy in the field than those of the other chieftains of the Highlands. The means taken to intimidate and compel them are strongly characteristic of the state of society in Scotland at that period. [94] The reluctance of his clan must have been a subject of deep mortification to Lord Mar, when, in one evening, the summons of the Fiery Cross, paraded round Loch Tay, a distance of thirty-two miles, could assemble five hundred men, at the bidding of the Laird of Glenlyon, to join the Earl of Mar. [95]

A few days after the assembling of the forces, the Earl of Mar, assisted by his Jacobite friends, published a manifesto, asserting the right of James the Eighth, by the grace of God, King of Scotland, &c., and pointing to the relief of the kingdom from oppression and grievances. [96]

Whilst the adherents of James were thus assembling in the North, a brave but unsuccessful attempt was made to surprise the castle of Edinburgh. Ninety chosen men, under the command of Lord Drummond, were engaged in this undertaking, of which the design was, to seize the citadel and to place it under the command of Lord Drummond; then the artillery within the castle was to be employed in firing their rounds by way of signal to different posts, in concert. Fires were to be lighted up on the hills as a signal to Lord Mar to march and take possession of the city. The failure of this design was owing to the disclosure of one Dr. Arthur, a physician in Edinburgh, to his wife, who gave information of the whole plan to the Lord Justice Clerk, to whom she sent an unsigned letter the evening she had gained from her unwilling husband intelligence of the scheme. This failure, the first of those adverse events which disheartened the spirits of the Jacobites, was, however, less deplored than it would have been, had not the progress of the Earl of Mar's exertions borne the most flattering aspect. In September, the Earl marched to Logaret, where his forces still increased, and thence into the beautiful region around Dunkeld; here he was joined, with fourteen hundred men, by the Marquis of Tullibardine, and by five hundred Campbells from the Breadalbane territory, headed, not by their chief, but by Campbell of Glenderule, Campbell of Glenlyon, and John Campbell, the Earl's chamberlain. Enforced also by the addition of two hundred Highlanders from different quarters, the Earl of Mar resolved to make the town of Perth his head-quarters.

This was a wise resolution: the situation of that fine city presented the most important advantages to the General of the Jacobite forces. Seated on the river Tay, and near the sea-coast, it gave the Earl the control of the East Lowlands, of the rich counties of Angus, the Carse of Gowrie, Mearns, Murray, Aberdeen, and Banff, and also of the Shire of Fife. It also cut off the communication between the north and the south of Scotland, so that the friends of Government could neither act nor fly from the enemy. Thus all the usual posts were stopped. The revenues of the public fell into the hands of the insurgents who gave receipts for them in the name of James the Eighth, and the landowners in the counties subject to the Earl were taxed at whatever rate he chose to impose. Perth continued to be the head-quarters of the Lieutenant General until a few days before this disastrous contest was finally closed.

At the first general review at Perth, the forces of Lord Mar amounted only to five thousand men; but a few weeks afterwards, by the accession of his friends in the north, they were increased to the number of twelve thousand, both horse and foot, of well appointed men. That Lord Mar's hopes were high, and, at this period, not without reason of, at any rate, a partial success, the following letter addressed by him to Captain Henry Straiton, [97] at Edinburgh, is a proof. It relates, in the first instance, to the insurrection in Northumberland, under the guidance of Mr. Forster, a gentleman of suspected zeal and little discretion, to whom Lord Mar unwisely trusted the conduct of the gallant but ill-fated bands who fell at Preston: —

"From the Camp of Perth, October 12th, 1715. "[98]

"Sir,

"It was yesterday afternoon as I got yours of the ninth, which you may be sure was very acceptable, and also the others you sent me. Tom Forster tells me in his of the sixth, that they had taken the field that day with a hundred and sixty horse; that he had sent to the gentelmen of Lancaster who he expected to join him, and also the gentilmen from the scots side, that he expected two thousand foot from my camp and five hundred horse, that the town of Newcastle had promist to open their gates to them, and that they intended to take possession of Tinmouth.

"They have been better than their word in coming together so soon, and I would fain hope it has been occasioned by some consort with our friends further south, who are to join them, and that the Duke of Ormond is in England before this time, as I have reason to believe he is.

"My letters by Mr. E——ne[99] had not then reached those on the boarder, but when they do, I hope it will put the project of shooting themselves up in Tinmouth out of their thoughts; what good could they do there? I have wrote so fully by Mr. E——ne upon the subject of the way of their disposeing of themselves, that I need say little of it now. You certainly know of the detachment of two thousand foot, lying these severall dayes on the coast of Fife, to get over, if possible; but now that there's five men of warr in the Firth, I'm afraid it is not; however, they are stile about it, and will do what they can: but for finding horse that way, you will easily see is impracticable, unless the passage were open, and I hope our friends on the boarder will not want horse from us. I was very fond of the project of getting the passage of the whole armie opened, when I wrote by Mr. E——ne; but since that time, beside that of more men of warr comeing into the Firth, there's another thing I know since, which makes me alter my thoughts about it, at least of doing it soon, were it in my power. Mr. Ogilvie of Boin arrived here from France on the sixth, as perhaps you have heard, with my new commission, of which I send you a copie inclosed, and letters from Lord Bolingbroke; but I know you have accounts of a latter date at Edinb. so I need say the less of them. Lord Bolingbroke tels me, that in all probability, the King wou'd land very quickly in the north of Scotland; so until we be so happie that he comes to us, or at least we hear from him again, which by those letters I expect every day, I judge it were not prudent for me to pass the armie at Leith or Queensferry, were it in my power, for that wou'd be leaveing the enimie bewint the King and us, and he might have difficulty in passing over to us, and being in danger of the enimie; but this of passing the whole armie at any of these places seems not likely to be in our power.

"Lord Huntly and Earl Marishall are come up to us with their people in very good order, but Lord Seafort is not, being deteaned by forceing Earl Sutherland to submitt before he left that country, which he has done by this time, and will be with us soon. I make his not being come up the reason of our lying still here, but that of our expecting the King or one from him, is the true one; and I think we must do, until that happen, so as long as we loose no credit by it. I thought it was necessary to let you know this, the better to advise our friends in the South what meassurs to take; which they had best determine by the success of our detachment getting over to them, — what expectation they have of friends in England joining them, and what is to be expexted about Edinburgh. If they should be prest in England, which I hope will not be the case, and could do nothing at Edinbrugh, they can march throw the south and west of Scotland to Dumbartonshire, where before they can be, Generall Gordon's armie or a considerable detachment of it, will be before they can reach it, which they will aply join and be saif til we meet them. Glengarry is actually marcht from Auchalator that way alreddy. I have taken care to have detachments at all the places on the coasts, where I judge the King can land, so I hope all is safe for him when he comes on it; and so many of the cruisers being in the Frith make the coast pretty clear, which is one good our detachment in Fife has done, should they do no more. We have this day sent two gentelmen to France (I hope) a safe way with a letter to the Regent from the noblemen and gentelmen here, which we had resolved on before Boin arrived; but should the King be come off before it arrives in France it can do no hurt and may do good.

"I have wrote to Lord Bolingbroke (who is to remain in France to negotiate the King's affairs there during his absence,) a full account of things here; and if the King be come off, which I hope in God he is, he is to lay it before the Queen, to whom I have likewise wrote. I'm exceeding sorry for the loss of honest Keith's son, but these gentelmen will have it yet payd home to them.

"As to your going to the South, or staying at Edinbrugh, I scarce know what to say. I wish you could be in both places; but since that cannot be, I leave it to yourself to do which you think will be of most use to the service. If you go South I beg you may settle a correspondence 'twixt Edin[b] and this, and acquaint me with it.

"I heard to-day that my letters to our friends in the West, desireing they might go immediately South to join Lord Kenmore, came safe to hand, so I hope they will be with him soon. I have sent you some of the manifestos which were printed at Aberdeen, and are finely done: I wish they may come to you saif. I also send you encloset a letter to Sir Rich. Steele, which I leave open for you to read and take a copie of. Pray seal it and get it put into the post-house; and I wish you could get it printed at Edinburgh, tho' let me not seen it; and if you send a copie to any of your correspondants at London and Newcastle, to get if printed there it would do no hurt. I'm endeavouring to get a correspondence settled by barks from the point of Fife to Newcastle, which may be of use to us, especially if the communications twixt us and Edr should be stopt. "

On the very day of the Earl's arrival at Perth, Mr. James Murray, second son of Lord Stormont arrived from St. Germains, bringing assurances of support, and letters from the Chevalier, who had appointed him Secretary of State for the affairs of Scotland. Mr. Murray is said also to have presented the Earl of Mar with a patent, creating him Duke of Mar, Marquis of Stirling and Earl of Alloway: "And though, " observes an historian, "there was little more said about it, yet the relation seems justified by this, that in some of the papers printed at Perth, he is styled the Duke of Mar. "[100]

Extensive preparations were also declared to be in progress for the invasion of England. Twelve large ships were actually at that time at anchor in Havre, St. Malos, and other places. These vessels, with several frigates of good force, were loaded with ammunition, and manned with generals, officers, and soldiers. A particular account of the "Pretender's Magazine" is extant. But these preparations were all frustrated by the remonstrances of the Earl of Stair at the Court of the Regent of France. Admiral Byng was sent with a squadron to cruise on the coast of France, and the ships ready to sail for the enterprise against England were obliged, by command of the Regent, in order not to implicate the French Government, to declare that they were thus employed without the sanction or knowledge of the Regent. Thus, even whilst Mr. Murray was raising the sanguine hopes of the Jacobites to the highest pitch, their evil star had again prevailed. They were, indeed, singularly unhappy in those in whom they placed confidence. Their schemes perpetually got wind: whether it were owing to the irresolution of some of their partisans, or to the great participation which the female sex took in the affairs of the Chevalier's party, it is difficult to determine.

The Jacobite ladies were as fearless as they were persevering. The Duchess of Gordon, whose present of a medal to the Faculty of Advocates denoted her principles, and whose son, the second Duke of Gordon suffered a brief imprisonment on account of his share in the insurrection, was one of the most approved channels of communication between the two parties. She generally resided in Edinburgh, where she occupied herself as a mediator between some of the Presbyterians and the friends of James. Colonel Hooke mentions her as one of the depositories of all that was going on during his mission.

The Earl of Mar, in his letters, refers repeatedly to different ladies with approval of their zeal and courage, and mentions one of his fair confederates in the north of Scotland, through whose hands many of his letters were sent to different chieftains; but these channels may not, in all cases, have been so secure as the Earl conceived. [101]

The proceedings of the English Government were, meantime, marked with energy and judgment. The various movements of the insurgent party were met in every direction by a systematic resistance, the details of which have been minutely detailed by historians, and belong not to a narrative which is chiefly of a personal nature.

On the fourteenth of September, the Duke of Argyle, Commander in Chief of his Majesty's Forces in Scotland, and General of the army, arrived in Edinburgh. The interest of this able and powerful nobleman in the Western Highlands, his zeal for the Protestant succession, were sufficient reasons for his appointment to this important office. The following original letter from George the Second, then Prince of Wales, gives an insight into the views which were entertained by George the First upon the mode of conducting the warfare in Scotland. It is among various other papers in the Mar Correspondence.

"St. James's, 7th October, 1715. "

"I have learned, my dear Duke, by your two last expresses, the embaras you are in through the want of regular troupes. We have used such efforts that the King has consented last Wednesday to detach to you four batallions from Ireland, to reinforce your camp. Orders have been given to cause those marche who are nearest, and to cause them embarque as they come up, without waiting for their conjunction. It appeares yet by the departure of the Duke of Ormond, from Paris, that the malcontents continue in their wicked design of raiseing up troubles in this kingdom here, which is the cause that hinders me from sending you Campbell yet, untill that I see if he will not be necessary for his post, where I think that it is best every body should be fixed. As soon as all appearance of Rebellion is ended here, I shall dispatch you him, if you shall have need of him there. With respect to the orders you demand, it would be very difficult to give you them positive, not knowing the situation of your affairs, as you may judge yourself. The King remits himself entirely to your judgment, and to your conduct. All that I can say to you is not to hazard an action without a probable appearance of carrying it, —rather to shune an engadgment, and to yeild to them the ground, than to expose the affairs of the King to such ill consequences as would follow from a defeat. In case that my Lord Mar march into England before that you receive your reinforcement, I think you would do very well to allow him at least with your cavalery, and to harass him untill that we march to meet him. This last reasoneing is my own properly, but which you will judge yourself, if practicable or not. Farewell, my dear Duke; be assured of my esteem, and my sincere friendship. "

(Signed) "GEORGE P. "

The Earl of Mar now began to fortify Perth, and brought up fourteen pieces of cannon for that purpose from Dundee and Dunotter Castle.

His time and thoughts were at this time occupied in concerting and encouraging the movements of the southern insurrection conducted by Viscount Kenmure. There can be no better means of showing the state of the Earl's hopes and feelings at this time, than by giving them in his own words.

TO VISCOUNT KENMURE.

"My Lord,

"I wish your Lordship and Mr. Forster may have gott my letters, which I took all the care I could to send safe. I wrote last by a lady on the twenty-third, and she is so discreet and dextrous, that I make little doubt of its going right. I have since had two from an indisposed friend of ours on your side the water, and with them one of the twenty-second from Brigadier Mackintosh to him, where he tells of his being joined by your Lordship and five hundred horse with you, —Lords Withrington and Derwentwater, Mr. Forester, and about six hundred English gentlemen. Your Lordship may be sure this was very agreeable news to me, and now, with the blessing of God, if we do not mismanage, I think our game can scarce fail. By Brigadier Mackintosh's letter, it seems the English are all for your going to England in a body to put into execution a certain design, and our countrymen are for first having the Pass of Stirling opened, and our armies joined. I apprehended there would be difference about this before I saw that letter, as your Lordship would easily see by what the lady carried. It is indeed a difficult point to know or advise which of the two is the best for the King's affairs; and we on this side Forth being so ignorant of your situation on the other side, and also of the condition of England, that I could not take it upon me to determine in it, or to give any positive orders what your Lordship should do; but after stating the advantages of both, and what might happen according as the enemy should act, I left it to be advised and determined among yourselves on that side, who could not but know a great deal more, as you should judge it best for the King's interest in generall.

"I know our indisposed friend, for whose judgment I have a very great regard, advised coming to Dalkeith, and we have a report from Fife last night that you have done so.

"I long impatiently to know what resolution your Lordship and the noblemen and gentlemen with you have come to. It is of great consequence and deserves to be well weighed. If you are now come to Dalkeith, I will adventure to tell my thoughts in it, which I was not quite so clear in before when you were at a greater distance from it. That place was a far way from the other, where I judge the secret design was to be put in execution; and I am afraid before you can get there they'll have so strengthened the place, and filled it with troops, that the design would prove impracticable with the small army you have, —and it might prove, too, (especially if the Dutch troops come to England,) that you could not penetrate farther into that country with safety, and retiring back into Scotland would have many inconveniences.

"Dalkeith is but a short way from Stirling, where we on this side must pass (I mean near it), and I hope we shall attempt it very soon; and when we do, your being in the rear of the enemy could not but very much incommode them, and be of great advantage to us. The Duke of Argyle would be so hemmed in at Stirling by your being on the one hand of him and our being on the other, that I scarce see what I can do but to intrench myself, and by that our passage over Forth and joining of you might be very easy; nor do I see how the Duke of Argyle in those circumstances can subsist long there. Were we once past Forth and joined on the south side, we should soon make our way good to England, and then should be much more able to put in execution the project of our English friends, without being in any danger of returning back to Scotland. It would be of great consequence to have possession of Edinburgh, but I hear just now that the Duke of Argyle has sent two regiments of dragoons, so tho' perhaps that may prevent your getting possession of that town, yet I scarce believe that they will be able with all the detachments that the Duke of Argyle dare adventure to send from Stirling to make any attempt against you at Dalkeith, which is so strong a place naturally; and should the enemy return again from Stirling, you might either follow them in their rear without danger, or take possession of Edinburgh. Were once Lord Seaforth come up to us and General Gordon with the clans which I expect every day, I shall not be long of leaving this place, and I shall likewise be able to send more foot over the water, as I sent the last, if you want them, and your being at Dalkeith, they could easily join you. Should most of the Dutch troops come to Scotland, as is probable they will, it would be very hard for us here to pass Forth without your assistance, which would be a great loss and a grateing thing. I hear to-day from about Stirling that Sir William Blacish is upon the head of several thousands in the North of England, but your Lordship and our English friends will know the truth of this better: be it as it will, I do not think it alters the case much. The main and principal thing is for us to get soon joined all in one body, then I am sure we should be more considerable than all the force the Government, with the six thousand Dutch, can bring against us, and when once the British troops see so considerable a force together, asserting their King's and their country's cause, I cannot believe they will, but rather join us, and restore their country to peace and liberty.

"These, my Lord, are my humble thoughts, but they are with submission to your Lordship's and the King's friends with you who are equally concerned with us, and I know equally zealous, and you all certainly know a great deal more than me here.

"I beg your Lordship may make my compliments to our countrymen, with you, and to those noblemen and gentlemen of England who have so handsomely and generously joined you. I long impatiently to be with you, and with all the haste I can.

"I send copies of this three different ways, that one or other of them may certainly come to your hands.

"I also send by one of them, if not two, a power for your Lordship to raise money for the use of your armie, which my commission for the King fully empowers me to do and give.

"I wish this may come to your hand, and I long to hear from your Lordship, which it being necessary I should soon, I am, with all respect, my Lord, your Lordship's most obedient humble servant,

"MAR. "[102]

It was the intention of Lord Mar to remain at Perth until all the Jacobite clans should have joined his army; but having gained the intelligence that some arms for the use of the Earl of Sutherland were put on board a vessel at Leith, to be taken northwards, he determined to take possession of them. The master of the vessel had dropped anchor at Brunt Island, for the purpose of seeing his wife, who was there: Lord Mar sent a detachment to surprise the harbour, which succeeded in carrying off the spoil, back to Perth. A report was at the same time raised in Stirling: that the Earl was marching to Alloa, the Duke of Argyle forthwith ordered out the picquets of horse and foot, and, also, all the troops to be ready to march out to sustain them, if required. But the Jacobite army did not appear; and the report of their advance to Stirling was believed to be a false alarm, contrived by Mar in order to draw off the attention of the Duke of Argyle from the expedition to Brunt Island.

The insurgents were now masters of the eastern coasts of Scotland from Brunt Island to the Murray Frith, an extent of above one hundred and sixty miles along the shore. On the western side, the Isle of Skye, Lewis, and all the Hebrides were their own, besides the estates of the Earl of Seaforth, Donald Mac Donald, and others of the clans. So that from the mouth of the river Lochie to Faro-Head, all the coast of Lochaber and Ross, even to the north-west point of Scotland, was theirs: theirs, in short, was all the kingdom of Scotland north of the Forth, except the remote counties of Caithness, Strathnaver and Sutherland beyond Inverness, and that part of Argyleshire which runs north-west into Lorn, and up to Lochaber, where Fort William continued in possession of the Government.

The Earl of Mar had resolved to impose an assessment upon the large extent of country under his sway, to raise money for the use of his army. It was of course an unpopular, though doubtless a necessary measure. The sum of twenty shillings sterling was to be paid by each landholder upon every hundred pounds Scots of valued rent; and, if not paid by a certain day, the tax was to be doubled. In levying this assessment, the friends of the Government were far more severely treated than those of the Chevalier; and the Presbyterian Ministers, who had dared to raise their voices in their churches against the Pretender, as they called the Chevalier, were commanded to be silent on that subject; their houses were plundered, and many of them were driven by tyranny from their homes. [103]

The northern clans were now on their march to join the camp at Perth. First came the famous Laird of Mackintosh, better known as Brigadier Mackintosh, chief of that numerous clan in Invernesshire. His regiment, composed of five hundred men, whom he had persuaded to join in the insurrection, was considered the best that the Earl of Mar could boast. The Marquis of Huntley, with five hundred horse and two thousand foot, next arrived; and the Earl Marischal shortly afterwards brought a thousand men to the camp. But Lord Seaforth, afraid lest in his absence the Earl of Sutherland should invade his country, was still absent; and the anxiety of the Earl of Mar for his arrival is expressed in more than one of his letters.

The whole strength of the army amounted to sixteen thousand seven hundred men; this number was afterwards diminished by the detachment sent southwards by the Earl, and by the number of three thousand who were dispersed in garrisons. But it was no common force that was now encamped at Perth.

At this critical moment where was the individual for whom these great and gallant spirits had ventured their all, the hills so dear to them, their homes, the welfare of their families, to say nothing of that which Highlanders least consider, their personal safety? At this moment, the ill-advised and irresolute James Stuart, was absent. What could have been his counsels? who were his advisers? of what materials was he made? why did he ever come? are questions to which the indignant mind can scarcely frame a reply. The fact, indeed, seems to be that his heart was never really in the undertaking; that he for whom the tragedy was performed, was the only actor in it who did not feel his part; it was reserved for a nobler and a warmer nature to experience the ardour of hope, and the bitter mortifications of disappointment.

It was not until the middle of October that the Earl of Mar took any personal share in the contest between the Jacobite army and that of the Government. Hitherto he had remained at Perth, acting with an ill-timed caution, and apparently bestowing far more attention upon the ill-fated insurrection in Northumberland, aided by the low country Scots under Lord Kenmure, than upon the proximate dangers of his own army. The detachment of a body of troops under Brigadier Mackintosh, sent in order to assist the Lowlanders, who were marching back into Scotland, accompanied by the forces under Mr. Forster and the Earl of Derwentwater, was the immediate cause of the two armies coming to an engagement. The Earl of Mar in his narrative thus explains his plans and their failure.

The detachment under Brigadier Mackintosh having been sent, "occasioned, " Lord Mar says, "the Duke of Argyle's leaving Stirling, and going with a part of his army to Edinburgh. Now, had the Scots and English horse, who were then in the south of Scotland, come and joined the fifteen hundred foot, (under Brigadier Mackintosh) as was expected; had the Highland clans performed, as they promised, the service they were sent upon in Argyleshire, and marched towards Glasgow, as the Earl of Mar marched towards Sterling, he had then given a good account of the Government's army, the troops from Ireland not having yet joined them, nor could they have joined them afterwards. But all this failing by some cross accidents, Lord Argyle returned with that part of his army to Scotland, and the Earl of Mar could not then, with the men he then had, advance further than Dumblane, and for want of provisions there, was soon after obliged to return to Perth. "

"But immediately after that we had got provisions, and that the clans and Lord Seaforth had joined us, we marched again towards the enemy; and notwithstanding the many difficulties the Earl of Mar had upon that occasion with some of our own people, he gave the enemy battle: and, as you saw in our printed account of it, had not our left wing given way, which was occasioned by mistake of orders and scarcity of experienced officers, that being composed of as good men, and marched as cheerfully up to the field of battle as the other, our victory had been complete. And as it was, the enemy, who was advanced on this side the river, was forced to retire back to Sterling."[104]

Such is the Earl of Mar's comment upon the battle of Sherriff Muir, of which the friends of Government gave a very different representation.

The Earl had, it is evident, no disposition to risk a general engagement before the Chevalier arrived in Scotland. He had sent two gentlemen to the Prince to learn his determination, and had resolved to remain at Perth until their return. During his continuance in that city he employed himself not only in throwing up entrenchments round the town, but in publishing addresses to the people, to keep up the spirits of the Jacobites. Since the Earl was never scrupulous as to the means of which he availed himself, we may not venture to reject the declaration of an historian of no good will to the cause, that he ordered "false news" to be printed and circulated; and published that which he hoped would happen, as having already taken place. "The detachment, " he related, "had passed the Forth, had been joined by the army in the South, were masters of Newcastle, and carried all before them; and their friends in and about London had taken arms in such numbers, that King George had made a shift to retire. " These falsehoods were printed by Freebairn, formerly the King's printer at Edinburgh, whom the Earl had established at Perth, and provided with the implements brought by the army from Aberdeen. [105]
In the beginning of November, the Earl of Seaforth arrived at Perth, and the Mac Invans, the Maccraws, the Chisholmes of Strath-Glass,

and others, completed all the forces that Lord Mar expected to join him. Truly might the Earl say, "that no nation in such circumstances, and so destitute of all kind of succour from abroad, ever made so brave a struggle for restoring their prince and country to their just rights. "[106] But the usual fate of the Stuarts involved their devoted adherents in ruin: or rather, let us not call that fate, which may be better described by the word incapacity in the leaders of their cause.

The want of ammunition, which was to have been supplied from abroad, was now severely felt. "I must here add one thing, " says Lord Mar, "which, however incredible the thing may appear, is, to our cost, but too true: and that is, that from the time the Earl of Mar set up the Chevalier's standard to this day, we never received from abroad the least supply of arms and ammunition of any kind; though it was notorious in itself, and well known, that this was what from the first we mainly wanted; and, as such, it was insisted upon by the Earl of Mar, in all the letters he writ, and by all the messengers he sent to the other side. "[107]

On the ninth of November it was determined, at a great council of war, to march straight to Dumblane with the ultimate view of following the Brigadier Mackintosh into England, with the main body of the army, amounting to nine thousand men, whilst a detachment of three thousand should, if possible, gain possession of Stirling.

The engagement which ensued, and which was called the battle of Sherriff Muir, was fought on a Sunday; after both armies had been under arms all night. No tent was pitched for the Duke of Argyle's men, either by officer or soldier, on that cold November evening. Each officer was at his post, nor could they much complain whilst their General sat on straw, in a sheepcote, at the foot of the hill, called Sherriff Muir, which overlooks Dumblane, on the right of his army. In the dead of the night, the Duke, by his spies, learned where the enemy were; for, although on account of the hills and broken ground, they could not be seen, they were not at two miles' distance. This was at Kinback; at break of day, the army of Argyle was completely formed, and the General rode up to the top of the hill to reconnoitre the foe. [108]

The Earl of Mar, meantime, had given orders for his army to form to the left of the road that leads to Dumblane, and whilst they were forming in front of the town of Dumblane, they discovered the enemy on the height of the west end of the Sherriff Muir. A council of war was then held, and it was resolved, *nemine contradicente,* to fight.

The Earl of Mar's forces had also been ready for combat during the whole of the night. To the Highlanders the want of shelter was of little consequence. It was usual to them, before they lay down on the moor to dip their plaids in water, by which the cloth was made impervious to the wind; and to choose, as a favourite and luxurious resting-place, some spot underneath a cover of overhanging heath. So late as the year 1745, they could not be prevailed on to use seats. [109] It was therefore with unimpaired vigour that they rushed on to the combat.

The Earl of Mar placed himself at the head of the clans: perhaps a finer, a more singular, a more painful sight can rarely have been witnessed than the rush of this great body of Highlanders to the encounter. It was delayed by the Earl of Mar's despatching his aide-de-camp, Colonel Clephan, to Lord Drummond, and to General Gordon, with orders to march and attack immediately. On their return, pulling off his hat, he waved it with an huzza, and advanced in front of the enemy's formed battalions. Then was heard the *slogan* or war-cry, each clan having its own distinctive watch-word, to which every clansman responded, whether his ear caught the sound in the dead of night, or in the confusion of the combat. Distinguished by particular badges, and by the peculiar arrangement and colours of the tartans, these devoted men followed the Earl of Mar towards the foe.

But the action cannot be described in a manner better adapted to this narrative, than in the words of Lord Mar himself, in his letter on the very day of the engagement, to Colonel Balfour, whom he had left in command of the garrison at Perth. It is dated Ardoch, November 13th, 1715.

"Ardoch, Nov. 13th, 1715. "

"I thought you would be anxious to know the fate of this day. We attacked the enemy on the end of the Sherriff Muir, at twelve of the clock this day, on our right and centre; carried the day entirely; pursued them down to a little hill on the south of Dumblane; and there I got most of our horse and a pretty good number of our foot, and brought them again into some order. We knew not then what was become of our left, so we returned to the field of battle. We discerned a body of the enemy on the north of us, consisting mostly of the Grey Dragoons, and some of the Black. We also discovered a body of their foot farther north upon the field where we were in the morning; and east of that, a body as we thought of our own foot, and I still believe it was so. I formed the horse and foot with me in a line on the north side of the hill, where we had engaged and kept our front towards the enemy to the north of us, who seem'd at first as if they intended to march towards us; but upon our forming and marching towards them, they halted and marched back to Dumblane. Our baggage and train-horses had all run away in the beginning of the action. But we got some horses and brought off most of the train to this place where we quarter to-night about Ardock, whither we march'd in very good order: and had our left and second line behaved as our right and the rest of the first line did, our victory had been compleat: but another day is coming for that, and I hope ere long too.

"I send you a list of the officers' names who are prisoners here, besides those who are dangerously wounded and could not come along, whose words of honour were taken. Two of these are the Earl of Forfar, who I'm afraid will die, and Captain Urquhart, of Burn's Yard, who is very ill wounded. We have also a good number of private men prisoners; but the number I do not exactly know.

"We have lost, to our regret, the Earl of Strathmore and the Captain of Clan Ranald. Some are missing, but the fate we are not sure of.

"The Earl of Panmure, Drummond of Logie, and Lieutenant Colonel Maclean are wounded.

"This is all that I have to say now, but that I am,

"Yours, &c. MAR. "

"P. S. We have taken a great many of the enemy's arms. "

Lord Mar, on this occasion, showed a degree of personal bravery worthy of the great name which he bore. He had placed himself on the right, and, as he was giving orders to the Macdonalds to charge that battalion of the enemy opposite to them, he encountered a very close fire. "The horse on which my Lord was, " writes an eye-witness on the Jacobite side, "was wounded, for he fell down with him upon the fire, and got away, and my Lord immediately mounted another horse: he exposed his person but too much, and showed a great deal of bravery, as did the other lords about him. "[110]

The army of the Duke of Argyle lay on their arms all night, expecting that the next day the battle would be resumed; but, on Monday the fourteenth of November, the Duke went out with the piquet guard to the field to view the enemy, but found them gone: and leaving the piquet guard on the place, he returned to Dumblane, and thence to Stirling, carrying off with him fourteen of the enemy's colours and standards, and among them the royal standard called the Restoration, besides several pieces of artillery, and many prisoners, some of them men of rank and influence.

Both sides claimed the victory of Sherriff Muir as their own; but, however it may be argued, it is certain that with only three thousand effective troops, Argyle had contrived "to break the heart of the rebellion, " and to subdue an army such as could never again be reassembled. Between six and eight hundred of the Jacobites are stated to have fallen on the field, [111] and several, among whom was the brave Earl of Panmure and Colonel Maclean, were among the wounded. Lord Mar, nevertheless, celebrated the engagement as if it had been a victory.

Thanksgiving-sermons were ordered to be preached at Perth, and a Te Deum sung in the church; and ringing of bells, and other demonstrations deceived the hearts of those who knew little of the real injury done to the cause, or amused others whose nearest interests had not suffered in the Sherriff Muir. A paper was also circulated containing a report of the battle, of course highly favourable to the Earl of Mar's part in what he called his victory. The following is the statement which he sent to the Chevalier.

THE EARL OF MAR TO THE CHEVALIER. [112]

"Nov. 24, 1715.

"Sir,

"It was but yesterday that I had accounts of your being at sea, and I thought myself obliged to do all in my power to let you know the state of affairs in this island before you land in it, so that you may not be disapointed upon your comeing.

"I had the certain account yesterday of those who had appear'd in arms besouth Forth, and in the north of England, all being made prisoners at Preston in Lancashire, which I'm affraid will putt a stop to any more riseings in that country at this time.

"Your Majesty's army, which I have the honour to command, fought the enime on the Shirreff-Muir, near Dumblain, the thirteenth of this moneth. Our left behav'd scandalously and ran away, but our right routed the enimies left and most of their body.

"Their right follow'd and pursued our left, which made me not adventure to prosecute and push our advantage on our right so far as otherwayes wee might have done, however wee keept the field of battle, and the enimie retir'd to Dumblain.

"The armie had lyen without cover the night before, and wee had no provisions there, which oblidg'd me to march the armie back two milles that night, which was the nearest place where I could get any quarters. Next day I found the armie reduced to a small number, more by the Highlanders going home than by any loss wee sustained, which was but very small. So that and want of provisions oblidg'd me yet to retire, first to Auchterarder, and then here to Perth. I have been doing all I can ever since to get the armie together again, and I hope considerable numbers may come in a little time; but now that our friends in England are defeated, there will be troops sent down from thence to reinforce the Duke of Argyle, which will make him so strong, that wee shall not be able to face him, and I am affraid wee shall have much difficultie in makeing a stand any where, save in the Highlands, where wee shall not be able to subsist.

"This Sir, is a melancholy account, but what in duty I was oblidg'd to let you know, if possibly I can, before you land; and for that end I have endeavour'd to send boats out about those places where I judg'd it most probable you would come.

"Ther's another copie of this upon the West Coast, and I wish to God one or other of them may find you if your Majesty be upon the coast.

"By the strength you have with you, your Majesty will be best able to judge if you will be in a condition, when join'd with us, to make a stand against the enimie. I cannot say what our numbers will be against that time, or where wee shall be, for that will depend on the enimie, and the motions they make; but unless your Majesty have troops with you, which I'm affraid you have not, I see not how wee can oppose them even for this winter, when they have got the Dutch troops to England, and will power in more troops from thence upon us every day.

"Your Majestie's coming would certainly give new life to your friends, and make them do all in their power for your service; but how far they would be able to resist such a formed body of regular troops as will be against them, I must leave your Majestie to judge.

"I have sent accounts from time to time to Lord Bolingbroke, but I have not heard once from any of your Majestie's servants since Mr. Ogilvie of Boin came to Scotland, nor none of the five messengers I sent to France are return'd, which has been an infinite loss to us. I sent another, which is the sixt, to France, some days ago, with the account of our victory, who I suppose is sail'd ere now.

"May all happiness attend your Majestie, and grant you may be safe, whatever come of us. If it do not please God to bless your kingdoms at this time with your being settled on your throne, I make no doubt of its doing at another time; and I hope there will never be wanting of your own subjects to assert your cause, and may they have better fortune than wee are like to have. I ask but of Heaven that I may have the happiness to see your Majestie before I die, provided your person be safe; and I shall not repine at all that fortune has or can do to me.

"Your Majestie may find many more capable, but never a more faithful servant than him who is with all duty and esteem, Sir, your Majestie's most dutiful, most faithfull and most obedient subject and servant,

"MAR. "

"From the Camp of Perth, Nov. 24, 1715. "

A fortnight previously the Earl of Mar had addressed the following curious letter to Captain Henry Straiton, [113] at Edinburgh, to whom many of Lord Mar's epistles are written. The allusion to Margaret Miller refers to Lady Nairn, the sister-in-law of the Marquis of Tullibardine, and wife of Lord Nairn, who, in compliance with a Scottish custom, took his wife's title, she being Lady Nairn in her own right. The allusion to "a dose" which will require the air of a foreign country to aid it, seems to offer some notion of the Earl's subsequent flight.

"Novemb. 8th, 1715.

"Sir,

"I had yours of the fourth this forenoon, which was very wellcome. And I hope we shall soon see the certainty of what the accounts makes us expect of these folks' arivall. I sent of a pacquet yesterday with an answer to Margaret Miller's of the second, and in it I sent a copie of my last to Mr. H——n, which was dated the second and third, of which I sent him copies two different wayes, so I hope he'll get one of them at least. They were pressing them to go into England; and now that they are actually gone their, and in so good a way, I am easie as to that. I hope God will direct and assist them.

"I thought to have marcht from this to-day. The foot are mostly gone, and I march with the horse to-morrow morning. Our generall revew is to be at Auchterardor on Thursday morning, and then to march forward immediately. It is of great use to hear often from you, and to have accounts of our friends in the north of England, and what is doing in England beside; so I know you'll write as often as you can find occasions. I fancie I may hear to-day from our friends in the north of England, for I hope they had some days ago a way of sending directly. It seems the Duke of Argyll's absence from London is not like to do his own court of interest there much good. I hope our manifesto's being disperced at London, will have good effect; and I long to see what the prints call the Pretender's declaration, and the declaration of the people of England. The run upon the bank, I hope, will not lessen. The public credit must not be once ruined to make it raise again, and I hope that time may be sooner than we think of. We have rainy weather, but that is an inconveniencie to the enimie as well as to us. My humble service to Margaret Miller: I thank her for the information she gives me, of one about me giving intelligence; but other friends may be easie about it, for I am sure there is nothing in it; and I know what made them belive, which I confess had colour enough. I wish she would get the Doctrix to send a new dose to the patient she knows of, for there was a little too much of one of the ingredients in the last, which toke away the effect of the whole. It is the ingredient that has the postponeing quality in it; and the patient's greatest distemper is the apprehentions he has of a perfect cure being long of comeing, and that it is not to be til he get the air of another country. The dose must be carefully made up, and no appearance of its comeing from any other hand but the Doctrix' own. Ther's some copies herewith sent of a paper printed on this side the water, of which I hear severall are at Stirling. The other two papers I got to-day are given to revise, and are to be printed soon. I send you a copie of a letter was wrote t'other day, and sent to the Cameronians in the west. I wish you could send this one to some of them in the south. This is all I will trouble you with; but I hope both to get from you and give you good news soon, and I ever am, with all sincerity and truth, yrs. &c.

"Perhaps Capt. R——n will not be found to have done so much hurt as was thought he designed; but this is not to bid trust him yet. "

By two manuscript letters among the Mar papers, it appears, however, that the account soon afterwards published by Lord Mar was not so full of artifice and untruths as his enemies represented. "He kept the field of battle until it was dark, " says one writer, in a letter dated from Perth (November the 19th, 1715); "and nothing but want of provisions prevented us from going forward the next day. We hear the Whigs give various accounts of the battle, to cover the victory; but the numbers of the slain on their part being eleven or twelve hundred, and ours not above fifty or sixty, and our keeping the field when they left it, makes the victory incontestable. Your friends that I know here mind you often, and they and I would be glad to have the opportunity to drink a bottle with you beyond the Forth. "

Another eye-witness gives a still more detailed account. [114] "I have yours of the seventeenth, with the paper inclosed, wherein that gentleman has taken the liberty to insert many falsehoods relative to the late action, a true and impartial account of which I here send you, which is but too modest on our side, and many things omitted that will be afterwards made publick, particularly their murdering Strathmoir, after he had asked quarters, and the treatment they gave to Panmuir and several others, who, I hope, will be living witnesses against them. The enclosed is so full that I have little to say, only that we have not lost a hundred men in the action, and none of note, except Strathmoir, and the Captain of Clan Ronald. "

The cruel spirit of party destroyed the generous characteristics of the soldier, during the excitement of the combat: but how can we palliate the conduct of one of the King's generals, Lord Isla, after the fierceness of the encounter was over? The letter referred to discloses particulars which were hushed up, or merely glanced at, in the partial annals of the time.

"So soon as they saw us coming down upon them, they marched off in great haste towards Dumblain, and left several of our people they had taken, among which was Lord Panmuir, who offered to give his parole, not knowing what had passed upon the eighth; but he was told by the person he sent to Lord Isla, that he could not take a parole from a rebel, and they were in such haste that they lost him in a little house, with several others near the field, where we found them when we advanced and brought him along with us to Ardoch, two miles furder, where we stayed all night and next day, until that we heard the enemy were marched off to Stirling. He is now pretty well and in no danger. Earl Loudoun passed him as he lay in the field, without taking any notice of him, and he was wounded there by the dragoons after he had surrendered to them; but I hope there will be one other day of reckoning for these things. My Lord Mar sent off two or three people to take care of Lord Forfar when he heard he was wounded, and one of them waited of him to Stirling. He expressed a good dale of consern that he should have been ingadged against his countrymen, and sent a breslet off his arm to Lord Mar, so that we all wish he may live. A good pairt of our baggage and the provisions we had, were distroyed by our own people who went of from our left. We are now getting provisions and every thing ready as soon as possible; and I am hopefull we will be in a condition in a very few days to pass forth without oposition.

"We have got accounts this day of a victorie obtained by our friends in the south, the particulars of which we long for. I have sent you some copies of the printed account of the action to give our friends.

"So adieu. "

Notwithstanding the humane attentions shewn by the Earl to Lord Forfar, that brave and generous nobleman died of his wounds. After lingering more than three weeks, he expired at Stirling on the eighth of December. He was wounded in sixteen different places, but a shot which he received in his knee seems to have been the most fatal injury. The conduct of the Earl appears in strong contrast with that of the Earl of Isla; but we must remember that each party had its own chroniclers. It is, nevertheless, a result of observation, more easily stated than explained, that through the whole of the two contests, both in 1715 and 1745, the generous and somewhat chivalric bearing of the Jacobites was acknowledged; whilst a spirit of cruel persecution marked the conduct of some of the chief officers on the opposite side. The Duke of Argyle indeed, in his own person, presented an exception to this remark, which chiefly applies to those secondary to him in command and influence.

The conduct of Lord Mar, in retreating to Perth after the affair of Sherriff Muir, has been severely censured. But, as Sir Walter Scott has observed, he met with that obloquy which generally follows the leader of an unsuccessful enterprise. According to Lord Mar's own account (and it has been corroborated by others), his retiring to Perth was unavoidable. The Highlanders, brave as they were, had a custom of returning home after a battle; and many of them went off when the engagement was ended. The Earl of Mar was not, therefore, in a condition to pursue the advantage which he had gained, but was forced to await at Perth the arrival of the Chevalier, or of the Duke of Berwick; on the notification of which, the Highlanders would have rallied to his standard. No supplies had been sent; the gentlemen of the army, as well as the men, had been long absent from their homes, and were living at their own expense; and therefore were impatient for leave of absence. To add to the general discouraging aspect of affairs, the fatal result of the English insurrection, under the command of Mr. Forster, was communicated at this time.

At first the result of the battle of Preston was represented to the Jacobites at Perth in a very different light to that in which the defeat of the English Jacobites afterwards appeared. The following is an extract of a letter from Lord Mar, dated the twentieth of November. "This day we hear from good hands that they (the English Jacobites) have had a victory, for which we have had rejoicings, and I hope in

God they are in a good way by this time. Let me hear from you often, I beg it of you, and I'll long for the particulars of that affair.

"I am doing all I can to get us again in a condition to march from home. It will not be so soon as I wish, which is no small mortification to me, but our friends; you may depend on it, that it shall be as soon as I can, and no time shall be lost. It is wonderfull that neither the King nor the Duke of Ormond comes, nor that I have not accounts from them. Now that there is so considerable a party appearing in England, I hope they will put it off no longer. I hope all your friends in England are well in particular, but pray let me have an account of it.

"Lord Tullibardin and Lord George are well; they are gone again to Atholl to bring back their men, who went off that they might retrieve their honour, as I doubt not but they will. It is a great pity if poor Strathmore and Clanronald, and I'm afraid honest Auchterhouse, is killed, for we can get no account of him.

"I wish our prisoners may be as civilly treated as theirs are with us. They are all sent to Dundee (the officers I mean), where they have the liberty of the town, and wear their swords. My compliments to our sick friend, who I am sorry is still so; but he has had a good second and secretary.

"Pray let us have some good news now, and I am with all truth and esteem,

Yours, &c. "

"Perth, November 20, 1715. "

"Lord Panmure recovers pritty well. The enimie give out that he gave his parole when he was prisoner, but it was not so, he off'red it them but they wou'd not take it from a rebel as they call'd him, and neither did Strewan; so they were both resqued. "

These letters place Lord Mar in a somewhat more estimable light than the usual statements have done. The truth is, that we ought never to judge of a man's actions before we have had an insight into his real motives and circumstances at the time. Few individuals had greater difficulties to contend with than Lord Mar.

Harassed by cabals among the adherents of the Chevalier; unable to account for the continued reserve and absence of that Prince; and weakened greatly both by the secession of the clan of Fraser, who had joined the Insurgents with Mackenzie of Fraserdale, but who now went away, and joined him whom they considered as their real chieftain, the infamous Simon Fraser, of Beaufort, Lord Lovat; the Earl began to listen to those who talked of capitulating with the enemy. He found, indeed, that he was forced to comply with the wishes of the chieftains, some of whom were making private treaties for themselves. It must have been a bitter humiliation to Lord Mar to have sent a message to his former rival in politics, the Duke of Argyle, "to know if he had power to treat with him; " but the measure appears from the following letter to have been unavoidable. It was written after the news of the defeat at Preston had reached Perth. It bespeaks some degree of compassion and consideration for a man whose councils were distracted by dissensions, and who was embarrassed beyond measure by the absence of the Chevalier, to whose arrival he looked anxiously to give some hopes of revival to a sinking cause. The Master of Sinclair, to whom Lord Mar refers as a "devil, " and who, since the disaster at Preston was known, "appeared in his own colours, " was the eldest son of Henry, eighth Baron Sinclair, a devoted adherent of the House of Stuart, and one of those who had withdrawn from the Convention of 1689 when the resolution to expel James the Second was adopted. John, Master of Sinclair, was afterwards attainted, and never assumed the title of his father, although pardoned in 1726.

"November 27th, 1715.

"Sir,

"I had yours of the twenty-second, the twenty-fifth, and also spoke with the person you mention in it; I suppose he wou'd see you, as he returned. The disaster of our friends in England is very unlucky, both to affairs there and here. Since we knew of it here a *devil,* who I suspected for some time to be lurking amongst us, has appeared openly in his own colours. I forsaw this a-comeing some days ago. I have endeavoured to keep people from breaking amongst themselves, and was forced to go into the first step of it; but I hope we shall be able to have the manadgement of it, and prevent its doing any hurt, but to confounde in time comeing the designs of those who were the promoters of it. It was by the advise of all your friends what I have done, so let not our folks be alarmed when they hear of it from I——g. It is odd where the K——[115] can be all this time, since, by all appearance and all the accounts we have, he has left France long ago; but that must quickly appear, and I hope to get things staved off til it does. But without his comeing what can be done? Tho' I hope that will not be the case. It is odd that others write of Col. H——y and Doctor Abor—y, both at Parise, and that they do not write themselves, tho' I'm told to-day that there's a letter from them to me at Edinburgh, which I long for. We are told of troops comeing from Englande, both English and Dutch. I doubt if they'll ventur to quitt with both, and I would fain hope that none of them will come soon. God grant that the K—— be safe. If he go to England, as we are told he designed, I doubt not but he knows of support there. I confess there's a great deal lost by his long delay, but that certainly was not in his power to help, else it wou'd not have been so. If he still come here, I hope we will yet be able to make a stand for him this winter, but I thought I was obledged to let him know the true situation before he land, which I have done to the best of my pow'r, and lodged letters for him in the places where I thought it most likely he wou'd come, so that he may not be dissapointed by expecting to find things better than they are. He has been so long by the way that it wou'd seme he is not comeing to England, but that he is comeing round about Ireland to Scotland; and neither he nor D—— O——d[116] be in England. It wou'd seem that they will not stir there, which would make it a very hard task here; but I hope Providence will protect him, and yet settle him on his throne.

"I find it will be sometime before I can stirr from hence, and if the enemy get not reinforcments, I judge they will not stirr either; but as soon as they get them they certainly will, and I'm afraid we shall be oblidged to take the hills, which is a could quarter now. I wish you knew a great many particulars I have to tell you, but it is not safe writing them; there are some people with us who it had been good for the King they had stay'd at home, where they want not a little to be, and will leave us at last, but we must make the best of them, tho' there be but ill stuff to make it of as the saying is. Never had man so plaguie a life as I have had o' late; but I'll do the best I can to go threw it, and not be unworthy of the trust reposed in me. My service to Mr. Hall, and I hope he'll make my compliments to his correspondent at P——se, [117] who he mentions in his to me; but its odd that I have heard from none there myself ever sine B——n came, especially since other letters come through. I must own I have not had many encouragements, but that should be nothing if I had encouragements for others. Should it please God that the King's affairs should not succeed, but that people capitulated, I do not purpose to be a Scots or Englishman if they would let me, and all that I wou'd ask for myself is liberty to go abroad, for in that case I wou'd rather live in Siberia than Britain. If the King does not come soon, I find people will not hold out long; but if he does, there are honest men enough to stand by him and not see him perish. Pray let me hear from you as often as you can, and when you write to Mrs. Miller[118] make my compliments to her. I wish some of our men here had her spirit. I hope you are now perfectly recover'd, but pray take care that you fall not ill again. Adieu.

"Pray cause give the enclosed to my brother as soon as it comes to your handes. I beg you may apprise our friends at London and Parise of what has been done hear to-day; the sending to Argle at Stirling a message about articles of treaty, as appears from other papers, which I tel you I was forced to go into; —that they may not be surprised at it and think we have given all over, which might have very bad consequences in both places. Do this by the first post. All will come right again if the King come soon to Britain. "

The answer returned by the Duke of Argyle to Lord Mar's overture was this: that "he had no sufficient powers to treat with the Earl of Mar and his Council as a body, but that he would write to Court about it. "

To this reply, which was sent with much courtesy by the Duke, a rejoinder was made, "That when the Duke should let the Earl of Mar and his Council know that he had sufficient power, then they would make their proposition. " The proposal was sent up to St. James's, but no further notice was taken of it, nor were the powers of the Duke of Argyle extended to enable him to come to any terms with Lord Mar. But although the negotiation thus died away, the weakness it betrayed among the Jacobite party was highly prejudicial to their cause.

James, during all the recent events, had been engaged in making several attempts to leave St. Maloes. He had gone openly on board ships which were laden with arms and ammunition for his use, but had withdrawn when he found that his embarkation was known. He therefore changed his plans, and crossing to Normandy, resolved to embark at Dunkirk. Having lurked for several days, disguised as a mariner, on the coast of Brittany, he went privately to Dunkirk, where he embarked, attended by the Marquis of Tynemouth, the eldest son of the Duke of Berwick, Lieutenant Cameron, and several other persons, on board a French ship, which, according to some accounts, "was laden with brandy, and furnished with a good passport. " Thus at length having ventured on the ocean, the Prince set sail towards Norway; but changed his direction, and steered towards Peterhead, in Aberdeenshire. During all this time, the Earl of Mar suffered from the utmost anxiety and perplexity for one who was unworthy of the exertions made for his restoration. This is evident from the following letter, dated November the thirtieth, to Captain Straiton:

"The accounts of that person's[119] way of going on, and the danger he is in, confound me; but I hope Providence has not preserved him all this while to destroy him at last. I am doing all I can to make it safe; and perhaps what we thought our misfortune, (the men going home after Sheriff Muir,) may prove our happiness, they being where that person is to come, and I send troops there immediately. "

"I knew before I got yours that the Dutch troops were coming here. [120] Those by sea may come soon, but those by land cannot be here a long time. They will now power in all the troups from England on us; but I hope we may hold it this winter in spite of them, tho' we shall have hard quarters in the Highlands. In case of what Mr. H——ll writes me prove true, and happen, for fear of accidents after it does, were it not fitt that you should write to France to send some ships to cruise up and down the north-west coast to save the person Mr. H——ll writes of, if things should not prove right? and our friends in France can either send them from thence or Spain, round Ireland? I hear of but two little ships of warr on that coast; and the ships I would have sent may pass as marchant ships tradeing and putting in by accident therabouts, which they often do. Pray think of this, and write of it soon to France, as I intend to do to-night by an express I am sending; and were it not fitt you should write of it too to some trusty friend at London? But it must be done with the utmost caution, for fear of disheartning the English. Tho' the safty of that person is of such consequence that all ways is to be taken for it, and all accidents guarded against.

"I wrote to you the twenty-seventh, and in it I gave you account of an affair which happened amongst us, which obliged us to send a message to the Duke of Argyll. I hope this came safe to your hand.

His answer was very civil, and our return was in the words following, viz: 'We are obliged to the Duke of Argyll for his civility; that, since he has no powers to treat with us, we can say no more now; but if at any time he shall have them, and let us know it, we shall give our answer. '

"I hope this affair has been so manadgd that all the spirit of division amongst us is crusht; and pray take care to informe our friends at London and Parise about it, that it may not alarme them. I am affraid of its alarmeing the Regent, and keeping him from doing anything for the King; for which reason I send an express to Lord Bolingbroke to-night. I suppose it will be ten or twelve dayes at least before the Duke of Argyll will have a return, and we may know much before that time. If they agree to a treaty, it is still in our own power; and if not, I hope people will stand together for their own sake.

"You speak in your two last as if you were opresst about our divisions. All I shall trouble you further in relation to this, —there are odd people amongst us, and those of whom it should not have been expected; they had instild their spirit so farr into many, that there was no steming the tide but by going into it, or else breaking amongst ourselves, and, like them, make a seperat peace; but now those wise folk are ashamed of themselves, and are disclaimed by those who they said comissioned them. I do all I can to make others forgett this behaveour of those people, and I hope we shall be as unite as ever. If the King come, I am sure we shall; and if God is not pleased to bless us with his presence, whatever we do shall be in consert.

"I beg to hear often from you, and particularly what you can learn of the motion of the enimie and their designs.

"I send a reinforcement to-night to Bruntisland of a hundred men, and there was fifty in it before.

"Lord Seaforth went north some time ago, and severall of Lord Huntly's people; so I hope they togither will be able to keep Lord Sutherland from doing much mischife, and e'er long to reduce him and all the King's enimies there. We are not yet in so much apprehention of them as Mr. H——ll seems to be. I am mightily pleased you are so much recovered, which I know by your hand-writeing; but I can scarce conceave how you get yourself keept free of our enimies, —may you do long so, and

"I am sincearly yours, &c. Adieu. "

On the first of December, the Earl having still heard no tidings of the Chevalier, and being ignorant of his real movements, again writes in all the uncertainty, and with the circumspection of one who knows not whether his letter will be received. He seems always to have sent duplicates of his letters.

"I am in the utmost pain about the K— —, [121] and I have done all in my power to make him safe, but I hope Providence will protect him. I sent one for France this morning, and I hope he may sail in a day or two, but let that not keep you from writeing there too. I would fain hope that the Regent has altered his measurs, and is comeing into the K— —'s intrest, else I do not see how it had been possible for him to get thro' France: if so, I have good hopes, and I wish he may come to us; but if not, and that England do nothing, I wish he were safe again where he formerly was, for we shall never be able alone to do his bussiness, and he will be in the utmost danger after starveing a winter in the Highlands. Lord Huntley is still very much out of humour and nothing can make him yet believe that the K— —'s a-comeing. He intends to go north, under the pretext of reduceing Lord Sutherland, and his leaving us at this time I think might have very bad effects, which makes me do all I can to keep him. The Master of Sinclair is a very bad instrument about him, and has been most to blaim of any body for all the differences amongst us. I am plagued out of my life with them, but must do the best I can. I expect now to hear every day of the K— —'s landing; but should he be any time of comeing, and the Duke of Argyll get his powers and send us word of it before he come, our old work will begin again, and I am sure I shall be deserted by a great many. Some people seem so farr from being pleased with the news of the K— —'s comeing, that they are visiblie sorry for it; and I wish to God these people had never been with us for they will be our undoing! and what a plague brought them out, since they could not hold it out for so short a time? I shall be blamed, I know, over all Europe for what I am entirely innocent of. It will be my own ruin beside, but if that could advance the K— —'s affairs I am contented. In time I shall be justified when my parte in all this affair comes to be knowen, and I bless God I have witnesses enough who have seen all; and if accidents do not happen them, my papers will show it to conviction, for I have been pretty exact in keeping copies and a journall.

"Since I have wrote so fully to you, I do not write to Mr. H— —ll, for which I hope he'll forgive me. [122]

"I am anxious to know if my brother got my note that was inclosed to you in that of the twenty-seventh, which was to caution him in a thing that I was affraid his over great concern for me might make him do, and which would vex me extreamly if he did.

"I long to hear from you again, as I suppose you will from me; and as soon as I know of what you'll expect to hear of from me, you shall. Adieu. "

In a few days afterwards Lord Mar had gained more precise intelligence of the Prince's movements; on the delay at St. Maloes he puts the favourable construction of the vessel's having been wind-bound, as will be seen by the following letter. The dissensions in his counsels, aided, as he hints, by the influence which the Master of Sinclair exercised over the Marquis of Huntley, were, still, not among the least of his difficulties.

"December 6th, 1715.

"Sir,

"Last night one of the messengers I had sent to France returned, and there came with him to Montrose, Mr. Charles Fleeming and General Eclin; but they are not yet come here, nor some money that came along with them. I have a letter from the King, the fifteenth of November, N. S. from St. Malos; severall from Lord Bolingbroke, the last of which was the twenty-seventh, and he belived the King then to be saild, and he had been wind bound there three weeks; but he did not sail, as I understand from the messenger til the eighteenth inst., he having seen a letter from Col. Hay at St. Maloes, to Mr. Arbuthnot, two dayes after he sailed. God send him safe to us, for which I have done all in my power! It is in the hands of Providence, and I hope God will protect him. It is not to be known where he is to land, and indeed it cannot be known certainly. Even this has not quite cured all the whims amongst us. Lord grant a safe landing, and I hope that will. The Duke of Ormond is gone to England, and I believe he has some troops with him and arms and ammunition.

"I hear from Fife to-day that there landed at Leith on Sunday last four hundred of the Dutch troops. I hope that's all that are comeing by sea. I have the King's Declaration, which is to be reprinted here, and shall be dispers'd in a few days. The less that it be spoke that the King is to land soon, I believe the better, until he actually does, for that but make the Government more alert. Were he but once landed, I have reason to belive that there will be a new face of affairs seen abroad as well as at home in the King's favour, which is all I dare yet adventure to trust of it to paper; but I hope in God were the King once with us all will be well.

"There are more officers comeing to us from abroad different wayes, so it's likely they may be dropping in every day. The Duke of Berwick stays behind for a very good reason, and is to follow. The King has been pleased to confer new honours on me, but I do not think it fitt to take it on me til he comes, and if it pleases not God he come to us safe, I am indifferent what becomes of all I ever had, and this may go with the rest. It is goodness in him, and more than I askt or deserve. I will long to hear from you; and tho' I desire you not to let the news I write you be much talkt of, yet I suppose it will be no secret, for I am obliged to communicate what I get to so many that it cannot possible be keept, and yet I cannot help this. Tho' Lord Huntley said little to me to-day upon my shewing him my letters, yet I know it from good hands he is not a bitt in better humour and that he will now positively go north; which I suppose he'll write of to me to-morrow, for 'tis seldom now he'll either see me or let me see him, tho' I take all the ways I can to please and humour him, but all will not do: however, I hope will not have many followers. Master of Sinclair is gone this day to see his father upon a sharp letter he had from him yesterday about his behaviour. Some others are ashamed of the part they acted, but if the King come not soon all of them will relapse again. The clans stand firm, and I hope will to the last.

"Pray try to get notice of what private letters from London say upon our proposeing terms, and let me know as soon as you can. Adieu. "

It is curious to trace the revival of the Earl's hopes, and the increase of his confidence. The following letter contains, among other circumstances, a reference to the supposed attempt of the Earl of Stair, in France, to assassinate James.

"December 10th, 1715.

"Sir,

"Yesterday I had yours of the fourth and fifth, for which I thank you. I wrote to you on the eighth, which I hope you got safe, and in it I told you of one of the messengers I had sent to France being returned, and with him General Eclin and Mr. Charles Fleming, and some money: since that Doctor Abercromby is returned and Lord Edward Drummond is come with him and brought some more money. They come off the same day with the others, and landed the same day at Aberdeen the others did at Montrose. They only brought duplicates of the dispatches I had by the others, and a letter to me from the Q—— with a pacquet from her to the K——, by which you may be sure he is sail'd, and we hourly expect to hear of his landing. Since those people came, those amongst us who had been uneasy, are now comeing to be in good humour again, particularly Lord Huntley; and I have agreed to his going north with some of his horse to get all his people there together to suppress those about Inverness, and also to have them in readiness against the K. comes. Pray God send him safe and soon, and then I do not despair of things going right still. Our whole prisoners almost, I mean the private men, are like to take on since they heard of the K——g's being certainly a-comeing; and since they saw the two enclosed papers, they say that were he once come, there will be news of their armie and all those prisoners. Even those who do not lift with us, pray openly for the K——, and that God may keep him out of the hands of his enimies.

"The two enclosed are sent about to a great many places: it is better to delay dispersing the K——'s declaration til he arrive, since I hope that is near.

"I admear we hear no certain accounts of the Duke of Ormond, for the fifteenth inst. the K—— and Q—— too write to me that he was saild a second time for England.

"Pray God it may be well with him, and if he do not, then I wish he may come here with all my heart.

"We have heard nothing as yet of the Duke of Argyle's return from London, and I imagine we shall hear nothing from him upon it, when he does get it and I hope he shall never be askt for it more by us. The Duke of Atholl will himself send his men against Crafourd.

"I believe I forgot to tell you in my last that Colonel Hay mist very narrowly being murdered in France, takeing him for the K——

(being in one of his cheases), by Lord Stair's gang, and in their pockets Lord Stair's orders were found to go to such a place, and there obey what orders they should receive from Count Douglass[123] (Lightly), let them be never so desperate. This is something so horrid that I want words to express it. I tell it you just as those from France tell me. The fellow was imprisoned by the government there and reclaimed by Lord Stair. Lord Clairmont was actually reclaimed by the Regent before they come away; so his being brought to England after, may work something. I have just now a packet of news sent me by A. M., for which I thank you. Notwithstanding this great new General's being come, I see not how they can do anything at Stirling till the Dutch join them, and that cannot be yet for some time; pray Heavens the K—— come before them! I know by other accounts as well as yours, from abroad, that they are not above four thousand complete and some of these are lost. Our Highlanders have got in their heads a mighty contempt for them, which may do good. This goes by the Hole, [124] from when your packet yesterday was sent me. I have nothing further to add now, but I hope soon to send you agreable news. Pray give my service to I. H. and desire him to make my compliments to his landlady and tel her, I hope she is now right with her son, which I am exceeding glad of. Adieu. "

At length, on the twenty-second of December, James landed at Peterhead, after a voyage of seven days. His arrival dispelled many doubts of his personal courage, since, after all his deliberations, he adopted by no means the least hazardous course by traversing the British ocean, which was beset by British men-of-war. He had sailed from Dunkirk in the small vessel in which he had embarked, and which was followed by two other vessels, containing his domestics, and stores for the use of his army. His immediate attendants were disguised as French officers, and his retinue as seamen. It had been the Chevalier's original intention to have landed in the Frith of Tay; but observing a sail which he suspected to be unfriendly, he altered his course, and landed at Peterhead, where the property of the Earl Marischal was situated. The ship in which the Chevalier sailed was, however, near enough to the shore to be able, by signals, to make signs to his friends of his approach. At Perth the intelligence was received with the utmost joy, and produced a most favourable effect, even among the prisoners of war, which Lord Mar describes in the following letter. Up to the twenty-eighth of the month he had not seen the Prince:

"The 28th December.

"Yours of the twenty-second I have got just now by the Hole, and I sent one that way to you yesterday from our friend here, in which you have the joyfull news of the King's safe arival, which I hope in God will effectually sement what you recomend to us. Our friend went yesterday morning to meett his master, who I hope will be here with us again Friday; I pray God turn the hearts of his enemies, both for the sake of him and their poor country! It will be a monstruous crime never to be forgiven, if they now draw their swords against him, since he has been pleased to give them a most gratious indemnity for all that is past, without exception. All will now soon be dispersed in the North that opose him. Sutherland's men are deserting him, and the Frasers are all gone home. I make no doubt but that we are masters of Inverness, and so consequently the whole North before this time. I make no doubt but that the King's presence will forward everything: it has already had great effects here: and those that were for separate measurs have reason to be ashamed, and I hope they will make amends by their future behaveor. We have sent over some of the declarations, and ane other paket of them is gone this night. Now is the time for every body to bestir themselves, and that all resort here to their master. I ame persuaded you'l not be idle. Those that made a pretext of the King's not being landed, are now left unexcusable; and if those kind of folks now sit still and look any more on, they ought to be worse treated than our worst enemies. I beg of you to send us what accounts you can learn on your side, and what they are now to do upon this news. I hope in God we shall now be soon ready to give them a meeting! It will be of consequence for us to hear often from your side, and we have little other accounts than from you. I have sent yours by ane express this day to our friend, and I hope to hear from you soon in return to the last that went on Munday. The K—— lay on Saturday night at the Earl of Marischall's house; he had a very good and safe passage, and has given them fair slip, for I supose they did never rekon on his comeing the near way. I hear there is a great resort to him, since he landed, of all ranks.

"The Duke of Athol[125] sent a pairty of two hundered of his men yesterday morning, under the comand of his brother Lord Edward, and his son Lord James, to Dunkeld to have surprised our garison there, which consisted of about one hundred men of the clans; but it seems the garison had notice of it some hours before they came, and gave them such a warm reception, that they retired in great haste with the loss of two men killed by our out-sentinels and five or sixe wounded. I belive his Grace's men had no good will to the work, and were brought their against their inclinations. They had nott then gott the account there of the King's arival, els I belive they had not atempted it. I wish our garison were now at Brunt Island, but I hope that loss soon be made up. I hope you'll omitte no occasion in letting us hear from you. Adieu.

"The above is writte to H. S., [126] but it will serve you both to forward it to him. I got the money and the cloas safe. I expect to hear from you soon. I have yours of the twenty-third. I have sent over a paket to be dispersed, and some ane other way. Your letters are longer be the way than they need so order it. Fall on some proper way to gett the enclosed delivered by some person, but be not seen in it yourself. If ane answer can be got, send it. "

The Chevalier slept in the town of Peterhead on the first night of his landing, but on the second he was received at Newburgh, a seat of the Earl Marischal; and the adherents who welcomed him as their Prince, had there an opportunity of forming a judgment of one whom they had hitherto known only by the flattering representations of those who had visited the young adventurer, at his little Court in Lorraine.

In person, James is reported by the Master of Sinclair to have been "tall and thin, seeming to incline to be lean rather than to fill as he grows in years. " His countenance, to judge by the most authentic portraits[127] of this Prince, had none of the meditative character of that of Charles the First, whom the Chevalier was popularly said to resemble: neither had it the sweetness which is expressed by every feature of that unhappy Monarch, nor had his countenance the pensiveness which wins upon the beholder who gazes upon the portraits of Charles. The eyes of the Chevalier were light-hazel, his face was pale and long, and in the fullness of the lips he resembled his mother, Mary of Modena. To this physiognomy, on which it is said a smile was rarely seen to play, were added, according to the account of a contemporary, from whose narrative we will borrow a further description, "a speech grave, and not very clearly expressive of his thoughts, nor over much to the purpose; his words were few, and his behaviour and temper seemed always composed.

"What he was in his diversions we know not; here was no room for such things. It was no time for mirth. Neither can I say I ever saw him smile. Those who speak so positively of his being like King

James the Seventh, must excuse me for saying that it seems to say they either never saw this person or never saw King James the Seventh; and yet I must not conceal that when we saw the man whom they called our King, we found ourselves not at all animated by his presence; and if he was disappointed in us, we were tenfold more so in him. We saw nothing in him that looked like spirit. He never appeared with cheerfulness and vigour to animate us: our men began to despise him; some asked if he could speak. His countenance looked extremely heavy. He cared not to come abroad among us soldiers, or to see us handle our arms to do our exercise. Some said the circumstances he found us in dejected him. I am sure the figure he made dejected us; and had he sent us but five thousand men of good troops, and never himself come, we had done other things than we have done. At the approach of that crisis when he was to defend his pretensions, and either lose his life or gain a Crown, I think, as his affairs were situated, no man can say that his appearing grave and composed was a token of his want of thought, but rather of a significant anxiety grounded on the prospect of his inevitable ruin, which he could not be so void of sense as not to see plainly before him, —at least, when he came to see how inconsistent his measures were—how unsteady the resolution of his guides, and how impossible it was to make them agree with one another. "[128]

*****

It was at Glammis Castle, the seat of the Earl of Strathmore, that the Earl of Mar drew up a flattering account of the Prince, which he caused to be printed and diligently circulated. [129] The whole is here given, as affording an insight into all that was going on: —

"I have had three of yours since I left Perth, but I wonder I have no letters from London. I mett the King at Fetteresso on Tuesday se'night, where we stayed til Friday; from thence we came to Brichan, then to Kinnaird, and yesterday here. The King designed to have gone to Dundee to-day, but ther's such a fall of snow that he is forced to put it off til to-morrow, if it be practicable then; and from thence he designs to go to Scoon. There was no haste in his being there sooner, for nothing can be done in this season, else he had not been so long by the way. People every where as we have come along, are excessively fond to see him and express that duty they ought. Without any compliment to him, and to do him nothing but justice, set aside his being a prince, he is realie the finest gentelman I ever knew. He has a very good presence, and resembles King Charles a great dele. His presence, tho', is not the best of him; he has fine partes, and dispatches all his buissiness himself with the greatest exactness. I never saw any body write so finely. He is afable to a great degree w^{t} out looseing that majestie that he ought to have, and has the sweetest temper in the world. In a word, he is even fitted to make us a happie people, were his subjects worthie of him. To have him peaceablie settled on his thron is what these kingdomes do not deserve; but he deserves it so much, that I hope ther's a good fate attending him. I am sure ther's nothing wanting to make the rest of his subjects as fond of him as we are, but thus knowing as we now have the happiness to do. And it will be odd if his presence amongst us, after his running so many hazards to compass it, do not turn the hearts of even the most obstinat. It is not fit to tel all the particulars, but I assure you, since he arived, he has left nothing undone that well could be to gain every body, and I hope God will touch their hearts. His Majestie is very sensible of the service you have done him and he desires you may continue, for which he hopes he may yet be able to reward you. He wrote to France as soon's he landed, and sent it with the shipe he came in, which we hope got safe there long ago. It is not often that we can have opportunity of writeing or sending there, and the Queen and others will be mighty impatient to hear frequently; therefore his Majestie expects you should write there frequently, and give them all the accounts you can. I have reason to hope we shall very quickly see a new face on affairs abroad in the King's favour, which is all I dare comitt to paper. The Government will nott certainly send all the strength against us they can, but e'er long, perhaps, they may have ocasion for their troups else where.

"I belive one wou'd speak to you lately of a kind of comisary of the Dutch, that may be spoke to, which by no means ought to be neglected, and he being on your side the watter, it is left to you, and you must not stick at offering such a reward as he himself can desire, which I shall see made good: there should no time be lost in this, and I'll be glad to know soon if there be any hopes that way.

"Tho' the way of sending letters betwixt us be now much more difficult than ever, yet you must write as often as you possiblie can get any probable way of sending of them safe; and pray give us all the accounts you can. I have ordred some of the King's declarations for England to be sent you, and when they come to your hands you wou'd get some way of sending them to London and other places of England. Send the enclosed for my wife under a cover, as you used to do; by my not hearing from her, I am affraid my last has not come to her hands. When any comes from her for me, pray take care that you send them a safe way. We long to know what effects the news of the King's arivall had at London, Stirling, and Edinburgh. I suppose you still hear from Kate Bruce. I do not understand what she means by going to the country, which she mentions in her letter to you.

"I see in one of the prints that Lawrance is come off from London, so by this time he must certainly be in Scotland; pray let me know what you hear of him. If he be come, I suppose he'll understand himself so well as our prisoner, that he will immediately give himself up to us again.

"The King wears paper caps under his wige, which I know you also do; they cannot be had at Perth, so I wish you could send some on, for his own are near out.

"We are in want of paper for printing; is there no way to send us some from your side?

"Pray, send my wife one of the Scots and one of the English declarations at the same time my letter goes, but under another cover. Adieu.

"Since writeing I have yours of the thirty-first and first, for which I thank you, and am just going to read them to my master. "

Little dependance can be placed on the entire accuracy of either of these varying descriptions, —the one penned by a disappointed, and perhaps wavering, adherent, the other by a man whose personal interests were irrevocably involved with those of James. We must trust to other sources to enable us to form a due estimate of the merits of this ill-starred Prince.

James Stuart was at this time in his twenty-seventh year. From his very cradle he had been, as it might seem to the superstitious, marked by fate for a destiny peculiarly severe. His real birth was long disputed, without the shadow of a reason, except what was suggested by a base court intrigue. This slur upon his legitimacy, which was afterwards virtually wiped away by the British Parliament, was nevertheless the greatest obstacle to his accession, there being nothing so difficult to obliterate as a popular impression of that nature.

Educated within the narrow precincts of the exiled court, James owed the good that was within him to a disposition naturally humane, placable, and just, as well as to the communion with a mother, the fidelity of whose attachment to her exiled consort bespoke a finer quality of mind than that which Nature had bestowed on the object of her devotion. By this mother James must doubtless have been embued with a desire for recovering those dominions and that power for which Mary of Modena, like Henrietta Maria, sighed in vain, as the inheritance of her son; but the stimulus was applied to a disposition with which a private life was far more consonant than the cares of sovereignty. Rising as he does to respectability, when we contrast the good nature and mild good sense of the Chevalier with the bigotry of James the Second, —or view his career, blameless with some exceptions, in contrast with the licentiousness of Charles the Second, there were still no high hopes to be entertained of the young Prince; his character had little energy, and consequently little interest: he was affable, just, free from bigotry although firm in his faith, and capable of great application to business; but he wanted ardour. From his negative qualities, the pitying world were disposed to judge him favourably. "He began the world, " says Lockhart, "with the general esteem of mankind; but he sank year by year in public estimation: his Court subsequently displayed the worst features of the Stuart propensities, an intense love of prerogative; and his mind, never strong, became weaker and weaker under the dominion of favourites. "

The ship in which James had sailed returned to France immediately to give the news of his safe arrival, and at the same time Lieutenant Cameron, the son of Cameron of Lochiel, was dispatched to Perth to apprise the Earl of Mar of the event. Upon the spur of the moment the Earl, accompanied by the Earl Marischal and General Hamilton, and attended by twenty or thirty persons of quality, on horseback, set out with a guard of horse to attend him whom they considered as their rightful Sovereign. The cavalcade met the Chevalier at Fetteresso, the principal seat of the Earl Marischal. "Here, " says Reay, "the Chevalier dressed, and discovered himself, " and they all kissed his hand, and owned him as their King, causing him to be proclaimed at the gates of the house. At Fetteresso the Prince was detained during some days by that inconvenient malady the ague. Meantime, the declaration which he had prepared, and which was dated from Commercy, was disseminated, and was dropped in some loyal towns by his adherents in the night-time, there being danger in promulgating it openly. [130]

On the second of January, 1715-16, the Chevalier proceeded to Brechin, and thence to Kinnaird; and on Thursday to Glammis Castle, the seat of the Earl of Strathmore. On the sixth of January he made his public entry into Dundee on horseback, at an early hour. Three hundred followers attended him, and the Earl of Mar rode on his right hand, the Earl Marischal on his left. At the suggestion of his friends, the Prince shewed himself in the market-place of Dundee for nearly an hour and a half, the people kissing his hands. The following extract from a letter among the Mar Papers affords a more minute and graphic account of the Chevalier's demeanour than is to be found in the usual histories of the day.

"I hear the Pretender went this day from Glams to Dundee, and comes to Scoon to-morrow; and I am shourly informed that your old friend Willie Callender went to Glams on Wensday and kissed the Pretender's hand, of whom he makes great speeches, and says he is one of the finest gentlemen ever he saw in his life. Its weell that his landing is keept up from the army, for he has gained so much the good will of all ranks of people in this country that have seen him, that if it was made publick it's thought it might have ill effects among them. He is very affable and oblidging to all, and great crowds of the common people flok to him. When he toke horse this morning from Glams, there was about a thousand country people at the gate, who they say, gave him many blessings: he has tuched several of the ivil, as he did some this morning. He is of a very pleasant temper, and has intirely gained the hearts of all thro' the places he has passed. He aplyes himself very closs to business, and they say might very weell be a Secretarie of State. He has declared Lord Marischall one of his bedchamber. The toun of Aberdeen made him ane address, as did all the other touns as he passed; and I hear he is, at the request of the episcopal clergy in this country, to apoint a day of thanksgiving for his safe arival, and likeways a proclamation, to which will be referred his declaration, with something new, which shall be sent to you with first ocasion. There came a battalion of Bredalbins men to Perth on Tuesday, and ane other of Sir Donald McG Donalds this day; and they are now daily getting in more men.

"This is all the intelligence I can give you, and I hope to hear from you again soon, and lett me know what certain number are now come over, and what more designed. Deliver the enclosed and tell him these papers could not be gott him just now, but shall per next. I ame affraid poor W. Maxewell wild be dead before you get this, of a fever and a flux: he is given over this two days. Write soon. "

After the display at Dundee, the Chevalier rode to the house of Stewart of Grandutly, in the neighbourhood, where he dined and passed the day. On the following day he proceeded along the Carse of Gowrie to Castle Lyon, a seat of the Earl of Strathmore, where he dined, and went thence to Fingask, the seat of Sir David Threipland. On the eighth of January he took up his abode in the royal palace of Scoon, where he intended to remain until after his coronation.

For this event preparations were actually made by the Earl of Mar, whose sanguine spirit appears to have been somewhat revived by the presence of the Chevalier. The addition of a new dignity to his own ancestral honours had marked the favour and confidence of James. Before the arrival of the Chevalier in Scotland, the Earl of Mar had been informed that a patent of dukedom was made out for him; on which he thus expressed himself in a letter, written before the Chevalier's landing, full of gratitude and professions. [131]

"Your Majesty has done me more honour than I deserve. The new dignity you have been pleased to confer on me is what I was not looking for; and coming from your Majesty's hands is what gives it the value. The patent is not yet come, but tho' it had, I think I ought not to make use of it till your Majesty's arrival. "

The Earl of Mar had now had an opportunity of throwing himself at the feet of the King, which, as he expressed, "is the thing in the world he had longed most for. " But still, the difficulties in his path seemed to be rendered more insurmountable than ever by the arrival of James.

In the first place, the landing of the Chevalier evidently sealed the doom of those gallant and unfortunate noblemen who had been taken prisoners at Preston; and rendered all hopes of mercy futile. The sixteenth of January, which witnessed the forming of the Chevalier's council at Perth, was the day on which the unfortunate Derwentwater, Nithisdale, Kenmure, Wintoun, and Widdrington, petitioned for two days' delay to prepare for their trials. Their doom was hurried on in the general panic; and in the addresses from both Houses of Parliament to King George, it was declared by the members of those assemblies "that the landing of the Pretender in this kingdom had greatly encreased their indignation against him and his adherents. "

It is impossible that the Earl of Mar could have heard, without deep commiseration, and perhaps remorse, of the peril in which those ill-fated adherents of James were placed, although he may not have anticipated the full severity of the law. In one of his subsequent letters he remarks: "By the news I see the Parliament is to have no mercie on our Preston folks: but I hope God will send them salvation in time. " One of his greatest sources of anxiety had been respecting the movements of the Duke of Ormond, upon whose making a diversion in favour of James, in England, Mar had counted. The news that Ormond, after having been seen on the coast of England, had returned, disheartened, was brought by the Chevalier, who heard of it at St. Maloes. The only chance of success, the last hope, were centered in this resource. The failure of this expectation was fatal, as Lord Mar conceived, to the cause, and on it he grounded his own subsequent withdrawal from England.

The entrance of the Chevalier into Perth, on the ninth of January, was attended with far less enthusiasm than the previous portion of his progress. His reception was comparatively cold. On asking to see their "little kings" (the chieftains) with their armies, the Highlanders, diminished in numbers by the secession of the Marquis of Huntley and the absence of Lord Seaforth and others, were marched before him. James could not help admiring their bearing; but the small amount of troops in the camp filled him with a dejection which he could not conceal. When, a few days afterwards, the unfortunate Prince addressed his council for the first time, he said, with mournful truth, these words. "For me it will be no new thing if I am unfortunate: my whole life, even from my cradle, has been a constant series of misfortunes. " This sentiment of ill-presage was re-echoed in the address of the Episcopal clergymen.

"Your Majesty has been trained up, " said these divines, at Fetteresso, "in the School of the Cross, in which the Divine grace inspires the mind with true wisdom and virtue, and guards it against those false blandishments by which prosperity corrupts the heart. " And as this school has sent forth the most illustrious princes, — Moses, Joseph, and David, it was hoped that a similar benefit would accrue to the character of the Prince whom the Episcopal Clergy thus welcomed to their country.

Meantime the project of crowning the Chevalier at Scone amused the minds of the people, and continued to be the subject of diligent preparation by the Earl of Mar. Unhappily a ship laden with money and other aids, had been lost on its passage from France, close to the Tay, for want of a pilot. [132] The difficulties which were augmented by this misfortune, are alluded to in the following extract from one of Lord Mar's letters.

"January 15th, 1715-16.

"Sir,

"I wrote to you yesterday by one that used to come here from Mr. Hall, which I hope will come safe to your hands. At night I had yours of the fourteenth, and this night that of the tenth. The caps do pritty well, and I have orders to thank you for them. I send you one of his own; if you can get such paper t'is well, and if not, the other is what he likes best of any that you sent; so let some of either one or other come when you have an occasion.

"I am sorry Mr. Brewer[133] is ill, for his presence here wou'd be of great use; and as soon as he is able I wish he wou'd come, which I am ordered to tel you, and also that you may endeavour to get a copie of the coronation of King Charles the First and Second, which certainly are to be had in Edinburgh. Willie Wilson had them, and perhaps some of his friends may have got copies of them from him, which may be had.

"I spoke to one some time ago about makeing a crown in pices at Edinburgh and bringing it over here to be put togither, who, I believe, talkt to you of it. That man was here some days ago, but went away before I knew it is wisht that such a thing could yet be done, which is left to your care.

"In case there be occasion for it here, as I wish there may, bulion gold is what I'm afraid will be wanting, but it will not take much. Had not the misfortune I wrote to you of hapn'd to Sir J. Erskine[134] there had been no want of that. We have got no farther account of that affair, tho' we have people about it; but if they do not succeed this night or to-morrow when the spring tide is, it is lost for ever. There is more by the way tho', and I hope will have better fate. I have ordered more papers to be sent you, and certainly you have more of them before now. It is mighty well taken what that lady (the letters from London say) has ordered, as to those you sent her, which you are desired to let her have; and I do not doubt she will do the same as to those concerning E——d. Adieu. "

By the next letter it appears that the good opinion entertained by Lord Mar of the Chevalier was real; since the whole of the epistle has the tone of being a natural effusion of feeling, and is a simple statement of what actually took place, and not the letter of a diplomatist.

"Sir,

"I have seen a letter from Mr. S——g, who had spoke with you on the subject I formerly wrote to you of, concerning that fo—f—y of the D——h to a gentleman with us, Mr. S——q's friend, and upon it our master has thought fit to write the enclosed to him, and orders me to tell you that you must cause give him an hundred guineas at the delivery of the letter. The letter is left open for your perusal, and I wish it may have effect, as perhaps it may. There's no time to be lost in it, and I'll long to know what passes in it, and what hopes you have of him. I sent you credit for five hundred pounds, which I hope you got safe; but if by any accident it should not come to your hands, Mr. S——q there, is a certain goldsmith that will advance what there is occasion for this way. I send you enclosed a letter, which may be of use in an affair I wrote of in my last.

"We have got severall deserters since the K. came and last night nine came in with their clothes and arms, and says many more will follow soon, which I wish we may see. They say, too, that the two regiments of dragoons are marcht from Glasgow for England, and that two are to go from Stirling to replace them. Were they designing to march against Scoon, sure they would not do this, nor is it possible they can do anything in this weather; but if they, notwithstanding, attempt it, perhaps they may find frost in it.

"As I am writing I have received yours of the thirteenth. I read it to the K——g, and delivered him the enclosed letter from Mr. Holmes, which was very well taken, as you will see by the enclosed return, which you'll take care to forward safely; and pray do me the favour to make my compliments there.

"Perhaps you'll hear things of the two northern powers[135] that will look odd to your other friends, as no wonder; but all will come right again—the time they had taken being out in a few days. There's one sent some days ago to assist them, so I hope things will be soon right there, tho' they have done much to spoil them, and each of them makes an excuse of one another as they have done from the begining. The K——, you will see by all the enclosed, is not spareing of his pains. You must fall on the right way of having them all delivered.

"That to Seaforth he writes upon the great professions he made when in France; he is such a fellow that I'm afraid it will do little good.

"I have nothing else material to say just now, but I cannot give over without telling a thing which I'm sure will please you—that the longer one knows the King the better he's liked, and the more good qualities are found in him; that of good-nature is very eminent, and so much good sense that he might be a first minister to any king in Europe, had he not been born a king himself. He has allowed Neil Campbell to go to Edinburgh t'other day on his parole, he being ill, and it was with so much good nature that was evident in his doing of it, that it charmed me. I wish you could get notice how Neil represents it or expresses himself when he gets there; for I wrote it at length to the gentleman who wrote to me about him. Adieu.

"If people from S——q be designing to come to us, they should either do it soon or give us assurances of doing it soon as we are in view of each other; and these assurances must be such that we can depend on, for our conduct must in a great measure be regulated by what we expect that way.

"It were highly necessary that methods and measures were concerted for the right way of doing this, which you should let such of them as you know are so trusted know, and it is absolutely necessary that they either send one to me about this, or let me know it certainly some other way, that we may not be drawing different ways when we are designing the same thing.

"We have no return of the last message which was sent to the good man of the house you wrote of, and t'is above eight days ago. I believe he designs right, tho' t'is odd. "

The enthusiasm which was at first displayed towards the Chevalier was soon cooled, not only by his grave and discouraging aspect, but by his fearless and impolitic display of his religious faith. He never allowed any Protestant even to say grace for him, but employed his own confessor "to repeat the Pater nosters and Ave Marias: " and he also shewed an invincible objection to the usual coronation oath, —a circumstance which deferred the ceremony of coronation, —Bishop Mosse declaring that he would not consent to crown him unless that oath were taken. This sincerity of disposition—for it cannot be called by a more severe name—especially diminished the affections of the Chevalier's female episcopal friends, who had excited their male relations to bear arms in his favour. But the circumstance which weighed the most heavily against James, was the order which he published, on hearing that the Duke of Argyle was making preparations to march against him, for burning the towns and villages, and destroying the corn and forage, between Dumblane and Perth. This act of destruction, from the effects of which the desolate village of Auchterarder has never recovered, was determined on, in order that the enemy might be incommoded as much as possible upon their march; it added to the miseries of a people already impoverished by the taxes and contributions which the Jacobites had levied. It appears, however, from a letter of James's, since discovered, or perhaps, only suppressed at the time, to have been an act which he bitterly regretted, and the order for which he signed most unwillingly. He was desirous of making every reparation in his power for the ravages which were committed in his name. [136]

On the ninth of January a council of war was held by the Duke of Argyle at Stirling, where, by a singular coincidence, the council sat in the same room in which James the Second, then Duke of York, had, in 1680, been entertained by the Earl of Argyle, to whom he had proposed the repeal of the sanguinary laws against Papists. The refusal of Argyle to concur in that measure, the consequences of his conduct, and his subsequent death, are circumstances which, doubtless, arose to the remembrance of his descendant, as he discussed, in that apartment, the march towards Perth.

The country between Stirling and Perth was covered with a deep snow; the weather was one continual storm; it was therefore impossible for the army of Argyle to proceed until the roads were cleared, —a process which required some time to effect. It is asserted, nevertheless, by an historian, that upon Colonel Ghest being sent with two hundred dragoons to reconnoitre the road leading to Perth, that the greatest panic prevailed in that town: immediate preparations were made for defence, and nothing was to be seen except planting of guns, marking out breastworks and trenches, and digging up stones, and laying them with sand to prevent the effects of a bombardment. [137] The Earl of Mar, nevertheless, does not appear, if we may accredit his own words, to have even then despaired of a favourable issue. The following letter betrays no fear, but speaks of some minor inconvenience, which is far from being of a melancholy description. The difficulty of procuring the right sort of ribbon for the decoration of the Garter, is altogether a new feature among the adversities of royal personages. It seems strange that James should not have provided himself, before quitting France, with all that was necessary to preserve the external semblance of majesty.

"January 20th, 1715-16.

"Sir,

"I wrote to you the eighteenth, and sent severall others enclosed, which I hope will come safe to you. The inclosed, markt D. F., is from the King to Davie Floid at London, which he desires you may take care to gett conveid to him safly and soon, it being of consequence. The other is for my wife, which I beg you may forward as usewall.

"We are told that ther's some foot come to Dumblain, and that ther's more expected there. And they still talk as if they designed to march their whole armie against us nixt week. Perhaps they intend it, but with this weather I see not how 'tis in their power. If they do tho', upon their expecting we are to abandon Perth upon their aproach, as I'm told they believe, they will find themselves mistaken, for all here are resolved to stand it to the last, and perhaps we will not wait their comeing the lenth, but meet them by the way. We might have left it indeed, some time ago; but that time is past, and the King's being with us alters the case in every respect. After all, I cannot get myself to belive that they will actually come to us in haste, and if they do they may mistake their reckning. Sure I am, it were impossible for us to march to them in this snow, and our folks are as good at that as they. The snow puts me in mind of the children of Israel's pillar of smoke and pillar of fire; and to say truth, ther's something in the weather very odd and singular; I never saw such.

"My cloathes are almost all worn out, haveing left some at the battle: I know not if you could get me any made and sent from Edinburgh; but if you could, I should be glad of it. Ther's one Bird was my tayler and I belive has my measur, or some old cloathes of mine, that he could make them by. Perhaps he's a whig tho', and will not do it. I would have them deep blew, laced with gold, but not on the seams. I have but one starr and no riban, but 'tis no great matter for that, a better man than I is in the same case; he has only one scrub, one which he got made since he came, and no right riban. I believe ther's neither of that kind of blew nor green riban to be got at Edinburgh; but if you could get some tolorablie like it, you send some of both. Wine is like to be a more sensible want. We got a little Burgundy for the King, but it is out; and tho' we know of a little more, I'm affraid we shall scarce get it brought here; and he does not like clarit, but what you'l think odd, he likes ale tolorably well. I hope they will send us some from France, but with this wind nothing can come from thence. George Hamilton saild on Saturday last, and I belive is there long e'er now, which I heartily wish he may, and I hope you shall soon see the effects of his going with what he caried with him.

"I am affraid Macintosh's men in England may be in hard circumstances for want of money. The King has ordred some for them, which is this daye given to a friend of theirs who was sent to me from the North, who sayes he knows how to get it remitted to them.

"By the news I see the Parliament is to have no mercie on our Preston folks, but I hope God will send them salvation in time.

"I wish you would send us the newspapers oftner for we get them but seldome; the soonest way of sending them is by A. W. at Kirkaldy, who will find some way of sending them to us, notwithstanding of their garisons in Fife.

"I'm affraid what I wrote to you of formerly to be in danger will never be recovered, for it could not at this time, tho' it was try'd; and I fear shall not the next either, tho' we are to do all we can about it, and it was too much to go that way.

"We have heard nothing further as yet from the goodman of the house, as you call him, which I am surprized at. I can say no more now, so Adieu. "

If we may believe the public prints of the day, dissensions now arose between the Chevalier and the Earl of Mar: the former blaming his general for having urged him to come over, when he had so small a force to appear in his favour; the latter, recriminating that the failure of aid from the Continent had discouraged the Chevalier's friends. The Earl of Mar was severely blamed, to quote from the same source, for having deceived the Chevalier in making him believe that the forces in Scotland were more considerable than they really were, and for giving his Scottish friends reason to suppose that the Chevalier would bring over foreign auxiliaries. That the former part of these allegations against Mar was untrue, is shewn by the letter which has been given, explaining to the Prince the state of affairs; and rather discouraging him from his attempt. [138] That the whole report was groundless, was manifested by the favour and confidence which James long continued to extend to the Earl after his exile abroad.

For some time, the Earl of Mar and his party contrived to keep up their hopes. The season was indeed in some respects their friend, since it necessarily impeded the movements of Argyle's army against them. The winter of 1715-16 was one of the most severe that had been felt for many years, not only in Scotland, but abroad. In France and Spain the cold was so excessive, and the snow so deep, that the country people could not go to the market towns to buy provisions, whilst the plains were infested with bears and wolves, emboldened by the desolation, and ranging over the country in great numbers. [139]

Whilst the intense frost lasted, the three thousand Highlanders who were encamped at Perth were able to defy the English army, although now supplied with artillery and ammunition from Berwick. Their security was furthermore increased by a heavy fall of snow succeeding a partial thaw, and followed by a frost, which rendered the roads more impracticable than ever, especially for the foot-soldiers. This circumstance had even occasioned some deliberation whether it would not be advisable for the Duke of Argyle to defer his march to Perth until the winter should be ended. Until the middle of January, it was the full intention of the Highlanders, and also that of the Earl of Mar, to stand the event of a battle, let the enemy's force be what it might. That they purposed thus to maintain their ancient character for valour, was, even as those most adverse to them allow, the prevalent report. It is borne out by the Earl of Mar's correspondence. On the twenty-third of January he thus writes to Captain Straiton:

"The 23rd January.

"I have yours of the seventeenth and the twentieth both togather last night, and a paket from H. in the last. I wrote to you on Saturday the old way, and sent you a paket enclosed, which I belive is of consequence, so I hope it's come safe, and that H. has gott it. He has had two or three sent him from this of late, different ways, and one goes of this day by the near way he sometimes uses. We hear from all hands of the preparations against us, but we resolve to stand it, cost what it will, and if they come out we will certainly give them battle, lett their number be never so great. It must now be plain to all that will allow themselves to see, that nothing less is designed by the present managers than the intire ruin and destruction of this poor country, and of every honest man in it; and if this will not be an awakened people, I know nothing that will. Since this then is plainly the case, there can be no choise in dying honourably in the field for so just a cause, or leving to see the ruin and intire destruction of our country, our King, and our friends and relations. For my part, I shall prefer the first with all cheerfulness, and never desire to live to be a witness to the latter, which certainly will be the case if it please God our King should be defeat. "

The next paragraph of this letter speaks mournfully of disappointment in those on whose aid the Earl had counted.

"It must be a strange infatuation that has gott amongst people, especially those that always pretended to be friends to our cause, many of whom told before the King came that they wad certainly joyn him when he landed, and made his not being with us the only objection, and now when he is come they make some other shift; —I must say such people are worse than our greatest enemies; and if any misfortune should befal the King or his cause, (which God forbid!) I think they that pretended to be our friends have very much to count for, and are more the cause of it than any others, since no doubt the ashourances that many gave to joyn us when the King landed was a chief motive for his comming to us. I hope in God we shall be able to opose them tho' their numbers should be greater, and to their shame and confusion be it if they come against us. I hope very soon the King will have such assistance as will defeat all their designs, and that his affairs will take a sudden turn in other pairts. "

The most serious defection from the Jacobite cause was the submission of the Marquis of Huntley and the Earl of Seaforth to the victorious arms of the Earl of Sutherland, aided by Lord Lovat, in Invernesshire. Seaforth had collected, on the Moor of Gilliechrist, twelve hundred men, the remnant of those whom he had been able to save from Sherriff Muir; but finding that Lord Sutherland had resolved to force him into an engagement, he owned King George as his lawful Sovereign, and promised to lay down his arms. This had occurred early in December, and, according to Lord Mar, before the Earl of Seaforth, in those remote regions, could have heard of the Chevalier's landing. Mar therefore regarded it as a temporary cessation on the part of Seaforth and Huntley, for a given period, of hostilities against the Government.

As far as related to Lord Seaforth, the belief of Lord Mar was correct. At the end of the days agreed upon for the cessation of arms, Seaforth drew his people together, the influence of clanship enabling him to summon them at will, like a king; and again appeared in arms. This was the consequence of the news that James had landed having reached Inverness. But Seaforth could not retrieve the cause of James in the North, nor repair the effects of even a temporary submission. Eventually he returned to the party which he had espoused, and escaped to France. The Marquis of Huntley made his own terms with the Government.

At this critical juncture, unanimity still prevailed, according to Lord Mar, among the assembled chieftains at Perth. "I do assure you, " he writes, "that since the arms came here, there has not been a quarrel of any kind happened among us—not even among the Highland men, which is very extraordinary; and you may depend upon it there is the greatest unanimity here just now, and all fully resolved to stand to it, let what will come. I pray God preserve our King from the wicked and hellish designs of his enemies! I hope we will be apprized of their motions, so as to be in readiness to receive them. "

These expressions were written, but the letter which contained them was not sent, on the twenty-third of January. The postscript, written in a hurried hand, shows that the camp at Perth was not unprepared for the coming attack.

"Since writing of the inclosed, I have two from which I gott last night with the paket; and ane account of that detachment of horse comming out, who we hear came the lenth of Acterardie, [140] upon which account the whole army here were ordred to be in a readyness to march this morning, and we have no account they are returned: we hear it was to vew the roads, and to try if it was practicable to march their army, which they will find very hard to doe while this weather holds. The account you gave in yours of their motions and that detachment was very distinct. The K. read it himself, —it came prety quick. I entreat you fail not to lett us have what accounts you can learn, for what comes from you are among the best we can gett.

"The K. ordered a review of the whole army here this morning, and they are all to hold themselves ready at one half ane hour's advertisment. Lett me hear from you soon. Adieu. "

Again, on the twenty-fourth of January:

"What is above should have gone this morning, but was delyed. Six hundered of the clans are gone out this night to reinforce the garison of Braco and Crief. I hear they have orders to destroy the corn-yards and barns about Achterardir and Black Ford, which we hear were revewed by the enemy yesterday. The King signed thir orders, I can ashour you, most unwillingly; and caused put it in the order that every thing should be made good to the poor people, with a gratuity; and if any of them pleased to come to Perth, they should be maintained and all care taken of them. This you may take for truth, for no doubt they will make a great noise about it.

"We have just now got ane account of a ship being come into Montross, but we know not yett what she brings. Adieu, —writte soon. I am in haste. "

"Eleven att night. "

On the twenty-fourth of January, the Duke of Argyle marched to Dumblane, with two hundred horse, to reconnoitre the roads. The report that the enemy was approaching, was quickly conveyed to Perth; and now was the order to burn and destroy the village of Auchterarder, the contents of the houses, all stores of corn and forage, mournfully and promptly executed. It was supposed by this, that the march of Argyle's forces would be impeded; but it produced no other inconvenience to that army than obliging them to lie one night in the open air; whilst the unpopularity it brought on James and his advisers, was long the subject of comment to their enemies. It is consolatory to those who wish to judge favourably of James to find this declaration in Lord Mar's correspondence.

"The King was forced, sore against his will, to give these burning orders, as all of us were, could we have helped it; but this extraordinary manoeuvre of the enemy made it absolutely necessary. A finger must be cut off to save the whole body. I have ordered some copies of a proclamation to be sent you. There is about two of the places burnt, and there's another ordred about the rest. Adieu.

"It was not amiss that this proclamation were sent to London. "

In pursuance of the cruel and impolitic commands to which Lord Mar refers, three thousand Highlanders were sent forth to the act of destruction. Auchterarder, Crieff, Blackford, Denning and Muthel, were mercilessly burned; and the wretched inhabitants turned out at that inclement season to destitution without a roof to shelter them. Many decrepid people and children perished in the flames. [141] Had James sought, in truth, to prepare a way for the Government in the hearts of the people, he could not have adopted a more suitable means. In the Duke of Argyle, he had a generous and humane adversary to deal with, —one whose forbearance laid him under the imputation of a want of zeal for the cause of the Government, and rendered him no favourite at the English Court. The fashion at the Court of St. James's, according to a letter in the Mar Papers, was, to rail against the Duke, and even George the First and those about him joined in the unjust and ungrateful abuse.

Even so late as Sunday, the twenty-ninth of January, when Argyle's troops left Stirling and advanced to Braco Castle, Lord Mar appears to have been in ignorance of their actual movements. Perhaps, like the busy world of London politicians, he regarded the project of an attempt upon Perth in such weather as impracticable. Such was the opinion at St. James's. "Argyle's friends here, " writes one near the Court, "speak of the march and the attempt at present as madness. " And another individual writes, that "one half of their people must die of cold, and the other be knocked o' the head. So it seems Argyle is dragg'd to this matter. We cannot perceive, by all the letters that come up, any particular certainty as to Lord Mar's number and his designs. The Court are positive he will not stand; and they, as well as Ridpeath, assert strongly that the Pretender is gone already as far as Glammis. The Jacobites fancy that if he went thither, it was to meet and assemble these officers that were landed. "[142]

Whilst in this state of perplexity Lord Mar thus writes:

"Jan. 29th.

"Sir,

"I have keept the man that brought yours of the nineteenth and twentieth, from A. W., on Saturday, till now, that I might have a sure and speedy way of writeing to you when anything of consequence happened, which we were expecting every minut last night. I wrote one to you when I belived the enemie's front to be at Auchterarder, and despatcht it; but late at night getting intelligence of that party of the enemie who were marching towards Aucterarder haveing marcht back without comeing the lenth of that place to Dumblain, if not to Stirling, without halting by the way, I stopt my letter and kepp it till they actually march, and then perhaps I may yet send it to you, there being some other things in it necessary for you to know upon that emergance which is needless other wayes.

"In it I told you of my haveing received yours of the eighteenth on Sunday, and last night those of the fifteenth and twenty-first both togither.

"By all appearance the enemie resolve to march against us, as one might say, whether it be possible or not. They sent a party of horse and foot to Dumblain on Sunday, which came near to Auchterarder yesterday, I belive to try if the thing was practicable, but they returned to Dumblain as above. We shall be forced to burn and distroy a good deal of the country to prevent their marching, which goes very, *very* much against the King's mind, as it does mine and more of us; but ther's an absolat necessity for it, and I believe it will be put in execution this night or to-morrow morning, which grieves me. Could it be helpt? this way of their makeing warr in this, I may say, impracticable season, must have extraordinary methods to oppose it. And I hope in God, any that suffers now, it shall soon be in the King's power to make them a large reparation. After all, when they have no cover left them, I see not how it is possible for them to march. We are like to be froze in the house; and how they can endure the cold for one night in the fields, I cannot conceive; and then the roads are so, that but one can go abreast, as their party did yesterday; and ther's no going off the road for horse and scarce for foot, without being lost in the snow; but if, after all, they do march, we must do our best, and I hope God will preserve and yet prosper the King, who is the best prince I belive in the world.

"As for news in the kingdome of Fife, I suppose you wou'd hear that a party of the Mc Grigors some dayes ago from Faulkland attacquet a party of Swise and militia from Leslie and beat them, takeing thirty-two prisoners, wherof eleven horse, as I hear. I have not time to say more, so adieu. "

"January 29th, 1715-16. "

Again, in another letter on the same day, the Earl still seems to consider the game as not then lost. It is amusing to find how, in the carrying on of his projects, he availed himself of the aid of ladies, and how troubled he sometimes found himself with "busie women. " Whilst this letter was being penned, Argyle was employing the country people around Auchterarder in clearing the roads of snow: and on the following day, he had advanced towards Tullibardine, within eight miles of Perth. On that very Sunday, Lord Mar thus writes: it is evident he had at this time formed no plan of retreat.

"Sunday, 11 o'clock forenoon, Janu 29th, 1715-16.

"Sir,

"Since I wrote to you I have got yours of the twenty-second, one of the twenty-third, and two of the twenty-fifth; the last of which, tho' the first wrote, I got not til this morning. I wou'd have wrote to you these two dayes by post, but we have had so many alarms of the enimie's marching towards us, that I had not time, as I have very little to say anything just now, for I expect ivery minut to hear of their being marcht from Dumblain, where a considerable number of them have been these two dayes this way.

"The enclosed you must take care to send by the first post which is opened again on purpose for you to read, but I'm affraid you will not understand it all. As to that paper you sent me which came from England, there can be nothing said to it from hence just now, only that they are to do the best they can; and I hope shortly that country shall have sent them where withall to enable them to make a better figur than they have hitherto done. We are not in a condition here to give them any help just now. Ther's one Mrs. Lawson, who seems to be a diligent body, that complains a little that you do not allow her to see you often enough, which I take to be the complaint of an over busie woman, than which ther's nothing more uneasie; but just now such people must be humoured, and she has really been usefull. Before this goes 'tis very likely I may have occassion to inclose one I formerly wrote to you upon a certain occasion, but did not then send as I told you in another, the thing not then hapning, but we expect it every minut. Deserters of all kinds come in to us pritty fast, foreigners as well as subjects; and if they but give them time, I am perswaded great numbers will.

"'Tis now five o'clock and we have no accounts of any of the enimie being come further than Dodoch, where a partie of them came last night, so I'll detain the messenger. This goes by no stranger. Perhaps they may find the roads impracticable, and by the burning that they can advance no further, —at which, indeed, I shall not be much surprised; and if so, may be forced to delay their extraordinary march til more human weather for making warr. The King was forced, sore against his will, to give these burning orders, —as all of us were, could wee have helpt it; but this extrodinar manuver of the enimie made it absolutly necessary: a fingor must be cut of to save the whole body. I have ordered some copies of a proclamation to be sent you, there is about two of the places burnt, and ther's another order about the rest. Adieu.

"It were not amiss that this proclamation was sent to London. The little young letter enclosed is for Lady Wigton, which pray cause deliver. "

On Tuesday, the last day of January, the Duke of Argyle passed the river Eru, and took possession of Tullibardine. It has been stated by several historians that the Jacobites fled from Perth on the same day; but the following letter from Lord Mar, dated the first of February, shows that the flight could not have taken place until the following day. This curious letter, which was written at the early hour of six in the morning, is unfinished. It is the last in the series of that correspondence which has formed of itself a narrative of Lord Mar's life, from his first taking upon himself the office of General and Commander-in-Chief, to the hour when he virtually resigned that command. In the midst of pressing danger his sanguine nature seems not to have deserted him: his love of the underplots of life, the influence of "Kate Bruce, " and the arrangements for a coronation, were as much in his thoughts as in the more hopeful days before Sherriff Muir and Preston.

"Wednesday, about six forenoon, ffebruary 1st, 1716.

"On Monday evening I gave you the trouble of a greatly long letter, mostly on indifferent subjects, and sent it off yesterday to A. W. If I was too tedious upon what concerned a woman and a Prince, it was with a good intent, and to make matters plain. By what I hear from R. B., and the Hole, that Argyle's forces were yesterday forenoon at Stirling, and so was the regiments of dragoons there and St. Ninian's, for accounts of motions there and thereabouts, on both sydes of the river, —you may expect it best sent from R. B., the Hole, and a grave gentleman.

"By yesternight's post I sent of McQuart's letter; and indeed, in most or all letters I write to that quarter for ten weeks past, I alwayes requested that whatever was to be done might be quickly done. I lykeways sent to London between fyve or six, several honest hands, to put off the proclamation declaration about burning, and that paper of which I some days ago sent you two copies. And now I begin to think I have been in the wrong to Mr. S——g, in the short character I gave you of him, at least, if it be true that I am told, that he is not only author of that paper I sent you the two copies of, but has got a very great number of them printed; and tho' I may be an insufficient judge, I must acknowledge I am very well pleased with the paper, for I think it full of plain truths; and besydes other dispersings, I did indeed yesterday cause putt in fiftein copies of it in the Lords of Session's boxes.

"The litle letter to my good Lady W. [143] I caused carefully to be delivered. I wish all women had some share of her good, sweet, easie temper, for, as you will observe, over-busied women are most uneasie; and I have had much experience of it within these four months past in many instances, and with more persons than one or two. The only inconvenience I had by Kate Bruce lodging in the same house with me was, it brought in too many women upon me, and some of these brought in others, and to this minute I cannot with descretion get quit of them.

"A good time ago you were pleased to tell me you could not well conceive how I got myself keept free, but if you now knew what a multitude knows where I lodge, you would wonder more; and indeed it is no litle admiration to myself: but as soon as I have so much strenth, and can fynd a convenient place (which is not easie), I will change my quarters, if it were for no other reason than to be quit of useless people of both sexes, that interrupt me from busieness, or trouble with impertinent questions. And whyle I am accuseing others of indescretion, I wish I am not so myself in so much insisting upon and troubling you with such matters.

"At Perth I have gott a collection of all papers relating to the coronation of King Charles the First and Second, and shall send them whenever you think fitt; but I suppose it may be convenient to lett the present hurrie a little over before I send them to you.

"How the great Generalls can imploy their hors to great purpose in the deep snow, or how men and hors will long hold out in such weather, is what I do not understand. I hope a shorter time than they imagine will destroy, even without the help of an enemy, —at least, make many, both men and hors, inserviceable. "

Much had been going on in the meantime, to which Lord Mar, perhaps from the fear of spreading a panic, does not even allude to his correspondent in Edinburgh. When it became known in Perth that Argyle had left Stirling, the advisers of the Chevalier were dismayed and distracted by contending counsels. But the mass of the army expressed a very different sentiment, rejoicing that the opportunity of a rencontre with the enemy was so near: congratulations were heard passing from officers to their brother officers, and the soldiers, as they drank, pledged their cups to the good day near at hand. The council, meantime, sat all night: the irresolution of that body, towards morning, was disclosed to the impatient soldiery: the indignation of the brave men, and more especially of the Highlanders, burst forth upon the disclosure of what had passed in the council. The gentlemen volunteers resented the pusillanimity of their leaders: and one of them was heard to propose that the clans should take the Chevalier out of the hands of those who counselled him to retreat, and added that he would find ten thousand gentlemen in Scotland that would risk their lives for him. A friend of Mar, after remonstrating with these malcontents, asked "What they wished their officers to do? " "Do! " was the reply; "what did you call on us to take arms for? was it to run away? What did the King come hither for? was it to see his people butchered by hangmen and not strike a note for their lives? Let us die like men, and not live dogs. "[144]
On the thirtieth of January the Chevalier himself opened another council in the evening, and in a few words proposed a retreat. Lord Mar then addressed the meeting, and advocated the measure with a degree of ingenuity and eloquence which, at that moment, we are disposed rather to condemn than applaud; yet, his reasons for abandoning Perth were such, as in cool reflection were not devoid of justice, and they might be founded upon a humane consideration for

the brave adherents of a lost cause. He stated, first, as the cause of his proposal, the failure of the Duke of Ormond's invasion of England. Secondly, the accession of foreign troops to the Duke of Argyle's force. Lastly, the reduced number of the Chevalier's troops, which then amounted to four thousand, only two thousand three hundred of which were properly armed. Even in that weak condition the Chevalier would, according to Lord Mar's subsequent statement, gladly have maintained Perth, or ventured a battle; but when the enemy with an army of eight thousand men were actually advanced near to the place, it was found impracticable to defend Perth, the town being little more at that time than an open village; and the river Tay on one side, and the fosse on the other, being both frozen over, it would have been easy to enter the town at any quarter. Added to this, the mills had been long stopped by the frost, so that there were not above two days' provision in the town. There were no coals to be procured: the enemy had possession of the coal mines in Fife, and wood was scarce. The Earl also contended that the Highlanders, however able in attack, were not accustomed to the defence of towns.

Reasons equally cogent were employed against going out to fight the enemy, and a retreat northwards was at length proposed. But it was no easy task to bring the brave spirits who had hailed the approach of Argyle, to accord in sentiments which might spring from discretion, but which ill agreed with the Highland notions of honour. The council, after a stormy debate, was broken up in confusion, and adjourned until the next morning.

Some hours afterwards, a few, who were favourable to the abandonment of Perth, were summoned privately by Lord Mar; and it was then agreed not to fight, but to retreat. For a time this determination was concealed from the bulk of the army, but it gained wind; and on the evening of the thirty-first of January, eight hundred of the Highlanders indignantly left Perth, and retired beyond Dunkeld, to their homes. That very night, also, the Chevalier, who had far less of the Scottish Stuart within him than of that modified and inferior variety exemplified in the British line of the family, disappeared from the town, and repaired to Scone. He supped and slept in the house of the Provost Hay; and on the following morning, at an early hour, was ready for retreat. To do the Chevalier justice, there was, according to Lord Mar's journal, much difficulty in persuading him to this step: it was found necessary to convince him that it had become a duty to retire from the pursuit of the Government, which, as long as he was in the country, would never cease to persecute his followers, who could not make any terms of capitulation so long as he remained. He was obliged, at last, to consent: "And, I dare say, " adds Lord Mar, "no consent he ever gave was so uneasy to him as this was. "[145] Of that point it would be satisfactory to be well assured.

On the first of February, four hours after the unfinished letter of Lord Mar was written, the Jacobites abandoned Perth, and crossing the frozen stream of the Tay, took their route to Dundee. They went forth in such precipitation, that they left their cannon behind them, —a proof that they never hoped to oppose again the victorious arms of Argyle. About noon the Chevalier, accompanied by Lord Mar, followed his people towards the North. He is said to have been disconsolate, —and, shedding tears, to have complained "that instead of bringing him a crown, they had brought him to his grave. " This murmur and these tears having been reported to Prince Eugene, of Savoy, that General remarked "that weeping was not the way to conquer kingdoms. "[146]

The Jacobites marched direct for Dundee, along the Carse of Gowrie. The Duke of Argyle's forces entered Perth only two hours after the Highland army had entirely cleared the Tay, which, happily for their retreat, was frozen over with ice of an extraordinary thickness. At Dundee the Chevalier rested one night only; but leaving it on the second of February, was again succeeded by Argyle and his squadrons, who arrived there on the following day.

The unfortunate Prince pursued his way to Montrose. His route along the sea-coast gave credence to a report which had now gained ground, of his intention of embarking for France. The loudest murmurs again ran through the Highland forces, worthy of a noble leader, and the sight of some French vessels lying near the shore confirmed the general suspicion. This was, nevertheless, somewhat allayed by an order to the clans to march that evening at eight o'clock to Aberdeen, where, in accordance with the crooked policy and deceptive plan of Lord Mar, it was represented that large supplies of troops and arms would meet them from France. But a very different scheme was in agitation among those who governed the feeble James, and perhaps, with right motives, guided him to his safety.

A small ship lay in the harbour of Montrose, for the purpose, originally, of carrying over an envoy from James to some foreign court. This vessel was now pitched upon to transport the Chevalier; the size being limited, she could accommodate but few passengers: and therefore, to avoid confusion, the Chevalier "himself thought fit to name who should attend him. " "The Earl of Mar, who was the first named, made difficulty, and begged he might be left behind; but the Chevalier being positive for his going, and telling him that, in a great measure, there were the same reasons for his going as for his own, —that his friends could more easily get terms without him than with him, —and that, as things now stood, he could be of no more use to them in their own country, he submitted. "[147]

The Chevalier then chose the Marquis of Drummond to accompany him: this nobleman was lame from a fall from his horse, and was not in a condition to follow the army. He, as well as the Earl of Mar, the Lord Tullibardine, and the Lord Linlithgow had a bill of attainder passed against them. The Chevalier on that account was desirous of taking these other Lords with him; but both were absent: Lord Tullibardine was at Brechin with a part of the foot, and Lord Linlithgow at Berire with the horse. He ordered the Earl Marischal, General Sheldon, and Colonel Clephan to accompany him.

After these arrangements the Chevalier issued several orders which reflect the utmost credit upon his disposition. After appointing General Gordon Commander-in-chief, with all necessary powers, he wrote a paper containing his reasons for leaving the kingdom, and, delivering it to the General, gave him at the same time all the money in his possession, except a small sum which he reserved for his expenses and those of his suite; and desired, that after the army had been paid, the residue should be given to the impoverished and houseless inhabitants of Auchterarder. He then dictated a letter to the Duke of Argyle, in which he dwelt at some length upon his distress at being obliged "among the manifold mortifications which he had had in this unfortunate expedition, " to burn the villages. The letter, which was never delivered to the Duke of Argyle, is in the possession of the Fingask family. [148]
Having completed these arrangements, the Chevalier prepared to take leave for ever of the Scottish shores. The hour had now arrived which was appointed for the march of the troops, and the Chevalier's horses were brought before the door of the house in which he lodged: the guard which usually attended him whilst he mounted, were in readiness, and all was prepared as if he were

resolved to march with the clans to Aberdeen. But meantime, the Chevalier had slipped out of his temporary abode on foot, accompanied only by one servant; and going to the Earl of Mar's lodgings, he went thence, attended by the Earl, through a bye-way to the water side, where a boat awaited him and carried him and the Earl of Mar to a French ship of ninety tons, the Marie Therese, of St. Malo. About a quarter of an hour afterwards two other boats carried the Earl of Melfort and Lord Drummond, with General Sheldon and ten other gentlemen, on board the same ship: they then hoisted sail and put to sea; and notwithstanding that several of the King's ships were cruizing on the coast, they sailed in safety, and after a passage of seven days, arrived at Waldam, near Gravelines, in French Flanders.

The Chevalier sailed at nine o'clock. Some hours afterwards, Earl Marischal and Colonel Clephan arrived at the shore, but they could get no boat to convey them, for fear of the men-of-war that were cruizing near. The Marie Therese, nevertheless, got out of reach of these vessels before daylight.

With what reflections Lord Mar left his native country a prey to the power of an irritated Government, cannot readily be conceived. That he left it at such a moment, is a fact which for ever stamps his memory with degradation. The deserted adherents of James, being in no condition to make a stand against the Duke of Argyle, betook themselves to holes and caves, mostly in the remote parts of the Highlands, where many lurked until they could safely appear; but such as were most obnoxious took the first opportunity of ships to carry them into foreign countries; and vessels were, to this end, provided by the Chevalier with such success, that many escaped from the pursuit of justice.

James, accompanied by the Earl of Mar, proceeded to his former residence at St. Germains, where, in spite of the wishes of the French Government that he should repair to his old asylum in Lorraine, he wished to remain. In Paris, the Chevalier met two of his most distinguished adherents, —the faithless Bolingbroke, and the popular Duke of Ormond. Although aware of the unsoundness of Bolingbroke's loyalty, James received him cordially. "No Italian, " says Bolingbroke, "ever embraced the man he was going to stab with a greater show of affection and confidence. "

For some time the Chevalier lingered in Paris, hoping to see the Regent. "His trunks were packed, his chaise was ordered at five that afternoon, " writes Lord Bolingbroke, "and I wrote word to Paris that he was gone. Instead of taking post for Lorraine, he went to the little house in the Bois de Boulogne, where his female ministers resided; and there he continued lurking for some days, pleasing himself with the air of mystery and business, while the only real business which he should have had at heart he neglected. "[149]

Avignon was now fixed on as the retreat of the Chevalier; and thither, after some delay, he retired, to an existence politically forgotten by the Continental powers, until the war with Spain and the consequent declaration of the Spanish King in his favour recalled him to importance.

Lord Mar, meantime, occupied himself in fruitless endeavours to excite, once more, the struggle which had just ended so fatally. As far as France was concerned, all those schemes upon which Mar successively built were futile: no aid could ever be expected during the Regency. "My hopes, " said Bolingbroke, speaking of the Jacobite cause, "sunk as he [Louis the Fourteenth] declined, and died when he expired. The event of things has sufficiently shown that all those which were entertained by the Duke [of Ormond], and the Jacobite party under the Regency, were the grossest delusions imaginable. "[150]

Some of the remaining years of Lord Mar's life were, nevertheless, devoted to chimerical projects for which he received in return little but disappointment, ingratitude, and humiliation. One of his schemes was to engage Charles the Twelfth of Sweden on the side of the Chevalier. In a letter to Captain Straiton, the Chevalier's agent in Edinburgh, he signified that if five or six thousand bolls of meal could be purchased by the King's friends and sent to Sweden, where there was then a great scarcity, it would be of service to his master in conciliating the good will of Charles. This proposal was communicated by Mar's desire to Lockhart of Carnwath, to Lord Balmerino, and to the Bishop of Edinburgh. But it was the sanguine disposition of Mar which alone could lead him to suppose such a scheme practicable. It was, in the first place, found impossible to raise so large a sum from men, many of them exiles, or involved in difficulties from the expenses of the recent insurrection. It was also deemed folly to conceive that so large a quantity of Scotch meal as necessary could be exported without exciting the suspicion of Government.

The next plan which Lord Mar contrived was not so fully unfolded as the project of which Charles the Twelfth was to be the object. He wrote to Edinburgh soon after the failure of the first scheme, to this effect: that a certain foreign prince had entered into a design for the restoration of James: that it "would look odd if his friends at home did not assist him; " and he wished they would fall on some means to have in readiness such a sum as they could afford to venture in his cause when a fair opportunity occurred. The hint was taken up seriously by the zealous Lockhart of Carnwath, and assurances were sent from "several persons of honour, that they would be in a condition to answer his Majesty's call. " Among these, the Earl of Eglintoun offered three thousand guineas; and the others "would have given a good round sum. " The conduct of the English Government to the Duke of Argyle, who had been superseded as Commander-in-Chief in Scotland, and the strong personal friendship between Lockhart and the Duke, emboldened Mar to hope that a negotiation might be entered into with Argyle, and that he might be persuaded to join in their schemes. At the same time, Lord Mar enjoined the strictest secrecy in all these affairs, and with reason, for the letters of the exiled Jacobites abounded in false hopes and plans; many of their correspondents at home had not the discretion to conceal their delight, when the sanguine expectations of their party prevailed over despair.

The agent employed by Lockhart to treat with the Duke of Argyle was Colonel John Middleton. By him Lockhart was, however, assured that his Grace would neither directly nor indirectly treat with Mar for "he believed him his mortal enemy, and had no opinion of his honour; and, " added Middleton, "I cannot think Mar does, more seriously now than before, desire to see Argyle in the King's measures, lest he eclipsed him. " It was therefore resolved by Lockhart, that the correspondence between the Chevalier and Argyle should be contrived without Mar's cognizance. A letter was written to James, and was forwarded by Captain Straiton, enclosed, to the Earl of Mar, who was, in another epistle from Lockhart, "entreated not to be offended that the contents of the letter were not communicated to him, because he was bound to impart the same alone to the King. "

This letter, containing a proposal so important to the interests of James, is supposed never to have reached the Chevalier. Mar, distrustful and offended, is suspected of having broken it open, and given it his own answer in a letter to the Duke of Argyle, which tended to affront and repel the Duke rather than to invite him to allegiance. When, some time afterwards, Lockhart's son spoke on the subject to the Chevalier at home, and represented what a fair opportunity had been lost, the Prince replied, "that he did not remember ever to have heard of it before. "[151] Whether Mar was misjudged or not must be a matter of doubt, but this anecdote proves how little respect was entertained for his good faith, or even for his possessing the common sentiments of gentlemanly propriety, when the suspicion of breaking open a letter which had been entrusted to him was attached to his conduct.

In consequence of the difficulty of bringing any scheme to bear, from the want of a head, Lockhart had contrived a plan of having trustees in Scotland to conduct it, to be empowered by James to act during his absence, and in his behalf. This plan had the usual obstacles to encounter among a set of factious partisans, who were only united when the common danger pressed and common services were required, but discordant and selfish in the calmer days of suspense. Mar, perhaps, with greater wisdom than he was allowed to display, did not advance the scheme; his reluctance to promote it was ascribed to his love of power in Scotland; but since the plan was resented by Tullibardine, Seaforth, and Penmure, [152] as infringing upon their dignity, there is as good reason for believing that it was the suggestion of an intriguing ambition on the part of the proposer, as that Mar resisted it on selfish grounds. The notion was excellent, but the difficulty was to find men of sufficient fidelity, honesty, and prudence to exercise functions so delicate.

The spirit of Jacobitism seems scarcely, at this period to have been checked in the bosoms of the resolute people who had suffered so much; and the Netherbow and the High Street of Edinburgh still resounded at times with the firing of musquetry, directed against a harmless rabble of boys who betrayed the popular feeling by the white roses in their hats. [153] Nor was the lingering enthusiasm for the Jacobite cause confined to the lower classes in either country. It is almost incredible that men of Whig principles, who held high offices in the Government, should, at various times, have engaged in correspondence with the agents of James; yet such is the fact.

Among those who were involved in these dangerous negotiations, Charles Earl of Sunderland, the son-in-law of Marlborough, and at that time Prime Minister of George the First, was one with whom Lord Mar treated. Among the Sunderland Papers is to be found a singular letter from the Earl of Mar to the Earl of Sunderland, urging that nobleman to assist in inducing his royal master to accede to a proposal from which he might himself derive a suitable advantage. "We find, " says Dr. Coxe, "unequivocal proofs that Lord Sunderland, who was considered at the head of the new administration formed in 1717, was in secret correspondence with the Pretender and his principal agents. "[154]

The letter referred to from Lord Mar, on which Dr. Coxe has inscribed the word "curious, " began with professions of respect and confidence on the part of his Lordship, to whom it was quite as easy to address those expressions to a man of one party as of the other. It contained also a promise of secrecy, and an exaction of a similar observance on the part of Lord Sunderland. He then alluded to the misfortunes into which the British nation was thrown by the disputed succession, and the violence of party spirit in consequence. The subtle politician next touched on the subject of George the First, whom he delicately terms, "your master. "

"Whatever good opinion you may have of *your master*, and the way that things are ordered there at present, does not alter the case much; his health is not so good as to promise a long life, and he is not to live always even if it were good, nor will things continue there as they are, any longer than he lives at most. "

He then suggests that the Earl would have it in his power to prevent the dangers resulting from a disputed succession, "which can only be prevented by restoring the rightful and lineal heir. "

"I can assure your Lordship, " he continues, "my master has so many good qualities, that he will make the nation happie, and wants but to be known to be beloved; and I dare promise in his name, that there is not any thing you could ask of him, reasonable, for yourself and your friends, but he would agree to. My master is young, in perfect good health, and as likely to live as any who has pretensions to his crown, and he is now about marrying, which, in all appearance, will perpetuate rightfull successors to him of his own body, who will ever have more friends in those kingdoms, as well as abroad, than to allow the house of Hanover to continue in possession of their right without continual disturbance. "

The Earl then suggests that George the First should secure to himself the possession of "his old and just inheritance, and by the assistance of '*his master,*' and those who would join, acquire such new ones on the Continent as would make his family more considerable than any of its neighbours.

"Britain and Ireland will have reason to bless your master for so good and Christian an action; and Europe no less for the repose it would have by it: and your master would live the remainder of his life in all the tranquillity and splendour that could be required, and end his days with the character of good and just. "

Lord Mar was at this time on the borders of France, where he proposed to wait until he received Lord Sunderland's reply, in hopes that the Minister of George the First might be induced to give him a meeting, either in France or Flanders. "If you approve not of what I have said, " he adds, "let it be buried on your side, as, upon my honour, it shall be on mine. " "I am afraid, " he adds in a postscript, "you know not my hand; but I have no other way of assuring you of this being no counterfeit than by writing it myself, and putting my seal to it. "

The following remarks on this letter are interesting; they were penned by Dr. Coxe:

"Singular as this overture, made at such a period, may appear, we have strong proofs that it was not discouraged by Sunderland; for he not only procured a pension for the exiled nobleman, but even flattered the Jacobites with hopes that he was inclined to favour their cause. This we find by intelligence given at a subsequent period by the Jacobite spies. "

The following addition to the above-stated remark of Dr. Coxe is even yet more astonishing:

"On the death of Lord Sunderland the secret of this correspondence became by some means known to the Regent Duke of Orleans, and he hastened to make so important a communication to the King of England. The letter written on this occasion by the British agent at Paris, Sir Luke Schwaub, and the reply of his friend Lord Carteret, then Secretary of State, are highly curious, because they prove, not only the correspondence, but the fact that it was known and approved by the King. "[155]

How near were the unfortunate Stuarts to that throne which they were destined never to ascend!

Upon the disgrace of Bolingbroke, and on his return to England, the Seals had been offered by James Stuart to Lord Mar, who refused them on the ostensible ground that he "could not speak French. " The actual reason was perhaps to be sought for in a far deeper motive. [156]

In 1714 the celebrated Lord Stair had been sent as Ambassador to France, chiefly to watch over the proceedings of the Jacobites, and to cement a friendship with the Duke of Orleans, on whom King George could not rely. The brilliant and spirited manner in which Lord Stair executed this commission, the splendour by which his embassy was distinguished, and his own personal qualities, courtesy, shrewdness, and diligence, contributed mainly to the diminution of the Jacobite influence, which declined under his exertions. It was from Lord Stair's address that Bolingbroke, or, as Stair calls him in his correspondence, Mr. York, was confirmed in his disgust to the Jacobite cause.

Between Lord Stair and the Earl of Mar an early acquaintance had existed. Agreeably to the fashion of the period, which led Queen Anne and the Duchess of Marlborough to assume the names of Morley and Freeman, Lord Stair and Lord Mar, in the early days of their confidence, had adopted the familiar names of Captain Brown, and Joe Murray.

Lord Mar had remained in Paris until October 1717; he then went into Italy with the Duke of Ormond; but previous to his departure he called on Lord Stair, and remained in the house of the Ambassador for four or five hours. He appears to have declared to Lord Stair that he then looked upon the affairs of his master as desperate. "He flung out, " as Lord Stair wrote, "several things, as I thought, with a design to try whether there was any hopes of treating. " Lord Stair, not liking to give an old friend false hopes, declined "dipping into particulars; " adding at the same time, in his account of the interview, "he would not have dealt so with me: but in conversation of that kind there is always something curious to be learned. "

They parted without explanation, and Lord Mar proceeded to Rome. The correspondence between these two noblemen ceased for nearly two years. [157] During that interval, James had married the Princess Clementina Maria, a daughter of Prince Sobieski, elder son of John King of Poland. The marriage could scarcely have been solemnized, since it took place early in May 1719, before we find Lord Mar at Geneva, on his way from Italy, resuming his negotiations with Lord Stair.

LORD MAR TO LORD STAIR.

"May 6th, 1719.

"Good Captain Brown will not, I hope, take amiss his old acquaintance Jo. Murraye's writing to him at this time; and when he knows the occasion, I am persuaded he will forgive him, and comply, as far as he can, with what he is to ask him. My health is not so good just now nor for some time past, as you would wish it; and I am advised to drink the waters of Bourbon for it, as being the likest to those of the Bath of any this side the sea, of which I formerly found so much good. The hot climate where I have been for some time past, by no means agrees with my health; and I am persuaded that where some of our company is gone will still do worse with me.

"The affair in which it might be thought my Captain would employ me being now, I suppose, over for this bout, there needs be, I should think, no objection to what I should ask.

"I am come part of the way already; but I would not go much further, without acquainting you with it. And now I beg that on the consideration of the health of an old friend, you will give me allowance or furlo to go to the waters of Bourbon, and to continue there so long as I may have occasion for them during the two seasons this year; and I promise to you I shall do nothing in any way, the time of my being there, but as you would have me; so that this allowance can be of no prejudice to the service. If you cannot give me the furlo yourself, I imagine your Colonel will not refuse it, if you will be so good as to ask it for me.

"But because the first season of the waters is going fast away, I should be glad you could do it without waiting to hear from your Colonel about it, who, I should think, will not take it amiss when you acquaint him with your having ventured to do so. Do not, I beg of you, think there is any fetch in this, or anything but what I have told you, which, upon honour, is nothing but truth, and all the truth.

"I hope there will be no occasion of your mentioning your having had this trouble from me to any, unless it be to your Colonel and one or two about him, and the person, it is like, you must speak to where you are. There is one with me, an old school acquaintance of yours too, Mr. Stuart of Invernethy, whom you have seen dance very merrily over a sword; and if the allowance is granted me, I hope it will not be refused to him, for whom I promise as I do for myself.

"When I have done with the waters, I hope there will be no objection to my returning to Italy again, if I have a mind; but I judged it fit to mention this to you.

"The person who delivers you this, will get conveyed to me what you will be so good to write. "

Whilst he was thus in treaty with his former friend, Lord Mar was stopped on his way to St. Prix, near Geneva, by the orders of the Hanoverian Minister: his papers were seized and sealed up; and among them, a copy of that which was written to Lord Stair as Captain Brown. Lord Mar, who had borne an assumed name, disclosed his real rank, and wrote to Lord Stair for assistance, — again urging permission to go to the waters of Bourbon, or, if not allowed to go into France, the liberty to return to Italy, "where, " he said, "I may end my days in quiet; and those, probably, will not be many in that climate. " Whilst awaiting the reply of Lord Stair, the Earl was treated with respect by the authorities of Geneva; and "had only to wish that he had a little more liberty for taking air and exercise. " He expected that Lord Stair's answer could not arrive in less than a fortnight: in the meantime, he adds, "I shall be obliged, on account of my health, to ask the Government here a little more tether. "[158]

His indulgent friend, Lord Stair, was, meantime, urging his cause by every means in his power. "I wish Lord Mar, " he wrote to the English Ministry, "was at liberty upon his parole to the town of Geneva, or he had permission to go to the waters of Bourbon. I should be glad to know what pension you would allow him till he be restored? "

Lady Mar was now in Rome, whither she had followed her husband soon after his leaving Scotland. Her jointure, it appears, was stopped by the Commissioners, and she was unable, without that supply, to travel from Rome to Geneva. She was, probably, aware of Lord Mar's intention to leave the Chevalier's service, for the Earl had written a long letter, explanatory of his situation and intentions, to her father the Duke of Kingston. "I have offered him for Lady Mar's journey, " says Lord Stair, "credit upon me for a thousand pounds. " Yet notwithstanding this liberality, Lord Mar now began to be extremely uneasy at Geneva, and to fear that the Government meant "merely to expose him. " In vain, for some time, did Stair plead for him, with Secretary Craggs and Lord Stanhope. They were evidently, from Lord Stair's replies to their objections, afraid to have any dealings with him. "As to Lord Mar, " writes Stair, "the things that shock you, shock me; but our business is to break the Pretender's party by detaching him from it, which we shall effectually do by letting him live in quiet at Geneva or elsewhere, and by giving him a pension. Whatever his Lordship's intentions may be, it is very certain, in a few months, that the Jacobites will pull his throat out, —you know them well enough not to doubt of it. The Pretender, " he adds, "looks upon Mar as lost, and has had no manner of confidence in him ever since Lady Mar came into Italy. They looked upon her as a spy, and that she had corrupted her husband. This, you may depend on it, is true. " Little more than a week afterwards, Lord Stair informed his friends that "Lord Mar was *outré* at the usage he had met with. He says our Ministers may be great and able men, but that they are not skilful at making proselytes, or keeping friends when they have them. I am pretty much of his mind. "

It was, doubtless, as Lord Stair declared, the full determination of Lord Mar at that time to leave the Chevalier's interests. "The Pretender, I know, " said Stair, "wrote him the kindest letter imaginable since his [the Pretender's] return into Italy from Spain, with the warmest invitations to return to his post. "

The letters which Lord Stair had received, in the course of this negotiation, from Lord Mar, were instantly sent to Hanover. They were in some instances written in his own hand, but without signature, and in the third person. In the first which he wrote to Lord Stair, Mar announced that he had quitted the service of James, and was desirous of making peace with King George upon the promise of a pardon, and the restoration of his estates.

"You are to consider, " says Lord Stair, writing to the Secretary of State at home concerning this proposal, "whether it will be worth the while to receive him. In my humble opinion the taking him on will be the greatest blow that can be given to the Pretender's interest, and the greatest discredit to it. And it may be made of use to show to the world that nobody but a Papist can hope to continue in favour with the Pretender. I wish, " adds the Ambassador, "you may think as I do. I own all his faults and misfortunes cannot make me forget the long and intimate friendship and familiarity that has been between him and me. " It is consoling to find any politician acting upon such good old-fashioned maxims, the result of honest feeling.

Lady Mar having now joined her husband, Lord Mar resolved to make his escape from Geneva. Lord Stair advised him against it; but adds, in his letters to his friends at home, "I could hardly imagine that a man of his temper, and in his circumstances, will refuse his liberty when he sees he has nothing but ill usage and neglect to expect from us. "[159]

Thus ended this negotiation, the main conditions of which were, provided Lord Mar kept himself free from any plots against the Government, an offer of the family estate to his son; and, in the interim, till an act of Parliament could be obtained to that effect, a pension of two thousand pounds sterling, over and above one thousand five hundred pounds paid of jointure to his wife and daughter. [160]

It was the fortune of Lord Mar on this, as on many other occasions, to reap the ignominy of having accepted this pension, without ever receiving the profits of his debasement.

During the absence of Lord Mar at Geneva, his Countess, who remained in Rome, received the following letters from the Chevalier and his Princess, Maria Clementina: these epistles show how desirous the Chevalier still was to retain Lord Mar in his interests. [161]

"Montefiascony, Sept. 9, 1719.

"The Duke of Mar's late misfortunes and my own situation for some months past, hath occasioned my being much in the dark as to his present circumstances, which touche me too nearly not to desire you will inform me particularly of them. The last letter I had from him was in the begining of May, from Genua, in which he mentioned to me his ill state of health, and something of your comeing to meet him at Bourbon waters; but the season for them now advanceing, or rather passeing, I reckon that whether he had gone thither or not, he will soon be here on ye receipt of the note I sent you t'other day for him, and by consequence that what measures he may have taken with you about your meeting him will be altered on sight of that. I thought it necessary to inform you of these particulars to prevent any thoughts you might have of a journey so expensive and now useless: for as to his liberty, I make no doubt but that it will immediately follow the certainty of my return to this country. I should think it not prudent to write any politicks to him now, not knowing what fate my letters might meet with; but there is no secret in your sayeing all that is kind from me to him. If you cannot exagerate as to my impatience to see him, after all our mutual misfortunes and adventures, and I am sure he will be glad to know and see me more happy in a wife than I can be otherwayes, in most respects.

"I hope soon to have the satisfaction of seeing you at Rome, when I believe I shall soon convince you that if you and your lord have in the world many false friends, I am and ever shall be a true one to you both.

JAMES R. "

LETTER FROM THE PRINCESS CLEMENTINA TO THE COUNTESS OF MAR.

"Montefiasconi, 23rd. Sept.

[162]"Je vien de recevoire, votre chère letre par Mr. Clepen, et vous sui bien obligé, de l'attention que vous avé eu, de mervoyer dutée, lequell ne sauroit que étre bon venant de vous; vous me marquez avoire de la peine á ecrire le fransoi, mai votre esprit vous, laprendera bientot. Le Roi me charge de vous faire, se compliment et soy et aussi persuadez, de l'estime que j'auray toujour pour votre merite.

"CLEMENTINE R.

"J'ambrase de tous mon coeure la charman petite, J'espere dan peu de le pouvoire faire personnellement, et a vous de même. Nous nous porton très bien; l'aire d'icy est foie bonne. "

A subsequent letter is addressed "A ma cousine La Duchesse de Mar"—and subscribed "votre affectionée cousine, Clementine; " yet notwithstanding these professions of confidence and affection, the seeds of distrust were, it seems, soon sown between James and the Earl and Countess of Mar. At first the suggestions to their disadvantage were repelled, "There has been enough pains, " writes James, "taken from Rome within these few days to do you ill offices with me, but I can assure you with truth they have made no impression upon me, nor will they produce any other effect than to make me, if possible, kinder to you. But when I see you I shall say more on this head, for 'tis fitt you should know your false from your true friends; *and among the last you shall ever find me.* [163]

"JAMES R. "

An order, dated the ninth of October, 1719, that all such boxes "as are in the Duchesse of Mar's custody should be first naled by her, and then delivered with their keyes to Sir William Ellis, " written in the Chevalier's own hand, shews either that Lady Mar was on the eve of her departure from Italy, or that a breach of confidence had taken place. [164]

Lord Mar, with impaired health, and writhing under the rejection of his offers, returned to Italy. There, had he adhered to a resolution which he had formed, of not interfering in public affairs, he might still have closed his days in tranquillity.

Notwithstanding the apparent continuance of the Chevalier's regard, he never forgot the treaty between Lord Stair and the Earl of Mar. The whole of this intrigue, discreditable as it was, has been reprobated by all who have touched upon this portion of Lord Mar's history. His accepting the loan of a thousand pounds from Stair, an old friend, for the purpose of ensuring Lady Mar's journey, has been censured, I think, with too great severity. But, although it be desirable to set to rights matters of fact, yet, it is always unsatisfactory to begin the defence of a bad cause. There is no evidence to show that Lord Mar ever received a pension: he was not thought worth conciliating; but that circumstance, in this case, and after a display of his willingness to receive all that could be granted, assists very little in his vindication, and rather adds to the degradation of one whom no party could trust.

Soon after Lord Mar's return to Rome, the seeds of disunion between James and his young and high-spirited wife began to disturb the minds of all who were really well wishers to the Stuarts.

Maria Clementina, reported by Horace Walpole to have been "lively, insinuating, agreeable, and enterprising, " had encountered, soon after her marriage with James, the too frequent fate of many who were sacrificed to royal marriages. She had quickly perceived that her influence was inferior to that of the Prince's favourites: she was shortly made aware of his infidelities: she became jealous, without affection; and her disappointment in her consort was that of a proud, resentful woman, to whom submission to circumstances was a lesson too galling to be learned.

The Prince, after the fashion of his forefathers, was governed by favourites: like Charles the First, he had his Buckingham and his Strafford; and his miniature Court was rent with factions. But the Chevalier had neither the purity of Charles the First, nor the charm of character which gilded over the vices of Charles the Second. His household was an epitome of the worst passions; and his melancholy aspect, his want of dignity and spirit, his bigotry and even his unpopular virtue of economy, cast a gloom over that turbulent region. It was bitterly, but perhaps truly said of him, "that he had all the superstition of a capuchin, but none of the religion of a Prince. "[165] Like most of his immediate family, his character deteriorated as he grew older. He did not rise under the pressure of adversity; and his timid, irresolute nature was crushed by the effects of his cruel situation.

Colonel John Hay, of Cromlix, the brother of the Earl of Mar's first wife, and of George, seventh Earl of Kinnoul, succeeded in obtaining mastery over his subdued nature. The lady of Colonel Hay, Margery, the third daughter of Viscount Stormont, was said, also, to have possessed her own share of influence over the mind of the Chevalier. Of the real existence of any criminal attachment between the Prince and Mrs. Hay, there is, however, considerable doubt; and it has been generally regarded as one of those amours raised for a purpose, during the continuance of a fierce contention for power.

Clementina had also her favourites; and a certain Mrs. Sheldon, who had had the charge of Prince Charles Edward, had acquired her confidence. This choice was peculiarly infelicitous.

Mrs. Sheldon was reported to be about as unworthy a favourite as the unhappy Princess could have selected. According to Colonel Hay, she was the mistress of General Dillon, one of the most ardent adherents of the Stuarts, and the spy of the Earl of Mar. [166] For four or five years, nevertheless, after Prince Charles's birth, she continued to be his governess, and to sway the feelings of his mother, in the same manner as confidants and dependants usually direct the angry passions of their mistresses into the most dangerous channels.

During the height of Colonel Hay's favour, the confidence of the Chevalier in Lord Mar visibly declined, as appears in the following letter to one of his adherents in Scotland.

"I have always been unwilling to mention Marr, but I find myself indispensably engaged at present to let my Scots friends know that I have withdrawn my confidence entirely from him, as I shall be obliged to doe from all who may be any ways influenced by him. This conduct is founded on the most urgent, strongest, and most urging necessity, in which my regard to my faithfull subjects and servants have the greatest share.

"What is here said of Marr, is not with a view of its being made publick, there being no occasion for that, since, many years ago, he put himself under such engagements, that he could not serve me in a publick capacity, neither has he been publickly employed by me. "

To this it was answered, by the confidential friend to whom the remarks were addressed, "It is some time agoe since your friends here had doubts of the Earl of Marr; and thence it was that I was directed to mention him in the manner I did in my last two letters, it being matter of no small moment to us to know in whom wee might confide thorowly, and of whom beware, —especially when a person of his figure was the object. "[167]

Affairs were in this state; the Chevalier distrustful of Lord Mar, and devoted to his rival, Colonel Hay; the Princess heading an opposite faction, nominally commanded by Mrs. Sheldon, but secretly instigated by Lord Mar; when, in 1722, the conspiracy of Atterbury was discovered by the British Government.

The Earl of Mar was at that time in Paris, and Lord Carteret who was at the head of affairs in England, remembering the Earl's former negotiations with Lord Stair, dispatched a gentleman to Mar, with instructions to sound that nobleman as to his knowledge of the plot. Lord Mar happening to be in Colonel Dillon's company when the messenger reached Paris, and soon divining after one interview the nature of the embassy, it was agreed between him and Dillon that they would do James's cause a service by leading the British Government off the right scent. They therefore drew up, in conjunction, an answer to Lord Carteret. What was the nature of that reply, [168] does not appear; but its result was such as to cast upon Lord Mar a degree of odium far greater than that which he had incurred in Lord Stair's business. He was accused by Atterbury with having, on that occasion, written such a letter as had been the cause of his banishment; with having betrayed the secrets of the Chevalier St. George to the British Government; and of several other charges of "base and treacherous practises, discovered by the Bishop of Rochester, that the like had scarce been heard of, and seem'd to be what no man, endued with common sense, or the least drop of noble blood, could perpetrate; and that the King's friends were at a loss in not knowing what credit to give to such reports, tho' they apprehended the worst, from the directions he had lately given of having no correspondence with Mar or his adherents, from whom he had withdrawn all confidence. "

Shortly after this declaration the Chevalier declared Colonel Hay to be his Secretary, and created the favourite Earl of Inverness; between whom and the Earl of Mar an antipathy, which had now become open hostility, prevailed. "The Duke of Mar, " wrote the Earl of Inverness to Lockhart, "has declared himself my mortal enemy, only because I spoke truth to him, and could not, in my conscience, enter into his measures nor approve his conduct, tho' I always shunned saying any thing to his disadvantage, but to the King alone, from whom I thought I was obliged to conceal nothing. "[169]

With respect to the treachery towards Atterbury, the justification of Lord Mar rests upon the testimony of Colonel Dillon, and other persons who saw the Earl's letter to Carteret. It is also certain that James accorded his approval to Mar's conduct in that affair. No positive intention of mischief can be made out against Mar; but his habit of rarely acting a straightforward part, his insatiable love of interference, and his mistaking cunning for policy, brought upon him the mournful indignation of the exiled Atterbury, and fixed upon him a grave imputation which it were almost impossible to wipe away.

Another charge brought by Atterbury against Lord Mar, was his advising James to barter his pretensions to the Crown for a pension. But this accusation is refuted by the two letters, of which vouchers are given in the Lockhart Papers, on which the allegation is founded. These letters were written from Geneva to the Prince and to Colonel Dillon. [170]

Lastly, Lord Mar stood charged with a scheme, discovered to Atterbury by Lord Inverness, for the restoration of the Stuarts, which, under pretence of replacing them on the throne, would for ever have rendered that restoration impracticable. From this allegation Lord Mar justified himself by referring to the scheme itself, which he was declared to have laid before the Regent of France with the intent to ruin James. Of this scheme, the two main features were, first to re-establish the ancient independence of Scotland and Ireland: secondly, that a certain number of French troops should remain in England, and that five thousand Scots, and as many Irish troops, should be sent to France and kept in pay by the French King, for a certain number of years. There is certainly a great deal of Mar's double policy, his being all things to all men, in such a scheme. He declared, however, and proved that he acquainted James with his plan in confidence, and that Colonel Hay sent a copy of it to the Bishop of Rochester. Little as one can approve of Mar's conduct, it is manifest that, by a deeply-laid intrigue, it was resolved for ever to uproot him from the confidence of James.

But the public career of Lord Mar had now drawn to its ignoble close. That he had his partisans, who repelled the charges against him by counter allegations, Lord Inverness soon found; and he began to think that "the less noise that was made about Mar, " the better. [171]

During the year 1725, James further evinced his distrust of Lord Mar, by dismissing Mr. Sheldon, his supposed spy, and placing Mr. James Murray, a Protestant, as preceptor to the young Prince.

The retirement of the Princess Clementina into a convent, followed this last step. The correspondence of the royal couple, their recriminations, furnished, for some months, conversation for the continental courts, and even for St. James's, until the dismissal of Colonel Hay and his wife appeased the resolute daughter of the Sobieski, and produced an apparent reconciliation.

From the close of this altercation, and after the disgrace of Colonel Hay, the name of Lord Mar occurs no more in the history of the period. He resided at Paris until 1729, when, falling into ill health, he repaired to Aix la Chapelle, where he died in May 1732.

His wife survived him twenty-nine years, only to be the victim of mental disease, and, as it has been said, of cruelty and neglect. She became insane, and was placed under the charge of her sister, Lady Mary W. Montague, who, it has been reported, from avarice, stinted her unfortunate sister of even the common necessaries of life, and appropriated the allowance to herself. But this statement has been disproved. [172]

The latter years of Lord Mar were passed neither in idleness, nor wholly in the intrigues of the Court at Albano. His amusement was to draw plans and designs for the improvement of Scotland, which he had loved "not wisely, " but to which his warmest affections are said to have ever recurred. In 1728 he composed a paper, in which he suggested building bridges on the north and south sides of the city of Edinburgh: he planned, also, the formation of a navigable canal between the Forth and the Clyde. His beloved Alloa was sold by the Commissioners of the forfeited estates to his brother, Lord Grange, who, in 1739, conveyed it to Lord Erskine, his nephew. Lord Mar's children were enriched by the gratitude of Gibbs, the architect, who bequeathed to the offspring of his early patron the greatest part of his fortune.

The Earl of Mar was succeeded by his son, Thomas Lord Erskine, who was deprived of the famed title of Mar by his father's attainder. Lord Erskine was appointed by Government, Commissary of Stores at Gibraltar. His marriage with Lady Charlotte Hope being without issue, the title was restored to the descendant of Lord Grange, and consequently to the children of the unfortunate Lady Grange, whose sufferings, from the effects of party spirit, seem to belong more properly to the page of romance, than to the graver details of history.

The conduct of John Erskine, Earl of Mar, has afforded a subject of comment to two men of very different character, John Lockhart of Carnwath, and the Master of Sinclair. Neither of the portraits drawn by these master-hands are favourable; and they were, in both instances, written under the influence of strong, yet transient impressions of disappointment and suspicion. The mind naturally seeks for some safer steersman to guide opinion than the intemperate though honest Jacobite, Lockhart, or the sarcastic and slippery friend, Sinclair. The worst peculiarity in the career of Mar was, that no one trusted him; towards the latter portion of his life he had even lost the power of deceiving: it had become impossible to him to act without mingling the poison of deception with intentions which might have been honest, and even benevolent. The habits of a long life of intrigue had warped his very nature. When we behold him fleeing from the coasts of Scotland, leaving behind him the trusting hearts that would have bled for him, we fancy that no moral degradation can be more complete. We view him soliciting to be a pensioner of England, and we acknowledge that it was even possible to sink still more deeply into infamy.

With principles of action utterly unsound, it is surprising how much influence Lord Mar acquired over all with whom he came into collision. He was sanguine in disposition, and, if we may judge by his letters, buoyant in his spirits; his disposition was conciliatory, his manners were apparently confiding. At the bottom of that gay courtesy there doubtless was a heart warped by policy, but not inherently unkind. He attached to him the lowly. Lockhart speaks of the love of two of his kinsmen to him: —his tenantry, during his exile, contributed to supply his wants, by a subscription. These are the few redeeming characteristics of one made up of inconsistencies. He conferred, it must be allowed, but little credit on a party which could number among its adherents the brave Earl Marischal, the benevolent and honourable Derwentwater, and the disinterested Nithisdale. When we contrast the petty and selfish policy of the Earl of Mar with the integrity and fidelity of those who fought in the same cause, and over whom he was commander, his character sinks low in the estimate, and acts like a foil to the purity and brightness of his fellow sufferers in the strife.

FOOTNOTES:

[7] See Wood's Peerage of Scotland.

[8] Histories of Noble British Families by Henry Drummond, Esq. Preface to Part I.

[9] Robertson's History of Scotland, ii. 32.

[10] Wood's Peerage. The year of his birth is not stated.

[11] Cunningham's History of Great Britain, i. 326.

[12] Dalrymple's Memoirs, vol. iii. p. 100.

[13] Chambers's Biography, art. Erskine.

[14] See Dr. Coxe's MSS. in the British Museum, vol. iii.

[15] Dalrymple's Memoirs, vol. iii. p. 98.

[16] Lockhart's Memoirs, vol. i. p. 114.

[17] Lockhart, vol. i. p. 45.

[18] Granger, vol. ii. p. 31. Somerville's Queen Anne, p. 184.

[19] Of Alloa the following account is given. "Alloa House, situated in the immediate neighbourhood of the town, in the midst of a fine park, the seat of the Earl of Mar, and the subject of a fine Scottish song, is a place worthy of visit. The principal part of the building was destroyed some years ago by fire, and with it the only certain original portrait of Queen Mary existing in the kingdom. The original tower, a building of the thirteenth century, the walls of which are eleven feet thick, and ninety feet high, alone remains. In it James the Sixth and his eldest son, Henry, were successively educated under the care of the Mar family. The cradle of the former, and his little nursery-chair, besides Prince Henry's golfs, were preserved in the tower till a recent period, when they fell into the possession of Lady Frances Erskine, daughter of the late venerable Earl of Mar, who, we understand, now preserves them, with the care and veneration due to such valuable heirlooms, in her house in Edinburgh. The country in every direction round Alloa is extremely

level and beautiful, interspersed with numerous fine seats, and abounding in delightful little old-established bower-like villages. Among the latter we would particularize one called the Bridge of Allan as everything which a village ought to be—soft, sunny, and warm—a confusion of straw-roofed cottages, and rich massy trees; possessed of a bridge and a mill, together with kail-yards, bee-skeps, colleys, callants, old inns with entertainment for man and horse, carts with their poles pointing up to the sky, venerable dames in drugget knitting their stockings in the sun, and young ones in gingham and dimity tripping along with milk-pails on their heads.

"Besides all these characteristics as a village, the Bridge of Allan boasts of a row of neat little villas for the temporary accommodation of a number of fashionables who flock to it in the summer, on account of a neighbouring mineral well. "—*Chambers's Picture of Scotland.*

[20] Wood's Peerage.

[21] Somerville's Queen Anne, p. 167.

[22] Somerville, p. 177. Memoirs of Scotland, London, 1714. Defoe's History of the Union, p. 64.

[23] Lockhart Papers, vol. i. p. 114.

[24] Lockhart.

[25] Lockhart, p. 116.

[26] Daniel De Foe on the Union, p. 64.

[27] De Foe, p. 322.

[28] Lockhart. Letter to one English Lord concerning the Treaty, 1702, vol. i. p. 272.

[29] Memoirs, p. 74. De Foe, p. 321.

[30] Memoirs, p. 74. De Foe, p. 371.

[31] Introduction to De Foe's History of the Union, p. 16.

[32] Memoirs of Scotland, p. 31.

[33] Mackay.

[34] Lockhart Papers, vol. i. p. 54.

[35] Memoirs of North Britain, p. 113.

[36] Wood's Peerage, vol. i. pp. 714, 717; also Mackay's Memoirs, p. 178.

[37] Lockhart Papers, vol. i. p. 115.

[38] Wood's Peerage, art. Erskine of Mar.

[39] Memoirs of Scotland, p. 224.

[40] Memoirs of Scotland, p. 340.

[41] Cunningham's Hist. Great Britain, p. 257.

[42] Ibid. p. 61.

[43] Swift's Works, edited by Sir W. Scott, pp. 14, 72.

[44] The motto on Queen Anne's coronation medal.

[45] Cunningham, p. 71.

[46] Memoirs of Scotland. Cunningham, p. 157.

[47] Swift's Letters, vol. ii. p. 488; also p. 487, note by Sir W. Scott.

[48] Wood's Peerage. Swift's Letters, p. 475. See note.

[49] Mackay's Characters, p. 94.

[50] Swift added, in his own hand, to this eulogium, this remark: "He was little better than a conceited talker in company. "

[51] The following letter shows that the Duke anticipated the result of the duel.

London, Nov. 14, 1712.

My dear Son,

I have been doing all I could to recover your mother's right to her estate, which I hope shall be yours. I command you to be dutiful towards her, as I hope she will be just and kind to you; and I recommend it particularly to you, if ever you enjoy the estate of Hamilton, and what may, I hope, justly belong to you, (considering how long I have lived with a small competence, which has made me run in debt,) I hope God will put it into your head to do justice to my honour, and pay my just debts. There will be enough to satisfy all, and give your brothers and sisters such provisions as the state of your condition and their quality in Scotland will admit of.

I pray God preserve you, and the family in your person. My humble duty to my mother, and my blessing to your sisters. If it please God I live, you shall find me share with you what I do possess, and ever prove your affectionate and kind father, whilst

HAMILTON.

I again upon my blessing charge you, that you let the world see you do your part in satisfying my just debts.

Addressed thus: "To my dear Son the Marquis of Chilsdale. "

Memoirs of the Life and Family of James Duke of Hamilton.

[52] The Lady Elizabeth Gerrard, the sister of Lady Mohun, and Duchess of Hamilton, is said to have been "a lady of great wit and beauty, and all the fine accomplishments that adorn her sex. " Through her the great estates in Lancashire and Staffordshire came into the family of Hamilton.

[53] Wood's Peerage; also "Life of the Duke of Hamilton, " a scarce tract, p. 102.

[54] Coxe MSS. 9128. Plut. cxxxviii. H. British Museum.

[55] Ibid. See a Letter in French, dated April 5, 1714, p. 1.

[56] Coxe MSS.

[57] Lord Mahon's Hist. England, vol. i. p. 139. See also a scarce little book to be met with in the Advocate's Library in Edinburgh (Atterbury's Correspondence, with marginal notes by Lord Hailes): "By what accident these Letters have been preserved, " says the noble Editor, "I know not: by what means they are now brought to light, I am not at liberty to explain. "

[58] See the Letter before quoted.

[59] Cunningham, vol. ii. p. 440.

[60] Lockhart of Carnwath, vol. i. p. 446; also "Notices of Lady Grange, " by Dr. Mackay.

[61] See "Notices of Lady Grange, " by K. Mackay, M.D., 3rd edition. Glasgow, 1819.

[62] Cunningham, vol. ii. p. 441.

[63] Lord Mahon, vol. i. p. 152.

[64] "A Collection of Original Letters relating to the Rebellion of 1715. " Edinburgh, 1730.

[65] Introductory Anecdotes to Lord Wharncliffe's Edition of Lady M. Wortley's Letters, p. 26.

[66] Reay, p. 135.

[67] Reay, p. 152.

[68] Reay, p. 171.

[69] This commission was long doubted, and was even denied by the Chevalier. It is, nevertheless, signed by his Secretary, and is among the valuable papers which, belonging to Mr. Gibson Craig of Edinburgh, have been liberally placed at the service of the author.

[70] Caledonian Mercury, 1722.

[71] Lord Mahon, p. 147.

[72] Lord Mahon; from the Master of Sinclair's MS.

[73] Burke's Peerage.

[74] Buchan's History of the Keith Family.

[75] Buchan's History of the Keith Family; also Scottish Peerage.

[76] See Patten's List of Chieftains.

[77] Secret History of Colonel Hooke's Negotiations, pp. 26, 110.

[78] Patten, p. 232.

[79] Buchan's History of the Keith Family, p. 153.

[80] Colonel Hooke's Negotiations.

[81] See "Genealogie of the Most Noble and Ancient House of Drummond, by the First Viscount Strathallan, " Appendix. For this curious and elaborate work I am indebted to the Rev. Arthur Drummond.

[82] MS. Account of Several Clans, by Mrs. Grant, of Laggan.

[83] Brown's Highlands, vol. i. p. 131.

[84] The Rev. Robert Patten, from whose animated narrative many other writers have implicitly copied, was a man of indifferent character, who accompanied Mr. Forster, in the insurrection in Northumberland, as his chaplain. He afterwards turned king's evidence, and appeared against those whom he had served. For this act of treachery his pension was raised (as I find by the Caledonian Mercury for 1722) from 50*l.* to 80*l.* a-year. He dedicates his History of the Rebellion to Generals Carpenter and Wills.

[85] Patten, p. 151.

[86] Mar Papers.

[87] Reay, p. 191.

[88] Reay, p. 191.

[89] It seems to have been the custom of that period to write in the third person when in memoirs and statements. Lord Lovat's manifesto is in the same style.

[90] Patten, p. 257.

[91] A copy from the original, for which I am indebted to Mr. Gibson Craig, is given for the confirmation of Lord Mar's assertion: —

"James the Eighth, by the grace of God King of Scotland, England, France, and Ireland, Defender of the Faith, &c., to our right trusty and well-beloved Cousin and Counsellor, John Earl of Mar, &c. We reposing especial trust & confidence in your loyalty, courage, experience, and good conduct, doe by these * * constitute and appoint you to be our General and Commander in Cheif of all our forces, both by sea and land, in our antient kingdom of Scotland. Whereupon you are to take upon you the said command of General and Commander in Cheif, and the better to support you in the said authority, our will and pleasure is, that you act in consert with and by our * * * * We doe likeways hereby empower you to grant commissions in our name to all officers, both by sea and land, to place and displace the same as you shall think fitt and necessary for our service, to assemble our said forces, raise the militia, issue out orders for all suspected persons, and seizing of all forts and castles, and putting garrisons into them, and to take up in any part of our dominions, what money, horses, arms, and ammunition and provisions you shall think necessary for arming, mounting, and subsisting the said forces under your command, and to give recepts for the same, which we hereby promise to pay. By this our Commission, we likeways here empower you to make warr upon our enemies, and upon all such as shall adhere to the present government and usurper of our dominions. Leaving entirely to your prudence and conduct to begin the necessary acts of hostility when and where you think most advantageous conducing to our restoration; and we doe hereby command all, and require all officers and souldiers, both by sea and land, and all our subjects, to acknowledge and obey you as our General and Commander as Cheif of our army; and you to obey such furder orders and directions as you shall from time to time receive from us. In pursuance of the great power and trust we have reposed in you.

"Given at our Court at Bar le duc, the seventh day of September, 1715, and in the fourteenth year of our reign.

"By His Majestie's command, Sic Subscribitur, THOMAS HIGGINS."

[92] Patten, p. 256.

[93] Note in Reay. From the *Weekly Journal*, Feb. 4th, 1715-16.

[94] Reay, p. 193.

[95] Brown's Highlands, vol. i. p. 129.

[96] Mar Papers. In these there is a copy of this Manifesto; but since it has been printed in Reay's History of the Rebellion, and others, I do not think it necessary to insert it here.

[97] The Chevalier's agent there.

[98] The orthography of this letter is copied from the original, with the exception of the abbreviations usual at that period.

[99] Erskine.

[100] Reay, p. 221.

[101] Mar Papers.

[102] Mar Papers, communicated by Mr. Gibson Craig.

[103] Reay, pp. 236, 237.

[104] The Earl of Mar's Journal, as printed at Paris. At the end of Patten's History of the Rebellion, and addressed by Lord Mar to Colonel Balfour, p. 259.

[105] Reay, p. 197.

[106] Earl of Mar's Journal.

[107] Earl of Mar's Journal.

[108] Reay, p. 308.

[109] Brown's Highlands.

[110] Mar Papers.

[111] Reay, p. 309.

[112] From the MS. letter in the possession of Archibald Macdonald, Esq.

[113] The agent of the Jacobites in Edinburgh.

[114] Mar Papers, in the possession of Gibson Craig, Esq.

[115] King.

[116] Duke of Ormond.

[117] Paris.

[118] Lady Nairn.

[119] The Chevalier.

[120] The Dutch auxiliaries, to the amount of 6000, demanded by the English government, as accorded by treaty, arrived, to the number of 3000, in the Thames, on the 16th of November, expressly to assist in suppressing the rebellion, and proceeded to Scotland on the 25th. They were afterwards followed by 3000 more, who, being obliged to put in at Harwich, marched on by land. Reay, p. 327.

[121] The King.

[122] Lord Grange.

[123] The following note is annexed to this letter. It is in the handwriting of Bishop Keith: —"Son of Sir Wm. Douglass, colonel of a regiment, and who had come over with the Prince of Orange to England, and was made Knight and Colonel by the said Prince, as says my Lady Bruce. The story Wm. Erskine, brother to the Earl of Buchan, told me, as the King and he were travelling through France at this period, they saw the Chevalier's picture set up in some of the post-houses, and they were told this was done by the desire of the English Ambassador, who had promised a reward to those who should stop and apprehend the person whom the picture resembled."

[124] A concealment in the House of Kineil, near Borrostowness.

[125] The younger brother of the Marquis of Tullibardine, but assuming the forfeited title as head of the house.

[126] Henry Straiton.

[127] I have had the advantage of seeing an original crayon portrait of the Chevalier, in the possession of Kirkpatrick Sharpe, Esq., of Edinburgh; also, a miniature painted at Rome, belonging to Mr. Sharpe. In the miniature the eyes are darker, and have more animation than in the crayon drawing. The portrait lately placed at Hampton Court gives a much more pleasing impression of James Stuart than either of these likenesses: the countenance is animated and benevolent.

[128] "A True Account of the Proceedings at Perth, " by a Rebel, supposed to be the Master of Sinclair.

[129] That portion of the letter only which refers to the Chevalier appears to have been printed. I have given the entire letter from which the account was taken. A portion of this letter is published in Brown's History of the Highlands, vol. iv. p. 332.

[130] Reay, p. 352.

[131] MS. Letter in the possession of Alexander Macdonald, Esq., of the Register Office, Edinburgh.

[132] Mar Papers.

[133] Thomas Bruce, afterwards Earl of Kincardine.

[134] The loss of the ship from France.

[135] An allusion to the Marquis of Huntley and Lord Seaforth.

[136] Mar Papers.

[137] Reay, p. 364.

[138] Flying Post, or the Post Master, for January 28 and 31, 1716.

[139] Evening Post, Feb. 2, 1716.

[140] Auchterarder.

[141] Reay, p. 364.

[142] Mar Correspondence.

[143] Probably Wigton.

[144] Brown's Highlands, vol. iv. p. 337.

[145] Patten, p. 248.

[146] Reay, p. 367.

[147] Lord Mar's Journal.

[148] A copy is given of the Prince's letter in Dr. Brown's work on the Highlands, vol. iv. p. 340. It is a sort of expostulation with the Duke, but mildly and sensibly expressed. "I fear, " he said, alluding to the British people, "they will find yet more than I the smart of preferring a foreign yoke to the obedience they owe me. "

[149] Bolingbroke's Letter to Sir William Wyndham.

[150] Letter to Sir Wm. Wyndham, p. 139.

[151] Lockhart, vol. ii. p. 17.

[152] Ibid.

[153] Lockhart, vol. ii. p. 64.

[154] Coxe's Papers in the British Museum, MS. 9129. Plut. cxxxviii.II.

[155] I find that the biographers of Lord Mar, in the short lives given of him, (see Chambers's Scottish Biography, Georgian Era, &c.) have overlooked this correspondence. The letter from Sir Luke Schwaub, in French, with a translation, and the answer of Lord Carteret, in the Coxe Papers, although not exactly relevant to my subject, are interesting. "A thousands thanks, " writes the generous Lord

Carteret, in reply to Schwaub, "for your private letter, which affords me the means of obviating any calumny against the memory of a person who will always be dear to me. " [That is, Lord Sunderland.] "I have shown it to the King, who is entirely satisfied with it. " The anxiety on the part of Government to secure the papers of Lord Sunderland, was extreme, and affords a collateral proof of this connivance. The mysterious documents were seized by order of the King, and inspected by Lord Townshend, and not a trace of the correspondence was left when the papers were restored to the family. The seizure occasioned a suit between the executors of the Earl of Sunderland and the two Secretaries of State. —*Coxe MSS.*

[156] Hardwicke Papers, vol. ii. p. 252.

[157] Hardwicke Papers, vol. ii. p. 565.

[158] Hardwicke Papers, p. 586.

[159] Hardwicke Papers, vol. ii. p. 600.

[160] Chambers, art. *Erskine.*

[161] From original letters, for which I am indebted to Alexander Macdonald, Esq., of the Register Office, Edinburgh.

[162] The spelling is preserved as in the original.

[163] These words were written in the Chevalier's own hand.

[164] Letters in the possession of A. Macdonald, Esq.

[165] Bolingbroke.

[166] Lockhart Papers, vol. ii. p. 221.

[167] Lockhart Papers.

[168] See various papers in the State Paper Office. Collections for 1722.

[169] Lockhart, vol. ii. p. 149.

[170] Id. p. 183.

[171] Lockhart, vol. ii. p. 198.

[172] Mr. C. Kirkpatrick Sharpe was good enough to inform me that he had seen some letters on this subject, which exculpated Lady Mary W. Montague. The correspondence was destroyed, but it conveyed to the mind of that accomplished and erudite gentleman, who saw it, the impression that the charge against Lady Mary Wortley was groundless.

JAMES, EARL OF DERWENTWATER.

JAMES RADCLIFFE,
EARL OF DERWENTWATER.

In the vale of Hexham, on the summit of a steep hill, clothed with wood, and washed at its base by a rivulet, called the Devil's Water, stand the ruins of Dilstone Castle. A bridge of a single arch forms the approach to the castle or mansion; the stream, then mingling its rapid waters with those of the Tyne, rushes over rocks into a deep dell embowered with trees, above a hundred feet in height, and casting a deep gloom over the sounding waters beneath their branches.

Through the arch of the bridge, a mill, an object ever associated with peace and plenty, is seen; and, beyond it, the eye rests upon the bare, dilapidated walls of the castle. Its halls, its stairs, its painted chambers, may still be traced; its broken towers command a view of romantic beauty; but all around it is desolate and ruined, like the once proud and honoured family who dwelt beneath its roof.

This was once the favourite abode of the Ratcliffes, or Radcliffes, supposed to be a branch of the Radcliffes in Lancashire, [173] from whom were, it is said, descended the Earls of Sussex, [174] who became the owners of Dilstone in the days of Queen Elizabeth.

During several generations after the Conquest, a family of the name of Devilstone was in possession of Dilstone, until the time of Henry the Third. The estates then passed to many different owners; the Tynedales, the Crafters, the Claxtons, were successively the masters of the castle; and it was not, according to some accounts, [175] until the tenth year of Queen Elizabeth's reign, that it first owned for its lord one of that unfortunate race to whom it finally belonged, until escheated to the Crown. But certain historians have asserted that, so early as the reign of Henry the Sixth, Dilstone was the seat of Sir Nicholas Radcliffe. [176] At this period, too, other estates were added to those already enjoyed by the Radcliffes. Sir Nicholas married the heiress of Sir John De Derwentwater, to whom had belonged, for several centuries, the manors of Castlerigg and Keswick, and who, since the time of Edward the First, had enjoyed great consideration in the county of Cumberland. This alliance with the Derwentwater family, although it brought to the Radcliffe the possession of a territory, which, for its beauty and value, monarchs might envy, did not for many years, entice them to a removal to the mansion of Castlerigg. That old dwelling-place, a gloomy fortress, among "storm-shaken mountains and howling wildernesses, " was far less commodious than the castle at Dilstone, then in great fame from the flourishing monastery which reared its head in the Vale of Hexham. Castlerigg, being, eventually, abandoned by the Radcliffes, went utterly to decay; the materials of the old manor-house are supposed to have been employed in forming a new residence on Lord's Island, in Keswick Lake; and the estate was divided into tenancies, which, in process of time, were infranchised. The ancient demesne of the De Derwentwaters has now passed into the hands of the Trustees of Greenwich Hospital, and the oaks of the park which skirts the lake have of late years supplied much valuable timber.

The family of Radcliffe continued, during several centuries after the intermarriage with the De Derwentwaters, to increase in wealth and importance. It was not, however, ennobled until the reign of James the Second, in 1688, when, in consequence of the eldest son of Sir Francis Radcliffe having married during his father's life time the Lady Mary Tudor, a natural daughter of Charles the Second, by Mistress Mary Davis, Sir Francis was created Earl of Derwentwater, Baron Dilstone, and Viscount Langley. [177] "This alliance to the royal blood, " says the biographer of Charles Radcliffe, "gave them a title to match with the noblest families in the kingdom, and was likewise the occasion of that strict attachment which the several branches of the Derwentwater family have inviolably preserved for the line of Stuarts ever since. "[178] There was also another reason for this act of royal favour on the one hand, and for this devotion on the other: Sir George Radcliffe, we find by the Macpherson papers, was Governor of James the Second when he was Duke of York, and during the troubles of the Great Rebellion; and, under his care, the young prince remained some time in the city of Oxford. [179]

Whatsoever may be thought of the effect of this connection with royalty, in ennobling an ancient and loyal race, the marriage produced a lasting influence on the fortunes of the family. That they were proud of the alliance appears from the circumstance that the children of that marriage used to wear the prince's feather, that plume which has, since the days of Edward the Black Prince, distinguished the heir apparent to royalty. But the consanguinity in blood to the Stuarts produced another, and a far more serious result. The sons of the Lady Mary Tudor and of Francis, second Earl of Derwentwater, were educated, like brothers, with the son of the abdicated monarch. James Radcliffe, who was born about the year 1692, and who afterwards became Earl of Derwentwater, passed his childhood at St. Germains with his royal namesake, James Stuart. The brother of the Earl, Charles, was also brought up in France; both of these youths, whose fate was afterwards so tragical, were reared in the faith of the Church of Rome, and under the tuition of the Roman Catholic clergy. They thus grew up, without perhaps hearing, certainly without entertaining, a doubt of those rights which they died to assert. "The late Earl of Derwentwater, " writes the biographer of Charles Radclyffe, "and his brother Charles were so strongly attached to the Pretender's party, that their advice or consent was not so much as asked in those consultations that were held among the disaffected previous to the Rebellion; neither did the party think it necessary, because they were always sure of them whenever they should come to action. "

In 1705, Francis, Earl of Derwentwater, died; and during a season of domestic tranquillity, whilst as yet the Jacobites were full of hopes that the succession would be restored to the Stuart line, his son James succeeded to the Earldom, and to the vast estates which had accumulated to give dignity and influence to rank. Besides the castle of Dilstone and Castlerigg, which Leland, who visited Cumberland in 1539, describes as still being the "head place of the Radcliffes, " many other valuable properties, had been gradually added to the patrimonial possessions.

It was the disposition of Lord Derwentwater to employ the advantages of wealth and birth to the benefit of others. He returned to England, English in heart, and became the true model of an English nobleman. "He was a man, " said a contemporary writer, "formed by nature to be beloved; for he was of so universal a beneficence, that he seemed to live for others. "[180] Residing among his own people, among them he spent his estate, and passed his days in deeds of kindness, and in acts of charity, which regarding no differences of faith as obstacles to the course of that heavenly virtue, were extended alike by this unfortunate nobleman to Protestant and to Roman Catholic. In his days, Dilstone was the scene of an open-hearted hospitality, "which, " observes the renegade Jacobite who has chronicled the events of the period, "few in that country do, and none can, come up to. " That castle-hall, now ruined and for ever deserted, was thronged by the distressed, who, whether the poor denizens of the place or the wanderer by the way side, found there relief, and went away consoled. The owner of the castle gave bread to thousands, who long remembered his virtues, and mourned his fate. He conciliated the good will of his equals, and disarmed the animosity of those who differed from him in opinion. Beloved, trusted, almost reverenced in the prime of youth, James Earl of Derwentwater held, at the period of the first Rebellion, the enviable position of one whose station was remembered only in conjunction with the higher dignity of virtue. To the solid qualities of integrity, he added a sweetness and courtesy of manner which must have lent to even homely features their usual charm. [181] Blessing and blest, he thus dwelt amid the romantic scenery of the Vale of Hexham.

Lord Derwentwater married Anna Maria, one of the five daughters of Sir John Webb, Baronet of Odstock in Wiltshire. An ancestor of Sir John Webb had first acquired the title in the reign of Charles the First for "his family having both shed their blood in the King's cause, and contributed, as far as they were able, with their purses, in his defence, " as is expressed in their patent. [182]

During the reign of Queen Anne, Lord Derwentwater took no part in the various intrigues which were carried on by the Jacobite party. He lived peaceably at Dilstone, where his name was long honoured after the tragical events which hurried him into an early grave had occurred. But this tranquil demeanour does not argue, as it has been supposed, that the early playmate of James had become indifferent to the cause of the Stuarts. The friends of the exiled family founded their hopes of its restoration on the well-known partiality of Queen Anne for her brother, and on the circumstance of her having seen the last of her children consigned to the tomb. There seems no reason to doubt but that, had Anne lived longer, she would have taken measures, in unison with the wishes of the bulk of the nobility, and in conjunction with her confidential ministers, to have placed the Chevalier St. George the next in succession. In this hope, the wishes of the most respectable portion of the Jacobite nobility were tranquillized. [183]

The sudden decease of Queen Anne disconcerted the hopes of those who had been thus waiting for the course of events; and the immediate change of ministry depriving those who were favourable to the house of Stuart of power, the succession of George the First was secured, under the aspect, for a few weeks, of the most perfect national repose. It has been well explained, that, unless some circumstances connected with the birth and education of the Chevalier had favoured the interests of Hanover, a very different result would have appeared. The notion so diligently spread abroad, of a supposititious birth—the foreign education of the young Prince—above all, the pains which had been taken to inculcate in his heart a devotion to the faith of both his parents, were considerations which strongly favoured the accession of the Elector of Hanover. [184]

A year passed away, and that tranquillity was succeeded by an ill-concerted, immature enterprise, headed by a man of every talent except the right sort; and chilled, rather than aided, by the presence of that melancholy exile who presented himself for the first and last time, to sadden by the gloom of his aspect, and the inertness of his measures, the hearts that yearned to welcome him back to Britain.

It was towards the latter end of August, in 1715, in the shire of Perth, that the people first began to assemble themselves in a body, until they marched to a small market town, named Kirk Michael, where the Chevalier was first proclaimed, and his standard set up. [185] Meantime several noblemen and gentlemen, both in England and in Scotland, influenced by the Earl of Mar, began to collect their servants and dependants from different places, and under various pretexts, for their proceedings. There were also measures concerted in London by the Chevalier's friends; and among the more active of the partisans, was a certain Captain Robert Talbot, an Irish officer, who, upon being acquainted with the projected insurrection, took shipping and sailed for Newcastle-upon-Tyne. By this agent, the resolutions which had been adopted by the Jacobites in London were conveyed to their friends in the north of England. This was part of the scheme of the Jacobites; London was the centre of all their conferences, and from the metropolis intelligence was secretly conveyed in various directions: measures were concerted; the parties who were to engage were furnished with means to act, and brought together; letters were carried by private hands to various confederates, and debates and correspondence were carried on some months before the Rebellion actually broke out.

The plot was managed with care and address. The common conveyance of letters was dangerous, and the office of delivering them was undertaken by gentlemen of Jacobite principles, who rode from place to place as travellers, pretending merely that they were viewing the country, and making inquiries to gratify curiosity: these travellers were all Irish and Papists.

Another class of agents, consisting of Mr. Clifton, a brother of Sir Gervase Clifton, and of Mr. Beaumont, both gentlemen of Nottinghamshire, and attended by Mr. Buxton, a clergyman of Derbyshire, rode like gentlemen, with servants, but were armed with swords and pistols. These emissaries also continued moving from place to place, and kept up a constant intercourse between the disaffected parties, until all things were ready for action.

Under these circumstances, Government took a decided step, which, as it turned out, brought the whole concerted plot into action sooner than the confederates had originally intended. Means were taken for the apprehension of several suspected Jacobites. Towards the end of September, Lord Derwentwater, among others, received notice that there was a warrant issued by the Secretary of State to apprehend him, and that messengers were actually arrived at Durham in order to seize his person. [186]

On receiving this information, Lord Derwentwater, who had at that time taken no ostensible part in the consultations of the Jacobites, and who, as it was thought by many who knew him intimately, was undecided whether to join the insurgents or not, adopted the line of conduct most suitable to innocence. He repaired to the house of a neighbouring justice of the peace, whose name has not been given at length and boldly placed himself in his hands. He demanded what were the grounds of his accusation. Unhappily the magistrate's loyalty was not unimpeachable. Had this gentleman been zealously affected to the Government, or had he been a true friend to Lord Derwentwater, he would either have persuaded that nobleman to surrender to the messengers of Government, or he would have detained him, and thus prevented the rash outbreak which afterwards ensued. Such is the opinion of one who knew all the parties concerned in the insurrection well. Such is the statement of Mr. Robert Patten, himself a Jacobite, and chaplain to Mr. Forster. He afterwards turned King's evidence, and received for that treachery, or, as he is pleased to call it, penitence, a suitable remuneration. [187]

Lord Derwentwater unfortunately adopted a course which could but have one termination. He concealed himself from those who were employed to apprehend him. Clear from any direct imputation, had he then given himself up, he would have been released; and he might have been deterred from a participation in the disastrous scenes which ensued. He had now two children, a son and a daughter. He had many valuable considerations to forfeit for the one abstract principle of indefeasible right to the throne. Few men had more to venture. Many of the Jacobites went into the field with tarnished characters, and with ruined fortunes: they might gain, — they could not lose by the perilous undertaking. Amid the bands of high-born and highly principled men who co-operated in both the Rebellions, adventurers would appear, whose previous lives shed dishonour upon any cause; but the irreproachable, the prosperous, the beloved, could desire little more for themselves than what they already possessed: they ventured their rich and glorious barks upon the current; and let those who sully every motive with suspicion, say that there was no virtue, no patriotism, in the Jacobite party.

By his own descendant, Lord Derwentwater is believed to have hesitated upon the verge of his fate, but to have been urged into it by his brother Charles. Young and ardent, courageous even to rashness, the first to offer himself where an enterprise was the most hazardous, seeming to set no value upon his life where glory was to be obtained, the darling of his party, and, to sum up the whole, only twenty-two years of age, Mr. Radcliffe rashly drew his brother into a confederacy, so agreeable to his own ambitious and fearless spirit. But there was another individual on whom the responsibility of that luckless movement in the North must chiefly rest. This was Mr. Thomas Forster the younger, of Etherston in the county of Northumberland, and member for the county. During the first thirty years of his life, this gentleman had scarcely been known beyond the precincts of his paternal estate. He became a member of Parliament, and was drawn into the vortex of party without talents to adorn or judgment to guide his conduct. Although a Protestant, Mr. Forster soon made his house the place of rendezvous for all the non-jurors and disaffected people of the county in which he lived; and he became involved in the dangers of their schemes, almost before he was aware of the perils which he was about to encounter. The party of the Jacobites was composed of very dissimilar materials. Whilst some adopted its projects to retrieve character, or to attain, as they vainly hoped, fortune, whilst others were actuated by genuine motives, there were many who mingled in the mazes of the intricate politics of that day from vanity, and the love of being at the head of faction: such was Forster; and his career was unsatisfactory and inglorious as his character was weak.

A warrant for Mr. Forster's apprehension having been sent forth, he was, like Lord Derwentwater, obliged to fly from place to place, until he arrived at the house of Mr. Fenwick, at Bywell. Lord Derwentwater, meantime, had been secreted under the roof of a man named Lambert, in a cottage, where he had remained in safety. His horses had been seized by one of the neighbouring magistrates, and had been detained in custody for several weeks, pursuant to an order in council; yet, when he had need of them they were returned. "I afterwards asked that lord, " Mr. Patten relates, "how he came so quietly by his horses from the justice's possession, whom the believing neighbourhood esteemed a most rigid Whig. I was answered thus, by that lord's repeating a saying of Oliver Cromwell's, 'that he could gain his ends with an ass-load of gold, ' and left me to make the application. "[188]

Mr. Fenwick, of Bywell, was a secret, though not an avowed Jacobite; and it was soon agreed that at his house should be collected all those who were favourable to the cause. A meeting of the party was accordingly held: it was decided that finding there was now no longer any safety in shifting from place to place, and that since, in a few days they might all be hurried up to London, and secured in prisons, where they might be separately examined, and induced to betray each other; —it was now time to appear boldly in arms, and to show the loyalty of the confederates to King James.

In pursuance of this resolution, the place and hour of meeting were appointed the very next morning; the sixth of October was named, and all were to assemble at Greenrig. Here those who rode from Bywell were met by Mr. Forster, with a party of twenty gentlemen. The meeting might have recalled the days of the Cavaliers: the winding of the river Tyne in the valley; the rural village of Bywell; on the rising ground to the right a ruin, once the fortress of the vale, and held in former times by the Baliols, presented a scene of tranquil beauty, which some who met that day were destined never to look upon again.

The low situation of Greenrig was deemed inconvenient for the purpose of the insurgents, and the party ascended a hill called the Waterfalls, from which they could see the distant country. This spot is thus described: "As you look upon Bywell from the most pleasing point of view, the landskip lies in the following order: —from the road near the front of the river, the ruined piers of a bridge become the front objects; behind which, in a regular cascade, the whole river falls over a wear, extended from bank to bank, in height above eight feet perpendicular; a mill on the right hand, a salmon lock on the left: the tower and the two churches stretch along the banks of the upper basin of the river, with a fine curvature; the solemn ruins of the ancient castle of the Baliols lift their towers above the trees on the right, and make an agreeable contrast with the adjoining mansion-house. The whole background appears covered with wood. "[189]

On this height Mr. Forster and his party paused; but they had not been long there before they saw the Earl of Derwentwater, who came that morning from Dilstone, advancing. He was attended by several friends and by all his servants, some mounted on his coach-horses, and all well armed. As they marched through Corbridge, this gallant troop drew their swords. They were reinforced by several other gentlemen at the house of Mr. Errington, where they stopped; and they then advanced to the spot where their friends awaited their approach. They now mustered sixty horse, mostly composed of gentlemen and their attendants. After a short council it was decided that they should proceed towards the river Coquet, to Plainfield: here they were joined by several stragglers: they marched that evening to Rothbury a small market-town, where they remained all night, and continued their march on the following morning, the seventh of October, to Warkworth Castle.

In thus assembling his friends and his tenantry, Lord Derwentwater was not blameless of undue influence and oppression. The instances, indeed, of threats and absolute compulsion being used to augment the forces of the Jacobites, and to draw unwilling dependants into participation, are very numerous; they may be collected from various petitions, borne out by evidence, among the State Papers for 1715 and 1716. It is true that such excuses were certain to be alleged by many persons unjustly; but, where the charges were substantiated, we must with pain confess that the virtues of the Earl of Derwentwater, as well as those of other Jacobites, are sullied by a violent exercise of power over their tenantry. One man, named George Gibson, afterwards, in memorialising Lord Townshend from Newgate, affirms that upon his refusal to carry a message from Lord Derwentwater to Mr. Forster, two days before the insurrection, and returning to his own house instead, he was one night dragged out of bed by seven or eight men, and hurried off to serve in the said insurrection without a single servant of his own attending him. It was proved also, by King's evidence, that the unfortunate man did all in his power to escape from Kelso, and really made the attempt; but it was defeated, for he was ever an object of suspicion to the Earl of Derwentwater and Mr. Forster, whose watchfulness kept him among the rebel troops. [190] Party may do much to blunt the feelings; yet there was too much of what was good in the character of Lord Derwentwater for him, in the solitude of his own prison, not to remember in after days the heavy responsibilities which even by one act of this nature he had incurred, in compelling a man to act against his will and conscience.

Warkworth was probably chosen as a resting-place for the insurgents, on account of its strength. Situated only three-quarters of a mile from the sea, on the river Coquet, over which is thrown a bridge, guarded by a lofty tower, the Castle of Warkworth, which guards the town, commands a view both varied with objects of interest and importance.

From a lofty turret of the castle a great extent of land and ocean is to be seen. The great Tower of the Percys, from which this turret rises, is decorated with the lion of Brabant, and is seated on the brink of a cliff above the town. From this lofty structure the eye, stretching along the coast, may discern the castles of Dunstanbrough and Bamborough: the Fern Islands, dotted upon the face of the waters, the Port of Alemouth, and, at a little distance, the mouth of the river Coquet, with its island and ruined monastery. To the north, a richly cultivated country extends as far as Alnwick; to the south lies a plain, interspersed with villages and woods; the shore, to which it inclines, is indented with many ports and creeks; the smoke rising from many scattered hamlets, and the spires of churches enliven the smiling prospect.

In this secure station the rebels remained for two days; and here Mr. Forster assumed the rank of General of the Forces in the North, a title which had been bestowed on him by the Earl of Mar. On the day after his arrival at Warkworth, Mr. Forster sent Mr. Buxton, who was chaplain to the troops to desire Mr. Ton, the parish clergyman, to pray for the Chevalier as King; and, in the Litany, for Mary, the Queen Mother, and to omit the petition for King George, the Prince and Princess of Wales, &c. Mr. Ton declining to make this alteration, Mr. Buxton took possession of the reading-desk, and performed the service, whilst the deposed clergyman took flight, and, hastening to Newcastle, gave notice there of what had occurred. This was the first place where the Chevalier was prayed for in England; and Mr. Buxton's sermon, observes our historian, "gave mighty encouragement to his hearers, being full of exhortations, flourishing arguments, and cunning insinuations to be hearty in the cause. " These incentives were aided by a "comely personage, " and considerable eloquence and erudition.

On the following day, after proclaiming James King of England with all due formality and with the sound of trumpet, Mr. Forster attending the ceremony in disguise, the troops marched to Morpeth, their numbers increasing as they went. At Felton Bridge, they were joined by seventy horse, composed of gentlemen from the borders; and by the time they reached Morpeth, their number had augmented to three hundred: these were all horse-soldiers: Mr. Forster refused the foot as auxiliaries, otherwise the increase would have been considerable. The reason assigned for this rejection was the impossibility of supplying the men with arms; but the fairest assurances were given to the friends of the cause that arms and ammunition would soon be procured, and regiments listed forthwith.

The spirits of the Jacobite army were now high; their hopes were raised by the daily increase of their party. Newcastle was their next object, and thither they prepared to march, having first proclaimed the Chevalier, —Mr. Buxton taking upon himself the office of herald. Newcastle was, however, on her defence: the city gates were closed against the troops, and they turned towards Hexham, and thence marched to a moor near Dilstone Castle, and here they halted for some days. This was a feint, as they intended, it is thought, to have surprised the town of Newcastle. But the news they received from that place were far from encouraging. The gentry in the neighbourhood had rallied for its defence; and Lord Scarborough, the lord-lieutenant of the county, had entered the town with a body of men. Still there was a powerful High Church party, who, as the Jacobites hoped, would declare for the Chevalier. It was from Newcastle that Lord Derwentwater had been apprised, in the first instance, that there were messengers sent to apprehend him. The insurgents therefore, continued near Hexham, where they seized on all the horses and arms they could, read prayers in the churches for King James, and proclaimed him in the market-place.

The Earl of Derwentwater had appointed his brother to the command of his troop, whilst Captain Shaftoe was under Mr. Radcliffe. This, in some respects, was an unfortunate step: the young and brave commander had never even seen an army before: he was inexperienced, and ignorant of all military discipline: what he wanted in knowledge, he is said, however, to have made up for by the influence he acquired over his men, and by the power he had of inciting them to great exploits. [191]

Whilst the rebel forces lay at Hexham, they received the intelligence that Lord Kenmure, the Earls of Nithisdale, of Carnwath, and Wintoun, had risen in Nithisdale, and had marched thence to England to join the troops in Northumberland, and had even advanced as far as Rothbury. On the nineteenth of October, Mr. Forster joined the Scottish army at Rothbury, and afterwards marched with an increasing force to Kelso. Here prayers were read in the great kirk by Mr. Buxton; "and I, " relates Mr. Patten, "preached on these words, Deut. xxi. 17, —the latter part of the verse: 'The right of the first-born is his. '" The service of the Church of England was then read for the first time on that side of the Tweed. [192]

William Gordon, Viscount Kenmure, had the command of the Jacobite army until they had crossed the Tweed. Like the Earl of Derwentwater, this unfortunate nobleman is declared to have shewn reluctance to take up arms. On having been solicited by the Earl of Mar to command the forces, and assured that he would join him, he at first refused the offer, but had finally acceded, and had set up the standard of the Chevalier at Moffat, in Annandale. The standard was made, for this occasion, by Lady Kenmure, the sister of Robert, sixth Earl of Carnwath. It was very handsome; one side being blue, with the arms of Scotland wrought in gold; on the other side a thistle, — the words so often uttered during the Rebellion, and re-echoed in many a Scottish heart, "No Union, " were wrought underneath the thistle. Above it were the words NEMO ME IMPUNE LACESSIT; white pendants were attached to the standard, on which were inscribed—"For our Wronged King and Oppressed Country! " "For our Lives and Liberties! "

But the nobleman who had taken this prominent part in the Rebellion of 1715, although possessed of extraordinary knowledge in politics and civil affairs, was an utter stranger to all military business. His mild temper and his unoffending character inspired compassion for his subsequent fate, but unfitted him for the office of command: his gentler qualities were united, nevertheless, to a resolute and lofty mind. The fate of this nobleman, like that of his most distinguished friends, was a brief tragedy.

Lord Kenmure had a troop of gentlemen with him, the command of which he gave to the Hon. Bazil Hamilton of Beldoun, and a nephew of the Duke of Hamilton.

Among other characters who were conspicuous on this occasion, was the celebrated Brigadier Mackintosh. The sixth regiment, named after the Brigadier as chief of the clan, was commanded by a kinsman. The Brigadier had served in Germany, and had there gained his military rank. Descended from the ancient house of Fife, the chieftain had increased his influence by marrying, while a minor, the heiress of Clanchattan, in right of whom he became chieftain of that clan, comprising many others. His motto, "Touch not the cat without a glove, " and the coat-of-arms supported by two wild cats, with a cat for the crest, were not inappropriate. No suspicion had been entertained of Mackintosh's adherence to the Chevalier, with whom he became acquainted abroad, until he actually joined the party.

The Earl of Carnwath, Lord Nairn, Lord Charles Murray, and the Earl of Wintoun, commanded the other Scottish regiments, which were generally better armed than those of the English. The Earl of Derwentwater, and the Lords Widdrington had the two principal English regiments, of which there were four. [193]

On the twenty-fifth of October, the united army of Scots and English left Kelso, and marched to Jedburgh. On their march, some of the Scots, taking umbrage, left the army under the guidance of the Earl of Wintoun; and although that nobleman afterwards returned with his troop, above four hundred Highlanders deserted, and returned to their country.

During the progress of the insurgent forces, there is little reason to conclude that Lord Derwentwater took a very active or important part in the various consultations which were held, always with great disunion, and with a melancholy want of judgment, between the General, Mr. Forster, and his military council. The amiable nobleman appears to have assigned to his less discreet brother the entire guidance of his troop. "His temper and disposition, " as he expresses it in his defence, "disposed him to peace. He was totally inexperienced in martial affairs; that he entered upon the undertaking without any previous concert with its chief promoters, —without any preparation of men, horses, and arms, or other warlike accoutrements, " was at once an instance of his imprudence and a mitigation of his error. [194] There was, indeed, no doubt but that Lord Derwentwater might have brought many hundreds of his followers to the field, even from one portion of his estate only; for he possessed the extensive lead mines on Alstone Moor, where a large body of men were daily employed, and received from him their sole means of support. [195]

But whether or not this unfortunate nobleman failed in energy or in zeal; whether he entered with his whole heart into the cause of James Stuart; or whether, with the conscientious scruples of a gentle nature, he shrank from involving in the risk of this insurrection the majority of his humble dependants, he acted throughout the whole of this brief campaign with the consideration for others so characteristic of his mind. He truly affirmed on his trial, that no one could charge him with any cruel, severe, or harsh action during his continuance in arms: and his conduct in the last extremity corresponded to his previous forbearance. Such dispositions appear to have been cherished, indeed, by the rest of the Jacobite party. The merciful temper of the Chevalier, and his known aversion to destructive measures, may have had its influence over those who asserted his claims. There was something like the spirit of the cavalier of the Great Rebellion in Mr. Forster's reply to some of his officers, who wished to put down or burn a Presbyterian meetinghouse at Penrith: "It is by clemency, and not by cruelty, that we are to prevail. "[196]

After the insurgent troops had marched from place to place for some time, it was decided that the English regiments should recross the border; and after many disputes and much loss of time, they resolved on a march into Lancashire, a country abounding at that time in Roman Catholic gentry, and strongly Jacobite. [197] This decision, like most of the other military movements of the unfortunate Jacobites, was the work of a strong party in the camp, and was founded upon the alleged authority of private letters, which gave the assurance of a general insurrection taking place on the appearance of the insurgent force. The unlucky change of plans superseded a meditated attack upon the town of Dumfries. "Nothing, " observes Mr. Patten, "could be a greater token of a complete infatuation, —that Heaven confounded all their devices, and that their destruction was to be of their own working, than their omitting such an opportunity. " After a rapid march from Langholm in the west of Scotland, across the borders, and through Penrith, Appleby, and Kendal, to Kirby Lonsdale, the combined force entered the county of Lancaster; and having entered Lancaster without opposition, they resolved to proceed to Preston. It is now that the last disastrous events of Lord Derwentwater's brief career brought to light his excellent qualities, his pure and amiable motives of action. It is not possible to read the account of the battle of Preston, in which he was engaged, without a deep regret for the personal misfortunes of one so young, so well intentioned, and so esteemed, as this ill-fated nobleman.

The forces of the Jacobites amounted, after being joined by a party of volunteers under the Lords Rothes and Torpichen, and since their separation from the Highlanders, to about two thousand men. The foot was commanded by Brigadier Mackintosh; and six hundred Northumbrian and Dumfriesshire horsemen, by Lord Kenmure and Mr. Forster. [198]

On the ninth instant the march to Preston was commenced; the cavalry troops reached that town on the same evening; but the day proving rainy, and the roads heavy, the foot regiments were left at a small market-town called Garstang, half-way between Manchester and Preston. Two troops of Stanhope's dragoons, formerly quartered at Preston, having retired as the rebels approached, the spirits of the Jacobite officers and the ardour of their men were greatly encouraged. On the following day, Thursday the tenth of November, the Chevalier was proclaimed at Preston, and here the rebels were joined by many country gentlemen, their tenants and servants: this was the first accession to the party since their entrance into Lancashire. The new allies were chiefly Roman Catholics, a circumstance which aroused the instinctive dread of the Scottish volunteers to persons of that persuasion. The High Church party hung back from joining the cause. The Roman Catholics began, according to the historian of the Rebellion of 1715, "to show their blind side, " being never right hearty for their cause until they are "mellow, " as they call it "over a bottle or two. "[199]

The town of Preston seated on the river Ribble, was a place from which an enemy might, in the year 1715, have been easily repulsed. About a mile and a half from the town, a bridge over the river offered an admirable stand for a besieged garrison; it might have been so easily barricadoed, that it would have been impracticable to pass that way if the commonest precautions had been adopted. The river in this part was not fordable for a considerable distance on either side of the bridge, and it could have been easily rendered impassable. From the Ribble bridge to the town, the road ran between two steep banks; and this way, or lane, was then so narrow, that in several places two men could not ride abreast. It was here that Oliver Cromwell had met with a famous resistance from the King's forces in 1648, large mill-stones having been rolled down upon him from the rising grounds, so that the republican general was in considerable danger, and he only escaped with life by making his horse plunge into a quicksand.

This lane formed a curious natural outwork; and might easily have been barricadoed, but the deficiencies of Mr. Forster's generalship were fatal to so simple and obvious a plan of defence. He confined his exertions to the town, barricadoed the streets, and posted men in the bye-lanes and houses. The Jacobite troops formed four main barriers: one in the churchyard, commanded by Brigadier Mackintosh. This barrier was to be supported by four noblemen, who, at the head of the volunteer horse, (as in many instances in the army of Charles the First,) composed of gentlemen solely, was planted in the churchyard of Old St. Wilfred, as the parish-church of Preston was then called: their leaders were the Earl of Derwentwater, Lord Kenmure, the Earl of Nithisdale, and the Earl of Wintoun, —a truehearted band as ever braved the terrors of an encounter with their countrymen. At a little distance from the churchyard and at the extremity of a lane leading into the fields, Lord Charles Murray defended another post. The third was at a windmill, and that Colonel Mackintosh was appointed to command. The fourth was in the town.

Lord Derwentwater and his brothers were the objects, even before the action began, of universal approbation. Whatever may have been the real or supposed reluctance of the former to engage in the cause, it vanished as he came into action. There he stood, having stripped off his clothes to his waistcoat, encouraging the men, giving them money to induce them to cast up the trenches, and animating them to a vigorous defence. His brother addressed the soldiers also, and displayed all the ardour of his fearless spirit. "No man of distinction, " wrote a Scottish prisoner in the Marshalsea to his friend in the North, "behaved himself better than the Earl of Derwentwater. He kept himself most with the Scots, abundantly exposing himself. "[200] But all this was in vain, if we dare to call any manifestations of heroic devotion in vain.

With singular incapacity, Mr. Forster had failed in procuring the necessary intelligence of the movements of the enemy. He had been assured by the Lancashire gentlemen, that General Wills, who headed the King's forces, could not come within forty miles of Preston without their knowledge. On Saturday, the twelfth of November, after he had ordered the forces to march toward Manchester, the intelligence reached him that General Wills had advanced as far as Wigan to attack the rebels. Even at this crisis affairs might have been retrieved: a body of the Jacobites was, indeed, sent forward to defend the Ribble bridge, whilst Mr. Forster went on with a party of horse to reconnoitre. He soon saw the enemy's dragoons; but instead of disputing the bridge, or allowing Colonel Farquharson, belonging to Mackintosh's battalion, to keep the pass, he ordered a retreat to the town. Then all was confusion, slaughter, disgrace. General Wills advanced; he remembered the disaster of Oliver Cromwell; he looked carefully around him, and caused the hedges and fields to be viewed; but no enemy appeared to dispute his progress. The dragoons advanced towards the town; at first, their General conjectured that it must have been abandoned. When he discovered his mistake, he ordered his troops to pass through a gate which leads into the fields at the back of the town, and immediately disposed his forces so as to prevent either a sally or a retreat.

The insurgents, meantime, were prepared to receive him. The ancient church of St. Wilfred, which has since 1814 been replaced by a modern structure, and endowed with another name, that of St. John, must have been shaken to its foundations with the explosion of the cannon, as it was discharged beneath its ancient walls. The besieged formed four main barriers; one a little below the church, commanded by Brigadier Mackintosh: the Earl of Derwentwater and his gallant volunteers were commanded to support that barrier in particular, and here the first attack was made; but it met with so fierce a reception, and such a fire upon the assailants, that the dragoons were obliged to retreat to the entrance of the town. Of this repulse Lord Derwentwater and his youthful brother gained the chief credit. The scene that followed is a detail of fruitless gallantry, and of an agonised but ill-concerted resistance. The fatality which attended the Stuart cause, and which rendered the bloodshed of its gallant champions unavailing to promote it, was here conspicuous. That fatality was doubtless resolvable into a want of common sense, in entrusting the command of the forces into incompetent hands. All night, indeed, the Jacobite forces met their opponents with a determined resistance, that made up, in some measure, for inequality of numbers: the besieged were in many instances sheltered from the enemy's shot, and they had also the advantage on their side of cannon, with which General Wills was not supplied. In the course of that night of horrors, whilst the brave were carried away, mangled or dying, Lord Charles Murray, who was attacked late in the evening, wanted a reinforcement of men. He sent Mr. Patten to the Earl of Derwentwater to ask for aid; it was granted; Mr. Patten passing in safety on account of his black coat, upon which neither party would fire, conducted a troop of fifty volunteers to Lord Charles, who maintained his post, and obliged the enemy to retire with loss. Had it not been for another of Mr. Forster's fatal blunders, the insurgents would still have remained in possession of the town of Preston, which has always, from its commanding situation, been deemed, in all the civil commotions of the kingdom, as a military post of great importance.

All Saturday night, the platoons of the King's forces were incessantly playing upon the insurgents from two principal houses which the besiegers had taken, but few persons of importance were killed. Several houses were set on fire by both parties, but the wind was still, otherwise the inhabitants and the Jacobite troops must have perished in the flames. Towards morning the information arrived in the town through some of the King's soldiers who had been made prisoners, that General Carpenter, with three regiments of dragoons was marching towards Preston, and that he had arrived at Clithero. This intelligence spread great consternation among the Jacobites; and a capitulation began to be mentioned among them; yet it is probable they would still have held out, had not one of the avenues into Preston, by an inexcusable oversight of the Jacobite General, been left unguarded.

It was discovered by some of the King's men that the street leading to Wigan had not been barricadoed. This weak point was thereupon attacked by Lord Forrester, at the head of that brave and old regiment, called Preston's regiment. The assailants marched into a straight passage behind the houses: then Lord Forrester came into the open street, and faced Mackintosh's barrier; there were many shots fired at him, and he was wounded; yet he went back, and lead his men fearlessly into the street, where many of that regiment fell a sacrifice to this dauntless assault. It prevailed; and from that time the fate of the heroes of the churchyard of Preston, of Derwentwater and his noble comrades was determined. But, during that appalling conflict, whilst the blood of the valiant was tinging the streets of Preston, where was the General, who should have shared the dangers with his officers? "I had almost forgot to tell you, " writes the plain-spoken Scottish soldier above referred to, "that in the hottest time of our little action, which was about eleven on Saturday night, Lord Charles Murray's men falling short of ammunition, Robertson of Guy, and another gentleman, were sent to the General, Mr. Forster, for a recruit. When they got access, they found him lying in his naked bed, with a sack-posset, and some confections by him; which I humbly judge was not a very becoming posture at that time for a General. He took all along particular care of himself. "[201]

Towards morning Mr. Forster in conjunction with Lord Widdrington and Colonel Oxburgh, proposed a capitulation. It was considered, that by submission, terms of mercy might be procured by the insurgent troops. Those who thus argued had had no experience of the temper of those to whom they trusted, or they would have willingly died sword in hand rather than have confided in such slender hopes of clemency. The Earl of Derwentwater was among those who counselled the surrender. From his general character, the reasons which he assigned afterwards in his defence, for such advice, have ever been credited. When the fury of the action was over, the amiable nobleman perceived that it was his duty to coincide in a step by which the lives of his countrymen might be spared: he trusted to the mediation of Colonel Oxburgh, who offered to go to the King's forces, and to request a cessation of arms; and who also promised, by his personal influence, to obtain fair terms of capitulation. As a guarantee for the suspension of hostilities, Lord Derwentwater volunteered to become one of the hostages until the morning, should General Wills require it. It appears that his offer was accepted, and that while the Earl was in the camp of General Wills, he received assurances of King George's being a prince of known clemency, —a virtue which was said to form a distinguishing mark in his character. [202] But Mr. Radcliffe, young and ardent, opposed the capitulation with the vehemence natural to his character. During the whole of the action, he had been in the midst of the fire, and had displayed the utmost intrepidity; and now he declared, that "he would rather die with his sword in his hand, like a man of honour, than be dragged like a felon to the gallows, there to be hanged like a dog. " He was, of course, obliged to submit to the majority. [203] The common soldiers joined in his declamations. "Never, " writes the Scottish soldier, "was a handful of men more ready to fight than those at Preston. " It was with difficulty that the gallant Highlanders could be restrained from sallying forth, with their claymores, at all hazards, upon the enemy. They chafed under the disappointment and humiliation of that day; but all was to little purpose. Perhaps no power of words could express the bitter feelings of that hour better than the homely phrases of an eye-witness of the scene.

"On Sunday, to our surprise, about three in the afternoon, " writes the Highlander from his prison, "we saw a drum of the enemy beating a chamade in the street. In an instant we were all called from our posts to the Market-place: the horsemen were ordered to mount. This made us believe the parley had been proposed by General Wills, and that we were to break out and attack them sword in hand, —at least, break through them at that end of the town; but we soon found it was proposed by Mr. Forster, and that there was a cessation till nine next morning, and a capitulation to be made. This was very choaking to us all, but there was no helping of it; for no sooner had we left our posts, than they made themselves master of them, and of our cannon. "[204]

Whilst the chamade was beating, Colonel Cotton, sent by General Wills, rode up the street, and alighted at the sign of the Mitre: the firing meantime had not ceased from several of the houses: the common soldiers were ignorant of the real state of the case, and believed that General Wills had sent to offer honourable terms, not knowing that the offer of a capitulation had proceeded from their own party.

Still there were obstacles to the capitulation raised by the Scottish party, who were represented by Brigadier Mackintosh. "He could not, " he replied, when urged for his consent, "answer for the Scotch, for they were people of desperate fortunes, and he had been a soldier himself, and knew what it was to be a prisoner at discretion. " When this demur was stated to General Wills, "Go back to your people again, " was his answer to those who stated it: "I will attack the town, and I will not spare a man of you. " At the subsequent trial of the rebels General Wills was able, with truth, to deny the charge of having given his unhappy prisoners any hopes, to induce them to sign the capitulation. "All the terms he offered them, " such was his assertion, "was, that he would save their lives from the soldiers till further orders, if they surrendered at discretion: (the meaning of which was, that by the rules of war it was in his power to cut them all to pieces, but he would give them their lives till further orders;) and if they did not comply, he would renew the attack, and not spare a man. "[205]

No sooner had the news of the capitulation been bruited about the streets, than it was received with a sorrow and indignation almost past description. Had the unlucky and pusillanimous Mr. Forster appeared at that moment, he "would certainly, " as Mr. Patten relates, "have been cut to pieces. " Even in his chamber, the General was attacked by his own Secretary, Mr. Murray, and a pistol which was aimed at him only averted by Mr. Patten's hand. The truth is, even Forster's fidelity has been doubted; and subsequently, the mild treatment which he received during his imprisonment, and his escape from prison, have been construed, with what justice it is difficult to say, into a confirmation of this charge.

On the morning after the surrender, the rebels were all made prisoners and disarmed, soon after daybreak. That day, so fatal to the Jacobites of 1715, witnessed also the battle of Sherriff Muir under Lord Mar, and the retaking of the town of Inverness by Lovat. It must have aggravated the regrets of those who then laid down their arms, to see the townspeople of Preston plundered, in despite of every hope to the contrary, by the King's forces, as they dislodged the dejected Jacobites from their quarters. But these irregularities were soon checked.

At last the sound of trumpets and the beating of drums were heard: the two Generals were entering the town in form. They rode into the Market-place, around which the Highlanders were drawn up with their arms. The lords and gentlemen among the rebels were first secured, and placed severally under guard in separate rooms at the inn. Then the poor Highlanders laid down their arms where they stood, and were marched off to the church, under a sufficient guard. Here the thrifty Scots amused themselves by making garments of the linings of the pews, which they ripped off from the seats.

Seven noblemen, besides one thousand four hundred and ninety others, including gentlemen and officers, were taken at Preston. [206] Generally speaking, they were treated well by the military: "The dragoons were civil to us, " writes the Highlander, "their officers choosing rather to want beds themselves than we should. "[207] At Wigan the prisoners were allowed to commune together, under the inspection of sentinels; and a warm altercation occurred between Lord Widdrington and Brigadier Mackintosh, in the presence of Lord Derwentwater, who took little notice of the Brigadier, but turning to another gentleman, said: "You see what we have brought ourselves to by giving credit to our highborn Tories—to such men as Fenwick, Tate, Green, and Allgood. If you outlive misfortune, and return to live in the North, I desire you never to be seen in converse with such rogues in disguise, who promised to join us, and animated us to rise with them. " The gentleman promised that he would observe his Lordship's counsels. "Ah! " said Lord Derwentwater, "I know you to be of an easy temper. "[208]

The prisoners were now carried on towards London by easy marches, Mr. Patten accompanying his patron, Mr. Forster. As they went, the undaunted Highlanders called out to the country people who came to gaze at them, "Where are all your high-church Tories? If they would not fight with us, let them come and rescue us. " This indiscretion redoubled the vigilance of the watch put upon the rebels. From Daventry to London, Mr. Forster and Mr. Patten were greeted by the common people with encomiums upon a warming-pan, in allusion to the supposed birth of the Pretender. When the prisoners arrived at Barnet, messengers came to meet them, and to pinion their arms with cords, —"More for distinction, " adds the subservient Mr. Patten, "than for any pain that attended. " Yet the indignity must have been cruelly galling to the highborn and gallant men who were thus mercilessly paraded to their doom amid the cries of the populace.

At Highgate a strong detachment of horse-soldiers and dragoons received the prisoners from Lumley's Horse, which had hitherto guarded them; and now they were separated into pairs, a foot-soldier holding the bridle of each horse; and in this manner the Jacobite peers, Lord Derwentwater among the rest, were conducted to London through "a hedge of a mob, " as the Highland soldier declares, hired, as he hints, at Lord Pelham's charge, to muster that day. Cries of "Long live King George! " and "Down with the Pretender! " greeted the ear as they passed on to their several destinations. A Quaker, fixing his eyes on Mr. Patten, and seeing his black dress, remarked, "Friend, thou hast been the trumpeter of rebellion to those men, —thou must answer for them. " The moralizer was touched by a grenadier with the butt end of his musket, so that the "spirit fell into the ditch. " But the Quaker was not rebuffed. "Friend, " he said to the soldier, "thou art, I fear, no true friend to King George. "

Even at the last, Mr. Forster had hopes, it is said, of being released by a Tory mob. The Jacobite noblemen had been, indeed, all along misled, or ignorant of the real inclinations of the mass of the people. The dread of what they term "popery" is a deep and engrossing passion in the hearts of the lower and even of the middle classes, and it formed an effectual barrier against the restoration of the Stuarts. The cause of those unfortunate Princes was never, in this country, as it was in Scotland, the cause of the people. The personal attachment of the Highlanders to the ancient race of Stuart, and their devotion to their clan, superseded their religious scruples; [209] but that was not the case in the South.

The Earl of Derwentwater and his brother were consigned to different prisons, —the former to the Tower, the latter to Newgate; a very strict guard was set upon the Earl, and no one was allowed to see him or speak to him. [210]

On the seventh of January, 1716, the case of the seven rebel lords[211] was brought before the House of Commons; and Mr. Lechmere moved that they should not be left to the ordinary method of prosecutions, but should be proceeded against by way of impeachment. [212] In a long and, as far as the report enables a reader to judge, able speech, he referred to the declaration of the Pretender, given under his sign manual and privy seal at Commercy, on the twenty-fifth of October, 1715. "This paper, " Mr. Lechmere observed, "which he held in his hand, was sufficient to fire the thoughts of every gentleman there; and the House could do no more than to resent this so far as to make themselves the prosecutors of those who avowed the cause of the Pretender, and set themselves at the head of armies, in the heart of his Majesty's dominions. " In conclusion, "he impeached James, Earl of Derwentwater, of high treason, which impeachment he undertook to make good. "

Six other members then severally impeached the other six Jacobite lords; and an impeachment was carried up to the Bar of the House of Lords, with an assurance "that articles to make good the charge against the Earl of Derwentwater and the other noblemen would shortly be exhibited. "

A committee of the House of Commons, with Mr. Lechmere as their chairman, was therefore formed; and the articles were framed, and read before the Bar of the House of Lords. On the tenth of January the Jacobite lords were summoned to hear the articles of impeachment: a few days were allowed to them to prepare their replies. On the following Saturday, the Earl of Derwentwater was brought by the Gentleman Usher of the Black Rod before the Bar, where he knelt, until told by the Lord Chancellor to rise. He then delivered his answer.

Those who, in perusing the annals of these times, look for strength of character in the state prisoners who were now brought before the tribunal of the House of Lords, or for consistency in those principles which had led them into the field, will be painfully disappointed. In two instances alone was there displayed an undaunted demeanour, and a resolute adherence to the cause which they had avowed; and these were shewn in the subsequent rebellion, by the brave and admirable Lord Balmerino, and by the unfortunate Charles Radcliffe.

The Earl of Derwentwater expressed, in his reply, the "deepest concern and affliction to a charge of so high and heinous a nature as that brought against him. " He acknowledged with sorrow that he had been in arms, and did march through and invade several parts of the kingdom; and that he was thereby guilty of the offence whereof he was charged in the articles. "But, " he continued, "if any one offence of that kind was ever attended with circumstances which might move compassion, the said Earl hopes he may be entitled to it. " He then referred to his peaceable disposition, and pleaded his youth and inexperience; the absence of all malice, of all concerted conspiracy; his having made no warlike preparations. He pleaded also, that he could not be justly reproached with any cruel or harsh conduct while he bore arms: he specified his advice to those with him to submit at Preston, and to trust to the King's mercy. He adduced his anxiety to save the lives of his Majesty's subjects by avoiding further bloodshed, and brought in proof a letter which he had written to those of his own party, conjuring them to capitulate. Under such circumstances, the Earl implored the mediation both of their Lordships and of the Commons for mercy on his behalf, "which will lay him, " so he declared in conclusion, "under the highest obligations of duty and affection to his Majesty, and perpetual gratitude to both Houses. "

The answer not appearing to the Lords to be sufficiently "express and clear, " the Earl was then asked by the Chancellor, whether he meant to plead guilty to the articles of the impeachment. The Earl replied that he did, and that he submitted to the King's mercy. His answer and plea were entered accordingly, and the Earl then withdrew. [213]

On Thursday, February the ninth, the Lords came from their own House into the hall erected in Westminster Hall, to pass sentence upon James, Earl of Derwentwater, and upon the five other noblemen who had pleaded guilty with him; the Earl of Wintoun, who had pleaded not guilty, being reserved for trial.

The Lord High Steward who presided on this occasion was William Earl Cowper, Lord Chancellor, who, for the time of trial, was called "your Grace, " and had the privilege of walking uncovered, his train borne, except whilst the commission was read by the Clerk of the Crown.

The usual proclamation rang through the Court, and the Sergeant-at-Arms, saying "Oyez! Oyez! Oyez! " enforced silence. Then another proclamation was made, commanding the Lieutenant of the Tower to bring forth his prisoners to the Bar, and accordingly the six rebel lords were brought to the Bar by the Deputy-Governor of the Tower, having the axe carried before them by the Gentleman Jailer, who stood with it on the left hand of the prisoners, with the edge turned from him. The prisoners after kneeling before the Bar, bowed to his Grace the High Steward, and also to the Peers, whose sad privilege it is to try those of the same rank in the scale of society as themselves, and often, from extensive intermarriages, connected by ties of blood. The articles of impeachment against James Earl of Derwentwater were read, and the prisoner's reply.

He was then asked if he pleaded guilty to the high treason in the said articles of impeachment. His Lordship replied, "I do. " He was ordered to withdraw; but was called before the Bar the same day to receive judgment. Upon being asked by the Lord High Steward "Why judgment should not be passed upon him according to law? " the Earl repeated a few circumstances mentioned in his answer to the articles. His voice was scarcely articulate as he proceeded to say, "But the terrors of your Lordship's just sentence, which at once deprive me of my life and estate, and complete the misfortunes of my wife and innocent children, are so heavy upon my mind, I am scarcely able to allege what may extenuate my offence, if any thing may do it. " He then again besought of their Lordships the mediation in his behalf.

After the Lords Widdrington, Kenmure, Nithisdale, and Carnwath had been severally addressed, and had replied to the Court, proclamation for silence was again made, and judgment was given. It was prefaced by a long and elaborate address; which, however elegant, however explanatory, however just, it may be considered, was strongly tinctured by the adulatory spirit of the day, and was calculated to wound and to harden the offending prisoners, rather than to unfold with dignity the reasons for condemnation. In conclusion, since nothing could, in the narrowing view of party, be too dictatorial for the unfortunate Jacobites, they were exhorted not to rely any longer on the usual directors of their consciences, but to be assisted by some of the pious and learned divines of the Church of England. This was addressed to men who were, with two exceptions, of the Church of Rome, and whose chief reliance must naturally be upon those of their own persuasion.

The terrible sentence of the law was then recorded. It was that usually given against the meanest offenders in like kind, the most ignominious and painful parts being remitted by the grace of the Crown to persons of quality. Judgment was, however, pronounced, according to the usual form for high treason. [214]

The prisoners were then reconducted to the Tower; the Lord High Steward, standing up uncovered, broke the staff of office, and declared the present commission to be ended. The Peers returned to the House of Lords.

Little is known of the dreary and solemn hours which intervened between the judgment and the execution of the sentence. But one brief expression, in an old newspaper, relative to the young and unhappy Earl of Derwentwater, speaks volumes: "The Earl of Derwentwater is so desponding, that two warders are obliged to sit up with him during the night. "[215] He was visited in his prison by Thomas Townshend, Viscount Sydney, then Under Secretary of State for George the First; [216] one of the most amiable men, as well as refined and elegant scholars of the day, and a nobleman whose sensibility and delicacy of feeling, which prevented his taking a share in the more active parts of public business, must have caused an interview with the Earl of Derwentwater to have been deeply touching. The Duke of Roxburgh also visited the condemned nobleman; but no record is left of these communications. The Duke was at that time Keeper of the Privy Seal for Scotland, and Lord-Lieutenant of the counties of Roxburgh and Selkirk. He had recently distinguished himself at Sherriff Muir: he was at this time a young man of twenty-five years of age, and one whom all parties have commended. "Learned, without pedantry, he was, perhaps, " says Lockhart of Carnwath, "the best accomplished young man of Europe. " To these acquirements were added a singular charm of manner. [217] One can hardly suppose the visits of two such men not to have had their source from some motive of kindness.

To the credit of the House of Lords, an address was voted to the King, petitioning that his Majesty would reprieve such of the rebel lords as deserved his mercy. The royal answer was couched in these terms: that "the King on this, and all occasions, would do what he thought consistent with the dignity of the Crown and the safety of his people. "[218] It was unfortunate that, both at this time and in the Rebellion of 1745, there was no Queen Consort. A woman's heart would, one may trust, have pleaded for the young, gallant, and beloved Derwentwater. The English Court was, at that time, insulted by the audacious intrigues of foreign mistresses. These women had no interest in the King's real fame, nor in the national credit. Such was the case in the first Rebellion. [219] In 1745 Queen Caroline, the wife of George the Second, was dead.

Accompanied by two courageous ladies, the young Countess of Derwentwater threw herself at the feet of the King, and implored mercy on her husband. [220] In the House of Commons, the First Lord of the Treasury declared, that he had been offered a bribe of sixty thousand pounds to save Lord Derwentwater. Sir Richard Steele spoke loudly in favour of the condemned lords, but the declaration of Walpole suppressed all hopes of mercy. "He was moved with indignation, " he said, "to see that there should be such unworthy members of this great body as to open their mouths, without blushing, in favour of rebels and parricides. " He adjourned the House until the first of March, it being understood that the peers would be executed in the mean time. It is some consolation to reflect that the Minister had, on this occasion, only a majority of seven.

At this juncture, when all hope seemed lost, Mary, Dowager Countess of Derwentwater, proffered the following petition in behalf of her sons. One can hardly suppose how it could have been disregarded; but the Monarch had few sympathies with his people of England.

"The humble Petition of Mary Countess of Derwentwater, 1716, to the King's most excellent Majesty, sheweth,

"That the Earl of Derwentwater and Charles Radcliffe (your petitioner's two and only sons) having been unfortunately engaged and surprised into a horrid and open Rebellion against your most sacred Majesty, have surrendered themselves at Preston, and submitted to your Majesty's great clemency and mercy.

"Their crimes are so enormous, that your petitioner can scarce hope for a pardon; yet the greatness of their offence doth not make your petitioner lay aside all hopes of mercy, when your petitioner and they, who are both very young, throw themselves, absolute and entirely, at your Majesty's feet for it; and as they have a just abhorrence and a sincere and true repentance for what is past, so they will give undoubted security and proof of their most dutiful behaviour to your Majesty's Government for the future.

"Wherefore your petitioner most humbly prays that your Majesty will, out of your royal clemency and boundless mercy and compassion, spare the lives of your petitioner's sons, and grant them your most gracious pardon.

"And your petitioner shall ever, as in duty bound, &c. "[221]

The petition was unavailing, and the unfortunate young nobleman prepared to meet his doom.

On the twenty-fourth of February, at ten o'clock, the Earl of Derwentwater, with Lord Kenmure, was carried in a hackney-coach from the Tower to the Transport Office in Tower Hill, where there was a room prepared for their reception, hung with black, and a passage or gallery railed in, which led to the place of execution. The scaffold was surrounded with the Guards. Lord Derwentwater suffered first. He was observed to turn very pale as he proceeded through the gallery and ascended the steps; but there was a modest composure observable in his demeanour. He held a book in his hand, from which he read prayers for some time; then, requesting leave of the Sheriffs to read a paper to the people, he went to the rails of the scaffold, and there delivered the following touching and beautiful address, which, how different soever may be the sentiments and opinions with which it is perused, can hardly fail to impress the reader as coming from a conscientious mind: —

"Being in a few minutes to appear before the Tribunal of God, where, though most unworthy, I hope for mercy, which I have not found from men now in power, I have endeavoured to make my peace with His Divine Majesty, by most humbly begging pardon for all the sins of my life; and I doubt not of a merciful forgiveness, through the merits of the passion of my Saviour Jesus Christ; for which end I earnestly desire the prayers of all good Christians.

"After this, I am to ask pardon of those whom I might have scandalized by pleading guilty at my trial. Such as were permitted to come to me, told me that, having been undeniably in arms, pleading guilty was but the consequence of having submitted to mercy, and many arguments were used to prove there was nothing of moment in so doing, —among others, the universal practice of signing leases, whereof the preambles ran in the name of the persons in possession.

"But I am sensible that in this I have made bold with my loyalty, having never owned any other but King James the Third for my lawful King: him I had an inclination to serve from my infancy, and was moved thereto by a natural love I had to his person, knowing him to be capable of making his people happy; and though he had been born of a different religion to mine, I should have done for him all that lay in my power, as my ancestors have done for his predecessors, being thereto bound by the laws of God and man.

"Wherefore, if in this affair I have acted rashly, it ought not to affect the innocent; I intended to wrong nobody, but to serve my King and my country, and that without self-interest, —hoping, by the example I gave, to have induced others to their duty; and God, who sees the secrets of my heart, knows I speak the truth. Some means have been proposed to me for saving my life, which I looked upon as inconsistent with honour and innocence, and therefore I rejected them; for, with God's assistance, I shall prefer any death to the doing a base unworthy action. I only wish now, that the laying down my life might contribute to the service of my King and country, and the re-establishment of the ancient and fundamental constitution of these kingdoms; without which, no lasting peace or true happiness can attend them. Then I should, indeed, part with my life even with pleasure; as it is, I can only pray, that these blessings may be bestowed upon my dear country; and since I can do no more, I beseech God to accept of my life as a small sacrifice to it.

"I die a Roman Catholic: I am in perfect charity with all the world (I thank God for it), even with those of the present Government, who are most instrumental in my death. I freely forgive all such as ungenerously reported false things of me; and hope to be forgiven the trespasses of my youth by the Father of Mercies, into whose hands I commend my soul.

J. DERWENTWATER. "

P. S. "If that Prince who now governs had given me my life, I should have thought myself obliged never more to have taken up arms against him. "

After delivering this address, the unfortunate nobleman thus spoke to the executioner: "You will find something for you in my pocket [this was two half-guineas], and I have given that gentleman [pointing to a person who held his hat and wig] somewhat more for you. Let me lie down once, to see how the block fits me. " This he did. Then, kneeling down again, and uttering a short prayer with the executioner, he arose, and undressed himself for execution, the headsman assisting him. After which, the Earl desired the executioner to take notice, that "when he heard the words 'sweet Jesus! ' then he should do his office so soon as he pleased. " After which, his Lordship laid himself down on the block, and said, "I forgive my enemies, and hope that God will forgive me; " and then, turning his head up towards the executioner, he exclaimed, "After the third time I cry *'sweet Jesus! '* strike then, and do what is most convenient to you. "

A solemn and appalling scene then ensued. The voice of Lord Derwentwater was heard to exclaim, and the watchful ear of the executioner caught these words: "*Sweet Jesus*, receive my spirit; *sweet Jesus*, be merciful unto me; *sweet Jesus*"—he seemed to be going on, when the sentence was broken and the voice for ever hushed, the executioner severing his Lordship's head from his body, which he did at one stroke. Then the executioner took up the head, and at the several quarters of the scaffold elevated it with both his hands, crying with a loud voice, "Behold the head of a traitor! God save King George! " When he had done so, the friends of the Earl not being provided with hearse or coffin, Sir John Fryer, the Sheriff, ordered the body to be wrapped in black baize, to be conveyed to a hackney coach, and delivered to his friends, one of whom had wrapped up his head in a handkerchief. [222]

On the day of the execution, Mary, Countess of Derwentwater, accompanied by another female, dressed herself as a fishwoman, and in a cart drove under Temple Bar, having previously bribed some people to throw the head of her lord into her lap, as she passed under the pinnacle on which it was placed. [223]

Various accounts have been given of the interment of the Earl of Derwentwater. He is generally believed to have been buried in the church of St. Giles-in-the-Fields, near the altar. But a popular tradition has found credence, that he was buried at Dilstone. This has arisen from the Jacobite ditty, called "Derwentwater's Good Night, " or has probably given origin to that lay, in which the Earl is made to say: —

"Albeit that here in London town
It is my fate to die,

O carry me to Northumberland,
 In my father's grave to lie:
There chaunt my solemn requiem,
 In Hexham's holy towers,
And let six maids of fair Tynedale,
 Scatter my grave with flowers."[224]

This is said to have been his last request, but to have been refused, for fear of any popular tumult in the North. Either a pretended burial in the church of St. Giles took place, or the Earl's body was removed, "for it was certainly, " says Mr. Hogg, "carried secretly to Dilstone, where it was deposited by the side of the Earl's father, in his chapel. " "A little porch before the farm-house of Whitesmocks, " adds the same authority, "is pointed out as the exact spot where the Earl's remains rested, avoiding Durham. " The coffin is said to have been opened during the present century, and the body of the Earl recognized, both by his appearance of youth, his features, and the suture round his neck. It is seldom satisfactory to state what has no other source than common report. In the North, the aurora borealis is still said to be called "Lord Derwentwater's lights, " because, on the night of his execution, it appeared remarkably vivid. It is, any rate, pleasant to reflect, that one who "gave bread to thousands" is remembered by this beautiful appearance in the county which he loved, and where his virtues are remembered and his errors forgotten.

His fate was hard. Let us not, contrary to nature, call up motives of state policy to vindicate the death of this brave and honourable man. The Earl of Derwentwater was one upon whom clemency might safely have been shown. Generous, liberal, sincere, a prince might have relied upon his assurance that, had mercy been shown to him, it would never have been repaid by treachery. His youth and inexperience, —his wife, his children, —should not have been forgotten: nor should it have been forgotten, that the principles of loyalty for which his life was forfeited, have dictated some of the most important services which have been rendered to the state, and have secured the existence of an hereditary government.

Of what the Earl of Derwentwater might have become, in character, in intellect, his early fate has prevented our judging. In person he was noble and elegant; his portraits do not give the impression of that beauty of feature which has been ascribed to him. In character he was irreproachable. He was, in one sense, one of those noblemen of whom it were well for this country to have more: he lived among those from whom he drew his fortunes—their benefactor and their friend.

The widowed Countess of Derwentwater died at Brussels in August, 1723. [225] The descendants of the Earl are now extinct, a son and daughter who survived him having both died. His Lordship's brother married a Scottish peeress, and is the ancestor of the present Earl of Newburgh, the rightful representative of the Earl of Derwentwater.

"The domains of the Derwentwater family in Cumberland are, " says Lord Mahon, "among the very few forfeitures of the Jacobites which have never been restored by the clemency of the House of Hanover. " In 1788, a clear rent of two thousand five hundred pounds was, however, granted out of these estates to the Newburgh family. "They were first, " says the same authority, "settled on Greenwich Hospital, but have since been sold to Mr. Marshall, of Leeds. "

The deeds of the Derwentwater estates were preserved in the following manner: "On the night when Preston surrendered, Lord Derwentwater found means, " as Mr. Hogg relates, "to send messengers to Capheaton, to prevent the family there from appearing in arms. By his orders, the family papers were removed to Capheaton, and they were laid between two walls and a chimney. A slater employed about the house discovered several chests with the Derwentwater arms engraved on the lids. Being a rigid Presbyterian, he informed old Sir Ambrose Middleton, of Belsay, who being Deputy-Lieutenant for the Duke of Somerset, searched Capheaton for arms, and under that pretence broke open the walls, and found the deeds, from the concealment of which Greenwich Hospital had been put to some difficulties. "

Such was the fate of the last memorial of the unfortunate Earl of Derwentwater. It is impossible to help regretting that a name once so honoured should have become extinct; and there appears to be an unaccountable injustice in that oblivion, whilst most of the Scottish forfeited titles have been restored.

FOOTNOTES:

[173] I write it Radcliffe, because the most careful historians and genealogists have given the preference to that mode of spelling the name.

[174] The fact has been rather surmised than proved.

[175] Hutchinson's View of Northumberland, vol. i. p. 171.

[176] Lysons' Magna Britannia, vol. ii. p. 85.

[177] Burke's Extinct Peerage, art. *Radcliffe*; also Wood's Peerage, 309. It has been erroneously stated, that Francis Radclyffe himself, who married Mary Tudor, was first ennobled. It was his father, Sir Francis Radclyffe.

[178] Life of Charles Radcliffe. "By a gentleman of the family, to prevent the public being imposed upon by any erroneous or partial accounts to the prejudice of this unfortunate gentleman. " London, 1746.

[179] Macpherson Papers, vol. ii.

[180] Patten's Hist. Rebellion, p. 47.

[181] In personal appearance the Earl is declared to have been distinguished for grace and comeliness. Neither the prints of this nobleman, nor an original picture in the possession of the Earl of Newburgh, at Hassop in Derbyshire, give the impression that the Earl was handsome. Yet he obtained the appellation of "handsome Derwentwater. "

[182] Kimber's Baronetage, vol. i. p. 517.

[183] Encyclopædia Metropolitana.

[184] Id. Annals of George I.

[185] Patten, p. 3.

[186] The following is a copy of the warrant, and affords a specimen, which may be novel to some readers, of the form in which such

affairs are couched. The original is still preserved by the present Earl of Newburgh, the descendant of Charles Radcliffe. I am indebted to the courtesy of the Earl of Newburgh for permission to copy this document, and also for several particulars concerning the family of Radcliffe, which I have interwoven with this biography: —

"James Stanhope, Esq., one of his Majesty's most Honourable Privy Council, and Principal Secretary of State.

"These are in his Majesty's name, to authorise and require you, taking a constable to your assistance, forthwith to make strict and diligent search in such places as you shall have notice, for the Right Honourable James, Earl of Derwentwater; and him having found, you are to seize and apprehend for suspicion of Treason, and to bring him, together with his papers, before me to be examined concerning the Premisses, and to be further dealt with according to law: for the due execution whereof, all Mayors, Sheriffs, Justices of the Peace, Constables, and all his Majesty's officers, Civil and Military, and loving subjects whom it may concern, are to be aiding and assisting to you as there shall be occasion. And for so doing, this shall be your warrant.

"Given at Whitehall the two-and-twentieth day of September, 1715.

"JAMES STANHOPE. "

"To Richard Shorman, John Hutching, and John Turner, three of his Majesty's Messengers in Ordinary. "

[187] His pension was raised for his services from fifty to eighty pounds per annum. —See Caledonian Mercury, 1722.

[188] Patten, p. 19.

[189] Hutchinson's History of Northumberland, vol. i. p. 131.

[190] State Papers. Domestic, No. 4, 1716.

[191] Life of Charles Radcliffe, p. 15.

[192] Patten, p. 31.

[193] Patten. Smollett.

[194] Parliamentary History, 2 Geo. I. vol. vii. p. 269.

[195] Patten, p. 47.

[196] Id. p. 65.

[197] An instance of this spirit is related by Lord Sunderland in the case of a Mr. Crisp, a Lancashire gentleman, who acted with such zeal for the Government during the Rebellion, that he was never able to live in his native country afterwards. —Lord Mahon's History of England since the Peace of Utrecht, vol. i. p. 253.

[198] Lord Mahon, vol. i. p. 248.

[199] Patten, p. 79.

[200] Letter from a Scots Prisoner. —See Weekly Journal, or British Gazette, for 1716.

[201] Weekly Journal, p. 354.

[202] Parliamentary History, p. 269.

[203] Life of Charles Radcliffe, p. 23.

[204] Patten.

[205] Patten, p. 96.

[206] Patten, p. 103.

[207] Weekly Journal.

[208] Patten.

[209] Patten.

[210] Caledonian Mercury for 1716.

[211] Earls of Derwentwater, Nithisdale, Carnwath, and Wintoun; Viscount Kenmure, and Lords Widdrington and Nairn.

[212] State Trials, vol. xv. p. 762.

[213] Parliamentary History, vol. vii. p. 269.

[214] State Trials.

[215] Caledonian Mercury for 1716.

[216] Beatson's Political Index.

[217] Douglas's Peerage of Scotland.

[218] State Trials, vol. xv. p. 802.

[219] Lord Mahon's History, vol. i. p. 291.

[220] Id.

[221] State Papers, 1716, No. 4; now, for the first time, printed.

[222] Or rather, a piece of red cloth, which is still preserved at Hassop, the seat of the Earl of Newburgh, the marks of blood being still visible.

[223] From a tradition current in the descendants of this family.

[224] Hogg's Jacobite Relics, vol. i. p. 31.

[225] See Caledonian Mercury, 1723.

THE MASTER OF SINCLAIR.

John Sinclair, called, in compliance with the custom of Scotland in regard to the eldest sons of Barons, the Master of Sinclair, was descended from the ancient family of Saint Clare, in France, on whom lands were bestowed by Alexander the Third of Scotland. In early times, the titles of Earls of Orkney and Caithness had been given to the first settlers of the Saint Clares; and the possession of the islands of Orkney and Shetland had been added to certain royal donations, by a marriage with an heiress of the sirname of Speire. One of the Sinclairs had even borne the dignity of Prince of Orkney; but this distinction was lost by an improvident member of the house of Sinclair, called William the Waster; and the prosperity of his descendants was due only to the favour of James the Sixth, who created Henry Sinclair, of Dysart in Fife, a Baron.

The family continued in honour and estimation, until the subject of this memoir, John, brought upon it disgrace, and incurred to himself lasting self-reproach.

The Master of Sinclair was the eldest son of Henry, seventh Lord Sinclair, and the representative, therefore, of an honourable family. But it was his fate to forfeit his birthright, not so much by his adherence to an ill-fated cause, as by the violence and brutality of his own temper and conduct.

He was, at an early age, engaged in the military profession, and bore the commission of Captain-Lieutenant in Preston's regiment under the great Marlborough. At the battle of Wynendale, fought on the twenty-eighth of September, 1708, the events which stamped the future character of the Master of Sinclair's destiny occurred.

Two brothers of the name of Schaw, Scotchmen, of an ancient race, and ancestors, collaterally, of the present family of Shaw-Stewart of Renfrew, had commissions also in Preston's regiment. These unfortunate young men were of the chief family of the Schaws, or Sauchie, who had flourished since the reign of Robert the Second.

By that singular coincidence which sometimes occurs, and which seems to stamp certain races with misfortune, the Schaws had already been nearly exterminated in feudal times by the violence of a neighbouring clan, the Montgomeries of Skellmorlie; and had been preserved from total destruction by what seemed to human comprehension to be the merest chance. By one of the Montgomeries, the Tower of Greenock was invaded and taken, and the Laird of Schaw and four or five of his sons were put to death. One child, then in his cradle, alone escaped, and grew up to manhood, with the resolution to avenge his father and his brothers rankling at his heart. Accordingly, he collected his friends and dependants, and invested, during a period of repose and security, the house of his enemy. Montgomery, finding his castle attacked, stood forth on the battlements, and, after demanding a parley with the besieger, "Are you not, " he cried out, "an ungrateful man to come hither with bow and brand to take the life of the man who made you young laird and auld laird in the same day? " Young Schaw, struck by the argument, drew off his forces, and left the castle of Skellmorlie standing, and its inmates uninjured.

The family of Schaw were zealous Whigs, the father of the two young officers in Preston's regiment having raised a regiment at the time of the Revolution, without any other expense to the Government than that of sergeants and drummers.

The eldest brother, Sir John Schaw, had been an active promoter of the Union; and, upon a threatened invasion of the French, and a consequent alarm of the Jacobites, Sir John had offered to join the army with five or six hundred of his followers. This decided political bias may, perhaps, in some measure, account for the disposition to affront on the side of Sinclair, and the quickness to resent on the other hand, which was shown between the parties.

During the battle of Wynendale, in the midst of the fire, it appeared, in evidence afterwards taken, that Ensign Hugh Schaw, the first of the victims to the Master of Sinclair's wrath, was heard to call out to the Master "to stand upright; " it was afterwards publicly stated by Ensign Hugh Schaw, that he had done so upon seeing Sinclair bow himself down to the ground for a considerable time. This alleged act of cowardice on the part of Sinclair appears, however, not to have really taken place; but it was made the groundwork of a calumnious imputation. It must, however, be acknowledged, that there was nothing in the subsequent conduct of the Master of Sinclair, as far as the battle of Sherriff Muir was concerned, to raise his character as a man of personal bravery.

Upon hearing of this injurious report, Sinclair sent a challenge to Ensign Schaw. It was dispatched through the medium of a brother officer, to whom the Ensign replied, at first, that he had just heard of his brother George's being wounded before Lisle, and that it was of far greater importance that he should go to him than accept the Master of Sinclair's challenge; besides, the young man added, that since his last misfortune, probably a fatal duel, he had pledged himself neither to receive nor to give a challenge. Should a rencontre happen, he would defend himself as he could; that, after all, he had said nothing but what he could prove. Upon these words being repeated to the Master of Sinclair, he fell into a violent passion, and swore that he would not give Schaw fair play; that his honour was concerned. The second whom he had employed then threatened to take the challenge to Colonel Preston; upon which the Master told him "he was a rascal if he did it. "

On the following day, the Master met Ensign Schaw, and taking a stick from underneath his coat, struck the Ensign two blows over the head with it. They both drew, and fought with such fury that the Master's sword was broken, and that of the Ensign bent; upon which Sinclair retired behind a sentinel, desiring him "to keep off the Ensign, as his sword was broken. " Schaw then said, "You know I am more of a gentleman than to pursue you when your sword is broken. " But the young soldier Schaw had at this time received a mortal wound, of which he died; but not until after the verdict of the court-martial ultimately held on Sinclair.

In the course of three days a second fatal rencontre succeeded this deadly contest; and another brother, Captain Alexander Schaw, fell a victim to the vindictive and brutal notions at that period considered in the army to constitute a code of honour.

Captain Schaw was naturally indignant at the death of his brother; he expressed his anger openly, and said, that the Master of Sinclair had "paper in his breast, " against which his brother's sword was bent; and that he had received the fatal wound after his sword had thus become useless. The Master of Sinclair having heard of these assertions, resolved to avenge himself for these imputations cast upon him. On the thirteenth of September, as Captain Schaw was riding at the head of Major How's regiment, the sound of his own name, repeated twice, announced the approach of the hated Sinclair. Captain Schaw turned, and inquired of the Master what he wanted. Sinclair replied, by asking him to go to the front, as he wanted to speak to him; to which Captain Schaw rejoined, that he might speak to him there. "Yes, " returned Sinclair, "but if I fire at you here, I may shoot some other body. " Captain Schaw answered, that he might fire at him if he pleased, he bore him no ill-will. "If you will not go to the front, " returned Sinclair, "beg my pardon. " This was refused, some words of further aggravation ensued; then the Master of Sinclair drew his pistol and fired at Schaw. The Captain was also preparing to fire; his hand was in the act of drawing his pistol when it was for ever checked, whether employed for good or evil; the aim of Sinclair was certain, and Schaw fell dead from his horse. Sinclair, without waiting to inquire how far mortal might be the wound he had inflicted, rode away.

Thus perished two young officers, described by their brother, Sir John Schaw, as "very gallant gentlemen. " To complete the tragedy, a third, wounded at Lisle, was brought to the camp at Wynendale, and expired in the same room with his brother, Ensign Schaw, partly of his wounds, partly of grief for his brother's death; so that the offender, as the surviving brother remarked, "was not wholly innocent even of his blood: " yet both these rencontres, to adopt the mild term employed by Sir Walter Scott, were viewed in a very lenient manner by the officers of the court-martial which afterwards sat upon the case, and even by Marlborough himself. The Master of Sinclair speaks of them in his narrative in terms which imply that one, whose hands were so deeply dyed in crime, regarded himself as an injured man; there can scarcely be a better exemplification of the deceitfulness of the heart than such a representation.

On the seventeenth of October, 1708, a court-martial upon the Master of Sinclair was held at Ronsales by the command of the Duke of Marlborough. Upon the first charge, that of challenging Ensign Hugh Schaw (in breach of the twenty-eighth article of war), Sinclair was acquitted, the court being of opinion that the challenge was not proved.

Of the second accusation, that of killing Captain Alexander Schaw, the Master of Sinclair was found guilty, and sentenced to suffer death. He was, however, recommended to the mercy of the Duke of Marlborough, in consideration of the provocation which he had received, —the prisoner having declared that, not only on that occasion, but upon several, and in different regiments, Captain Schaw had defamed him; that he was forced to do what he did, and that he had done it with reluctance.

The case was, however, afterwards referred to the Attorney General and the Solicitor General, who gave it their opinion that Sinclair was guilty of murder; for had the trial taken place in England before a common jury, the judge must have directed the jury to find him guilty of murder, no provocation whatever being sufficient to excuse malice, or to make the offence of killing less than murder, when it is committed with premeditation. How far the provocation was to be considered as a ground of mercy, these legal functionaries declined to judge.

Upon the publication of this sentence, Sir John Schaw addressed a petition to Queen Anne, praying for justice on the murderer of his brothers, and appealing to his Sovereign against the extraordinary recommendation of the court to mercy. He also wrote urgent letters to the Earl of Stair and the Duke of Argyle, praying for their intercession with the Duke of Marlborough that the murderer of his brothers might be punished. He next wrote to the Duke of Marlborough himself. The following letters show the earnestness of the pleader, and prove the caution and subtlety of the General. Some deep political motive lay beneath the mercy shown to Sinclair, otherwise it seems impossible to account for the conduct of so great a disciplinarian as Marlborough in this affair.

SIR JOHN SCHAW TO THE DUKE OF MARLBOROUGH.

"May it pleas your Grace,

"Amongst the misfortunes that attend the murthers of my two brothers, I thinck it's one to be constrain'd to appear importunate with your Grace. The case, by the depositions of the witnesses, being in the opinion of the learn'd lawyers of the most atrocius nature, and not pardonable by the law of the country whereof we are subjects, and such as indispensable requires my utmost applications for redress, I cannot forbear the repeating of my submissive prayers to your Grace for speedy justice. The blood of my brothers, the tyes of nature, and the sentiments of friendship, would render the least negligence on my part inexcusable with the world and with my own conscience.

"I should deliver my petition personally, rather than venture to give your Grace the trouble of letters, were I not sufficiently assured of your Grace's justice, and at the same time willing to gratifie my wellwisshers desires in staying here. Hoping your Grace wil, with a condescending compassion to my present circumstances, favourably admit the bearer, Capt. James Stuart, in Coll. M'Carty's regiment, who is my faithfull friend and near relation, to deliver this letter, and represent my case, that the whole matter may be sett in a true light for a finall decision, in the meantime, I remain, with a profound respect, my Lord, Your Grace's most humble, etc. "

"To the Duke of Marlborough, London, the 29th November, 1708. "

THE DUKE OF MARLBOROUGH TO SIR JOHN SCHAW. [226]

"Sir,

"Captain Stewart has delivered me your letter of the twenty-first of November; I had before, from the Secretary at Warr, the opinion of the Attorney and Sollicitor General upon the proceedings of the court-martiall, with the copie of the petition you had presented to the Queen, but no positive directions from hir Majesty, which I should have been very glad to have received, being without it under very great uneasiness, as Captain Steward will tell you; however, you may be sure I shall have all the regard you can desire for your just resentment against Mr. Sinclair, being truly, Sir,

"Your most humble servant, (*Sic subscribitur*) "MARLBOROUGH. "

"Copie letter Duke of Marlborrough to Sir John Schaw, dated at the Camp at Melle, the 16th December, 1708. "

After this correspondence, the unhappy brother of the two young officers had every reason to conclude that the delinquent would very soon be brought to justice. He wrote to Mr. Cardonnel, secretary to the Duke of Marlborough, in grateful terms for the kind intercession employed for him. What was afterwards his astonishment to find that Sinclair was allowed to serve in the British army in the sieges of Lisle and Ghent, and eventually received in the Prussian service! The evident favour of the Duke is fully shown in the following passage from the Master of Sinclair's narrative:

"I was obliged to quit [the army] for two misfortunes which happened in a very short time, one after the other, notwithstanding of the court-marshall's recommending me to the General, his Grace the Duke of Marlborough's mercy, which was always looked on as equal to a pardon, and which I can aver was never refused to any one but myself. Nor was his allowing me to serve at the sieges of Lisle and Ghent precedented on my giving my word of honour to return to arrest after these sieges were over, which I did and continued (prisoner) till his Grace the Duke of Marlborough sent his repeated orders to make my escape, which I disobeyed twice; but at last being encouraged by his promise to recommend me to any prince that I pleased, for these were his words, I went off, and procured his recommendation to the King of Prussia, from whose service, which I may say is of the strictest, I came back to serve in the Low Countries, where I continued until the end of the war, at which time her Majesty Queen Anne having, as it is said, turned Tory, vouchsafed me her pardon. "

These marks of indulgence to Sinclair fell heavily upon the heart of him who still mourned two promising brothers, sent to an untimely grave by brutal revenge. The following letter from Sir John Schaw is beautifully and touchingly expressed. [227] What effect it produced upon the great but not faultless man to whom it was addressed, can only be known by the impunity with which Sinclair, his hands being imbued in the blood of his countrymen, continued in the Prussian army, and afterwards returned to Scotland.

"It is with very great regrate that I give your Grace any further trouble on account of the melancholy story of my two brothers, who had the misfortune to be murthered in the space of three dayes by Lieutenant Sinclair, then in the regiment of Prestoun, in the year 1708. Your Grace was at the paines to be informed of the whole case, and the murtherer, being a man of quality, had many to intercede for him; your justice did overcome all other considerations and indeed nothing could be more worthie of the great character your Grace has, and the glorious name you must leave to posterity, than the punishment of so cruel and bloodie a fact; but the criminal escaped, and the sentence of death pronounced by the court-martial, and confirmed by your Grace, was not executed; and I, having done all I could to bring the murtherer of my unfortunate brothers to condign punishment, was satisfied to pursue him no further, tho' the atrocity of the crime committed against the law of nations would have affoarded me ground to have prosecuted him in any country where he could have been found. But to my surprize and sorrow, I have of late been informed that Lieutenant Sinclair has added to the repeated murthers the impudence of returning, an officer in a Prussian regiment, to the army, where he was condemn'd, as it were to affront justice, and glory in what he has done. I am wel persuaded, that if his guilt had been known to the King of Prussia or his Generals, his Majesty would not have suffered so odious ane offender to be entertained in his service. Nor can the Generals or Ministers of Prussia have anything to plead, why a sentence pronounced by a British court-martial against one of hir Majesty's subjects, and confirmed by your excellency her Generall should not now be executed. I am confident your Grace will not sufferr publick justice to be insulted in that affair, and I doe in the most humble and earnest manner begg that your Grace would cause apprehend the murtherer, that justice may be done upon him for his barbarous and bloodie crimes. I had about two years ago four brothers, of whom I may without vanity say, they were very gallant gentlemen; two were murthered by Lieutenant Sinclair; the third died in the roome with one of these, partly of his wounds received before Lille, and pairtly out of griefe for his brothers' misfortunes, so that the offender is not innocent even of his blood; the fourth was killed at the battle of Mons. The blood of these that were barbarously slain, call for vengeance; the law of God and nature requires it. They had, and I in their name have a claime, in a particular manner, to your Grace's justice, they having been all four under your Grace's command; forgive it to my natural affection, if I use arguments with your Grace to do an act of justice when the whole world, and I in particular, have such proofs of the greatness of your minde and virtue, I shall only add my most sincere and humble acknowledgement of your Grace's justice and dispatch in the melancholie affair, of which I shall ever retain the most gratefull sense; and remain under the strictest tyes of dutie, with the most profound respect, my Lord, your Grace's most humble, most obedient, obliged, and faithful servant, " &c.

With this letter, and some memorials of Sir John Schaw's public service, end all known appeals for justice on the murderer. But conscience avenged the crime. Many years afterwards, when living in opulence upon his patrimonial estate at Dysart in Fife, the Master received from an humble individual a bitter, though involuntary reproach. When preparing to cross the Frith, he stopped at an inn in order to engage a running footman to attend him. Detested by his neighbours, and ever in dread of the Schaws, Sinclair preserved a sort of incognito. A youth was presented for his approval. The Master inquired of the young candidate what proof he could give of his activity, on which this remarkable reply was given: "Sir, I ran beside the Master of Sinclair's horse when he rode post from the English camp to escape the death for which he was condemned for the murder of the two brothers. " "The Master, " adds Sir Walter Scott, "much shocked, was nearly taken ill on the spot. "[228]

During the insurrection of 1715, the Master of Sinclair took at first an active part, and became the commander of a company of Jacobite gentlemen of Fife. He joined the Earl of Mar at Perth, [229] and was employed in an expedition which gained some credit to the Jacobites. Some arms having been brought out of Edinburgh for the use of the Earl of Sutherland, and being put on board a ship at Leith, the Earl of Mar resolved to intercept these supplies. The wind being contrary, the master of the vessel thus loaded had dropped into Brunt Island, and had gone into the town on that island to see his family. A party of four hundred horse and as many foot was meantime detached on the second of October, 1715, and arrived at the island about midnight. They pressed all the boats in the harbour, and boarded the vessel, carrying off three hundred and six complete stand of arms, together with a considerable number which they found in the town. This expedition was skilfully contrived and managed, the horse surrounding the town whilst the foot ransacked it; and the invasion was made so silently that the Duke of Argyle gained no tidings of it. [230]

After this exploit the Master of Sinclair returned to the camp at Perth, there to promote, if not actually to originate, divisions which were fatal to the cause which he had espoused. Lord Mar, in his letters, charges him, indeed, distinctly with being the very source of the dissensions which soon sprang up among the Jacobite chiefs. [231] The temper of Sinclair could ill brook submission to the Earl of Mar, whom, as a General, he soon ceased to respect; and for whose difficult situation he had no relenting feelings. "The Master, " writes Sir Walter Scott, "who was a man of strong sense, acute observation, and some military experience, besides being of a haughty and passionate temper, averse to deference and subordination, soon placed himself in opposition to the general, whom he seems to have at once detested and despised. "[232]

The unfortunate result of the siege of Preston, soon brought to light the discontents which the Master had nourished among the followers of Mar. Parties had, indeed, for some time agitated the camp. When the disasters in England gave them a fresh impulse, and Lord Mar feelingly, and perhaps not too severely, described the influence of Sinclair when he bitterly describes him as "a devil in the camp, known in his true colours when calamity had befallen those with whom he was in conjunction. " It was henceforth in vain that Mar, to use his own expression, "endeavoured to keep people from breaking among themselves until the long-expected arrival of the Chevalier should, it was hoped, check the growing jealousies in the camp; " a party arose, headed by Lord Huntley, Lord Seaforth, and the Master of Sinclair, who soon obtained the name of the Grumbler's Club, and who rendered themselves odious to the sincere and zealous Jacobites.

Lord Huntley appears from Lord Mar's representations, "to have been completely under the influence of the Master. " "Lord Huntley, " writes Lord Mar, "is still very much out of humour, and nothing can make him yet believe that the King is coming. He intends to go north, under the pretext of reducing Lord Sutherland, and his leaving us at this time, I think, might have very bad effects, which makes me do all I can to keep him. The Master of Sinclair is a very bad instrument about him, and has been most to blame for all the differences amongst us. I am plagued out of my life with them, but must do the best I can. "[233]

Lord Huntley, however, continued to manifest the greatest disgust and suspicion of Lord Mar, often refusing to see him, and, though still lingering at Perth, threatening continually to leave the camp and go northward.

Lord Sinclair, meantime, having heard of these factions, and being sincerely affected to the cause of the Stuarts, wrote to his son "a sharp letter about his behaviour, " and a visit of explanation from the Master instantly followed. During his absence there was a revulsion of feeling among the Grumblers, and some contrition was expressed by them for the part that they had acted; but the fiend returned, and the malcontents quietly relapsed. [234]

The news of James's certain arrival silenced, for a time, all complaints; but again they revived. Lord Mar seems to have had some misgiving of this, when he wrote, "Those that made a pretext of the King's not being landed, are now left inexcusable, and if those kind of folks now sit still and look any more on, they ought to be worse treated than our worse enemies. " Yet it appears by a subsequent letter, that the grievances of which the General complained so bitterly, were not cured even by the presence of the Chevalier; that those who had made a pretext of his absence to complain and despond, desponded still, and that, in fact, the malady was so deep-seated as to be incurable.

It may be urged, in vindication of the Master, who obviously aggravated the spirit of the Grumblers, that the event proved that his apprehensions were well founded. It was, indeed, natural for an experienced officer who had served under Marlborough, to view with dissatisfaction and suspicion the feeble and tardy movements of Lord Mar. Yet a hearty well-wisher to any cause would have abstained from infusing distrust into those counsels which, whether wise or foolish, were destined to guide the adherents of the party. A man of honour will enter, heart and soul, into what he undertakes, or not enter at all. The conduct of Sinclair was that of a mean, morose spirit; and it is but fair to conclude that his motives for adopting the name of Jacobite were either those of personal advancement, or arose out of an enforced compliance with the wishes of his father.

Whilst Sinclair was thus undermining the welfare of the party to which he nominally belonged, his determined enemy, Sir John Schaw, after assisting the Duke of Argyle in defending Inverness against the insurgent troops, was marching with Lord Isla to rejoin the Duke of Argyle in his march towards Perth. It so happened that Lord Isla and his friends reached Sherriff Muir at the very moment when the Government troops and the Jacobites were about to join in battle. "Sir John, " says Sir Walter Scott, "though he had no command, engaged as a volunteer; and we may suppose his zeal for King George was heightened by the recollection that the slayer of his brothers fought under the opposite banners. " He behaved himself with distinguished courage, receiving a wound on his arm, and another in his side. [235] He was, at this time, the only surviving brother out of four, his brother Thomas having been slain at the siege of Mons a year after the death of the others. A month before Sir John Schaw had joined the Duke, Lady Schaw, the daughter of Sir Hugh Dalrymple, and a woman of singular energy and spirit, assembled the Greenock companies in arms, and telling them that the Protestant religion, with their laws, liberties, and lives, and all that was dear to them as men and Christians, were in hazard by that unnatural rebellion, exhorted them to conduct themselves suitably to the occasion.

The conduct of Sinclair at the battle of Sherriff Muir was not inconsistent with his former life. He remained, in that engagement, stationary, with the Marquis of Huntley, at the head of the cavalry of Fife and Aberdeen; hence the lines in the old song on Sherriff Muir.

"Huntly and Sinclair
They baith play'd the Tinkler,
With consciences black as a craw, man."

Upon the return of the Jacobite army to Perth, where they waited, as Scott remarks in a tone of mournful reprobation of Mar, "until their own forces should disperse, those of their enemy advance, and the wintry storm so far subside as to permit the Duke of Argyle to advance against them, " Sinclair was the chief promoter of a scheme formed by the Grumblers for a timely submission to Government. Instigated by their wishes, an attempt was made by Lord Mar to procure, through the Duke of Argyle's mediation, some terms with Government; but it failed, and those who had embarked in the cause were obliged to provide, as they best might, individually for their safety. The whole tenour of Sinclair's conduct was such as to draw down upon him the severest invectives of his party. In one of the poems of the day he is thus described:

"The master with the bully's face,
And with the coward heart,
Who never fail'd, to his disgrace,
To act a coward's part,
Did join Dunbogue, the greatest rogue,
In all the shire of Fife,
Who was the first the cause to leave,
By counsel from his wife."

The Master quitted the insurgent party at Perth, and joined the Marquis of Huntley at Strathbogie; thence he proceeded as a fugitive through Caithness and Orkney, with a few friends, who, like himself, were hopeless of pardon. After wandering in these remote districts for some time, the Master and his friends seized upon a small vessel and fled to the Continent. The Marquis of Huntley, more fortunate than his political ally, obtained his full pardon in consideration of his having left the rebels in time. [236]

The Master of Sinclair married, afterwards, the widowed Countess of Southesk, whom he probably met when on the Continent, since it appears that the Countess, for some time subsequent to the death of her husband, lived at Brussels. In referring to this union, it may not be improper to give some account of the family into connection with which it brought the Master of Sinclair.

James Carnegie, Earl of Southesk, the first husband of the lady whom the Master of Sinclair married, was descended from David Carnegie, an eminent lawyer, who in 1616 was raised to the dignity of Lord Carnegie of Kinnaird, and in 1623 was created, by Charles the First, Earl of Southesk. Like most of those families who had been elevated by the Stuarts to the peerage, the house of Carnegie retained a strong sense of their duty of allegiance to the Crown; and the first Earl of Southesk suffered for his principles by imprisonment and the extortion of a fine of three thousand pounds from his estates in the time of Cromwell.

James, the fifth Earl of Southesk, although nearly allied by his mother's side to the Maitlands, Earls of Lauderdale, had retained as great an affection for the Stuarts as his ancestors had manifested. Of the personal qualities of this nobleman little is generally known, except that he has been designated, "Brave, generous Southesk! "—of his fate, and of the subsequent fortunes of his family, still less is to be ascertained. Some few particulars which are to be derived from the State Papers are discreditable to the memory of this nobleman. Like several other Jacobite noblemen who have been mentioned elsewhere, Lord Southesk did not hesitate to summon his tenants to follow him to the field in the most peremptory terms. His commands fell heavily, in one instance, upon a poor man who lived on the Earl's estate, and bore also the name of James Carnegie. This unlucky man was a natural son of Charles, the late Earl of Southesk, and was therefore a brother of the present Earl James. Like all dependants in those days, he seems to have entertained a deep sense of his obligation to serve and to obey the head of the family; and his obedience was probably ensured by the tie of blood, however unacknowledged as constituting a claim between him and the Earl of Southesk. James Carnegie exercised the profession of a surgeon in the neighbourhood of Kinnaird, then the territory of Lord Southesk, and was employed by the Earl, who appears to have entertained considerable opinion of his skill. When the Insurrection of 1715 broke out, it would have been consistent with the character of a "brave and generous man" to have left this humble practitioner free to follow his own wishes, and not to have embroiled him in the dangers of that disastrous undertaking. A further claim upon the Earl's forbearance was the personal defect of the poor surgeon, who was lame, and short in stature. He was nevertheless ordered to meet

Lord Southesk, at a certain place of rendezvous, on a certain day. A compliance was expected as a matter of course, for James Carnegie was a yearly pensioner of his noble and powerful brother, and refusal was ruin. [237] Nevertheless, the surgeon ventured on this occasion to judge for himself. He had, it appears, from his subsequent declaration, been ever well affected to the reigning Government and attached to the Revolution interest and, by his disapprobation of the Insurrection of 1715, had given umbrage to his nearest relations. Upon the command of Lord Southesk being issued to follow him to the camp at Perth, Carnegie would have fled and hidden himself but for the illness of his wife; he afterwards took refuge in the house of Lord Northesk, but his seclusion was of no avail. The following letter from Lord Southesk, the original of which is in the State Paper Office, affords a curious insight into the despotism exercised by the little kings of the Highlands over their subjects: —

"James, —

"After what I both wrote and spoke to you, I did not think you would have made any furder difficultys of going to Perth with me. I know very well your wife's circumstances are to be pityd; however, since you have a pension from me, and served me since you have had any business, there is nobody of your employment in this country that I can put any confidence in, whatever may happen to me. Therefore I desire you may make no furder excuses; and if you can't be ready to wait upon me from Kinnaird upon Monday, I desire you may follow me upon Teusday; if you do not, you will for ever disoblige

"SOUTHESQUE. "

"Kinnaird, Sept. 17, 1715. "

"I desire you may come and speak with me this night, or to-morrow, at furdest. "

"The Case of James Carnegie, " also in the State Paper Office, furnishes a supplement to this peremptory summons.

"The Case of James Carnegie showeth, that though he lived in a country and amongst men the most notoriously disaffected of any in Scotland, he had, ever since his appearance in the world, espoused the Revolution interest, and given proofs of his affection to it, as would appear more fully in a declaration from the Presbytery of Brichen, in whose bounds he resided, and from another from Mr. John Anderson, his parish minister. That upon the first suspision of the treasonable designs of the rebells, Mr. James Carnegy would have set off and gone south, had not his wife's dangerous state (thought to be dying) obliged him to remain. That after the rebellion broke out, he firmly withstood all solicitations to join it, his neighbours and friends there threatening to burn house and land. He being disappointed of going south, attempted to retire to Ethie, Lord Northesk's house in Forfarshire. He could not remain concealed, the rebells being possessed of all the passes in the country. Finding himself blocked up amongst his enemies, to avoid the execution of the threatenings against him, he was induced, to his shame and regret, to go to Perth, but permitted none of his dependants or tennents to accompany him, and went with no arms but what gentlemen were in the habit of wearing. In order to give no support to those traiterous designs, he feigned illness at Coupar of Angus, but they forced him to go. "

The issue of this affair was mournful. At the battle of Sherriff Muir where the Earl of Southesk appeared with three hundred men, the unfortunate nobleman was supposed to be slain. His faithful, though reluctant attendant, James Carnegie, was taken prisoner as he was looking over the field of battle in order to find the body of his lord. He was carried into prison at Carlisle, whence considerable exertions were made for his release, not only by his own representations, but by the mediation of Sir James Stewart, the governor of the castle. What was the result, whether the blameless victim of the will of others was released, or whether he sank among the many who could not sustain the hardships of their fate, does not appear. [238]

The Earl of Southesk, although it was reported he had been killed, rallied his men, and retreated with the Marquis of Tullibardine, the Earl Marischal and several heads of clans to the mountains, to shelter themselves from the pursuit of the Government troops. Some of these chieftains afterwards made their escape to Skye, Lewis, and other of the north-western islands, till ships came to their relief and carried them abroad. [239] What was the fate of the Earl of Southesk afterwards is not known: neither what became of his descendant. [240] He had married the Lady Margaret Stewart, daughter of the Earl of Galloway, and by her, according to some accounts, he had two sons; according to a contemporary Scottish peerage, he had one child only. His widow also went on the Continent, and the mention of her name by her brother, the Earl of Galloway, in a letter written at Clery in France, [241] without that of her husband, in May 1730, appears to indicate that she was then a widow, and not married again. [242]

How long Lady Southesk lived, the wife of the Master of Sinclair, is dubious. He survived her, and married afterwards, Emilia the daughter of Lord George Murray, brother of the Duke of Atholl. This intimate connection with one of the principal leaders of the Rebellion of 1745, did not, however, induce the Master to enter a second time into a course towards which he had, perhaps in truth, no sincere good will.

Upon his flight to the Continent, the Master of Sinclair was outlawed, and attainted in blood for his share in the Insurrection of 1715. His father being still alive, and not having taken an active part, his estates escaped forfeiture, and Lord Sinclair endeavoured so to dispose of them as to prevent their becoming the property of the Crown. It was necessary, on this account, that Lord Sinclair should disinherit his eldest son; and "as it would, " says Sir Walter Scott, "have been highly impolitic to have alleged his forfeiture for treason as a cause of the deed, the slaughter of the Schaws was given as a reason for his exheredation. " The following is a clause of the deed by which the end was to be accomplished:

"This new diposition of the family estate is explained and qualified by the second deed, being a back bond running in the names of the said James and William Sinclairs, which set forth that their father had been induced to grant a disposition of his estate in their favour, and to pass over their elder brother, to prevent all inconvenience and hazard whatsoever which the rents of the said Lord Sinclair, his heritable estate, or his moveables, might be liable to, if they were settled in the said Master's person, '*on accompt of the said Master of Sinclair his present circumstances, by means of an unfortunate quarrel that some years ago fell out between the said Master and two sons of the deceased Sir John Schaw of Greenock*; therefore, " the deed proceeds to state, "it was reasonable that they, James and William Sinclair, should grant a back bond of settlement, binding themselves to manage the property, when they should respectively succeed to it by advice of friends, overseers, and managers, —viz. Sir John Erskine of Alva, Bart., Sir William Baird of New Baith, Bart., Mr. John Paterson, eldest lawful son to the deceased Archbishop of Glasgow, their brother-in-law—Sir John Cockburn of that Ilk, Bart., and Mr. Mathew Sinclair of Hermiston, their uncles. The said James and William Sinclair, as they should respectively succeed to the estate, were obliged to make certain necessary expenditure to the family for behoof of the Master; and the said James and William Sinclair became also bound, in case the Master, their brother, should become free of his present inconveniences, or should have a family of lawful children, then, and in that case to convey the estate to the said Master, or to his said children, at the sight of his trustees. "[243]

In the year 1726, the Master of Sinclair received pardon, as far as his life was concerned, but the forfeiture of his estates was not taken off, nor certain other incapacities reversed. He then returned to the family estate of Dysart in Fife, of which he was, by his father's disposition of affairs, the actual proprietor; and although the rents of the property were levied in his brother's name, they were applied and received by the Master. General James Sinclair, the second brother of the Master, was then the nominal owner only of the estates. But although thus returning to his patrimonial inheritance, the Master never recovered the good will of his former friends, nor the blessings of security, and of a calm and honoured old age. He seldom visited Edinburgh, living in seclusion and never going from home without being well guarded and attended for fear of the Jacobites, or of his enemies the Schaws. Under these circumstances it seems to have been a relief to his bitter and mortified spirit to have vented itself, in like manner with Lord Lovat, in composing memoirs of his own life. "These memoirs, " says Sir Walter Scott, who long had a copy of them in his possession, "are written[244] with talent, and peculiar satirical energy: so much so indeed, that they have been hitherto deemed unfit for publication. The circumstances attending the slaughter of the Schaws argue a fierce and vindictive temper, and the frame of mind which Sinclair displays as an author exhibits the same character. They are, however, very curious, and it is to be hoped will one day be made public, as a valuable addition to the catalogue of royal and noble authors. It is singular that the author seems to have written himself into a tolerably good style, for the language of the Memoirs, which at first is scarcely grammatical, becomes as he advances disengaged, correct, and spirited. "[245]

On the whole, it must be acknowledged that qualities more repulsive and a career more culpable, have darkened no narrative connected with the Jacobites so unpleasantly as the biography of the Master of Sinclair. A disgrace to every party, he appears to have joined the adherents of the Stuarts, only in order to disturb their councils, and to vilify their memory with personal invective. He has extorted no compassion for the errors and crimes of his earlier years by the courage and magnanimity of a later period: his character stands forth, unredeemed by a single trait of heroism, in all the darkness of violence and revenge.

The Barony of Sinclair, lost to the family in consequence of the attainder of the Master of Sinclair, was not assumed either by him, after his pardon in 1726, nor by his brother General James Sinclair. At the death of General Sinclair in 1762, the title reverted to Charles Sinclair, Esq., of Herdmanstown, a cousin, and after him to his son Andrew, who also allowed his claim to the Barony to lie dormant. It was, however, revived at his death in 1776, by his only son Charles, who is the present Lord Sinclair. [246]

FOOTNOTES:

[226] See Proceedings of the Court Martial held upon John, Master of Sinclair, with Correspondence, p. 27. 1828. Printed by Ballantyne and Company. Presented to the Roxburgh Club by Sir Walter Scott.

[227] It is printed in the interesting little collection before referred to, p. 35.

[228] Life of the Master of Sinclair, p. ix.

[229] His name is not among those who were assembled on the hunting-field of Braemar.

[230] Reay, p. 234.

[231] See Lord Mar's Life and Letters.

[232] Life of the Master of Sinclair, page v.

[233] See Lord Mar's Life, from the Mar Papers.

[234] Mar Papers.

[235] Reay's History of the Rebellion, p. 218.

[236] Reay, p. 387.

[237] See the certificate of the Justices of Forfar, in the State Paper Office, respecting the case of James Carnegie. Dated, Montrose, the first of October, 1716.

[238] See Papers in the State Paper Office for 1715 and 1716.

[239] Reay, p. 372.

[240] The title has remained in abeyance ever since. A mystery hangs over the fate of this family.

[241] See Letter.

[242] The letter from Lord Garlies, in which Lady Southesk is mentioned, is to be seen in the Murray MS. in the Advocate's Library at Edinburgh. It is addressed to the eccentric and imprudent Sir Alexander Murray of Stanhope. These papers were found on a floor of a room in Herriot's Hospital, and were rescued from destruction by Dr. Irvine of the Advocate's Library. After some remarks of no moment, Lord Garlies, afterwards the Earl of Galloway, observes—

"But now I hope that yours and all honest men's misfortunes are to have a turn, and since my cheif has had the good fortune to gett a young prince, I pray God his and all honest men's misfortunes may be at an end; and I hope before my young cheif dies, he shall have the name of Charles the Third. I beg of you to let me hear from you, and when I may expect to have the happinesse of seeing you in this countrey, which is what I both long mightily for, and expect as soon as you can conveniently. Besides, it will be a mighty obligation added to the many you have already done me, who am, dear Sandy,

"yours entirely whylst

"GARLIES. "

"May 12, 1730. "

"Sister Southesque and my spouse make their compliments to you. "

[243] Life of Master of Sinclair, page viii.

[244] The manuscript from which the life of the Master of Sinclair was taken, was found by Sir Walter Scott among the papers of his

mother, who was distantly related to the family of Greenock. The proceedings of the court-martial were attested by the subscription of John Cunningham, probably a clerk of the court.

[245] The MS. Memoirs of the Master of Sinclair are at present in the possession of the Countess of Rosslyn.

[246] Burke's Peerage.

CAMERON OF LOCHIEL. [247]

The clan Cameron, from whom were descended the chieftains who took an active part in the Jacobite cause, had its seat in Lochaber, of which one of their ancestors had originally received a grant from Robert Bruce. They sprang, according to some accounts, from the same source as that of the clan Chattan: they became, nevertheless, in the course of the fourteenth century, an independent state. In a manuscript history of the clan Cameron, they have been traced so far back as to the year 404; and their origin in Scotland ascribed to the arrival of a younger son of the royal family of Denmark, their progenitors acquiring the name of Cameron from his crooked nose.

The clan consisted of three septs; but the family of Lochiel were acknowledged as the chief, and, according to the singular system of clanship, the Camerons freely gave up their wills to that of their head. The history of this family, whilst it shows by what decision of character and intrepidity of conduct this superiority was maintained, presents little else than a tissue of successive feuds between the clan and its neighbours, until, during the seventeenth century, the events of history brought forth qualities of still greater importance to distinguish the house of Lochiel. From henceforth the disputes with the clan Chattan, and the long-standing feuds with the Mackintoshes, merged into obscurity compared with the more stirring interests into which the chieftains were now, fatally for their prosperity, intermingled.

The celebrated Sir Ewan Dhu of Lochiel, one of the finest specimens of the Highland chieftains on record, had passed a long life in the service of the Stuart family, for whom, even as a boy, he had manifested a sort of intuitive affection. This cherished sentiment had repelled the efforts of his kinsman, the Marquis of Argyle, to mould his youthful mind to the precepts of the Puritans and Covenanters. Sir Ewan Dhu combined a commanding personal appearance with a suitable majesty of deportment, and with a shrewd, dauntless, honourable, generous mind. His very sirname had an influence upon the good will of his superstitious and devoted followers. It denoted that he was dark, both in hair and complexion; and so many brave achievements had been performed by chieftains of the clan Cameron, who were of this complexion, that it had been foretold by gifted seers, that never should a fair Lochiel prove fortunate. Endowed with this singular hold upon the confidence of his people, Ewan Dhu eclipsed all his predecessors in the virtues of his heart and the strength of his understanding. His vigilance, his energy, and firmness were the qualities which had distinguished him as a military leader when, in the close of his days, the hopes and designs of the modern Jacobites began to engage the attention of the Highland chiefs.

The career of Ewan Dhu Cameron had been one of singular prosperity. At the age of eighteen, he had broken loose from the trammels of Argyle's control, and joined the standard of the Marquis of Montrose. He had contrived to keep his estate clear, even after the event of that unsuccessful cause, from Cromwell's troops. He next repaired to the royal standard raised in the Highlands by the Earl of Glencairne, and won the applause of Charles the Second, then in exile at Chantilly, for his courage and success. The middle period of his life was consumed in efforts, not only to abet the cause of Charles the Second, but to restore peace to his impoverished and harassed country. Yet he long resisted persuasions to submit and swear allegiance to Cromwell, and at length boldly avowed, that rather than take the oath for an usurper, he would live as an outlaw. His generous and humane conduct to the English prisoners whom he had captured during the various skirmishes had, however, procured him friends in the English army. "No oath, " wrote General Monk, "shall be required of Lochiel to Cromwell, but his word to live in peace. " His word was given, and, until after the restoration, Lochiel and his followers, bearing their arms as before, remained in repose.

At Killicrankie, however, the warrior appeared again on the field, fighting, under the unfortunate Viscount Dundee, for James the Second. As the battle began, the enemy in General Mackay's regiment raised a shout. "Gentlemen, " cried the shrewd Lochiel, addressing the Highlanders, "the day is our own. I am the oldest commander in the army, and I have always observed that so dull and heavy a noise as that which you have heard is an evil omen. " The words ran throughout the Highlanders; elated by the prediction, they rushed on the foe, fighting like furies, and in half an hour the battle was ended.

Although Sir Ewan Dhu was thus engaged on the side of James, his second son was a captain in the Scottish fusileers, and served under Mackay in the ranks of Government. As General Mackay observed the Highland army drawn up on the face of a hill, west of the Pass, he turned to young Cameron and said, "There is your father and his wild savages; how would you like to be with him? " "It signifies little, " replied the Cameron, "what I would like; but I would have you be prepared, or perhaps my father and his wild savages may be nearer to you before night than you may dream of. " Upon the death of Dundee, Sir Ewan Dhu, disgusted by the deficiencies of the commander who succeeded him, retired to Lochaber, and left the command of his clansmen to his eldest son, John Cameron, who, with his son Donald, form the subjects of this memoir.

Sir Ewan Dhu lived until the year 1719, enjoying the security which his exploits had procured for him; and maintaining, by his own dignified deportment, the credit of a family long upheld by a previous succession of able and honourable chieftains. The state and liberality of the Camerons were not supported, nevertheless, by a lavish expenditure; their means were limited: "Yet, " says Mrs. Grant of Laggan in her MS. account of the clan, "perhaps even our own frugal country did not afford an instance of a family, who lived in so respectable a manner, and showed such liberal and dignified hospitality upon so small an income, " as that of Lochiel.

The part which Sir Ewan Dhu had taken in the action at Killicrankie would, it was naturally supposed, draw down upon him the vengeance of those who visited with massacre the neighbouring valley of Glencoe. The forbearance of Government can only be accounted for by the supposition that King William, with his usual penetration, decreed it safer to conciliate, than to attempt to crush a clan which was connected by marriage with the most powerful of the Highland chieftains.

No arts could, however, win the allegiance of the Camerons from those whom they considered as their rightful sovereigns. Towards the end of William's reign, the young chieftain John was sent privately to France, where his early notions of loyalty were confirmed, and his attachment to the court of James enhanced, by the influence of the Duke of Berwick, who formed with him a sincere and durable friendship.

The character of the chieftain was softened in the young Lochiel. He was intelligent, frank, and conciliating in his manners, and had associated more generally with the world than was usually the case with the chieftains of those days. Among the circles with whom the young Lochiel mingled, Barclay Urie, the well known apologist of the Quakers, was also accustomed to appear. An attachment was thenceforth formed between John Cameron and the daughter of Barclay, and a matrimonial alliance was soon afterwards decided upon between the daughter of that gentleman and the young chieftain.

The choice was considered a singular one on the part of the young man. It was the customary plan to intermarry with some of the neighbouring clans; nor was it permitted for the chieftain to make a choice without having first ascertained how far the clan were agreeable to his wishes. This usage proceeded, in part, from the notion of consanguinity between every member of a clan, even of the lowest degree, to his chieftain, and the affability and courtesy with which the head was in the habit of treating those over whom he ruled. The clans were even known to carry their interference with the affairs of their chief so far as to disapprove of the choice of their abodes, or to select a site for a new residence. [248]

The sway which Sir Ewan Dhu had acquired over his followers was such that he dispensed with the ordinary practice, and, without the consent of the clans, agreed to receive the young Quakeress as his daughter. The marriage was completed, and eventually received the full approbation of the whole clan Cameron.

Meantime, great efforts had been made on the part of the English Government to detach Sir Ewan Dhu from his faith to James the Second. But the monarch who could attempt so hopeless a task as the endeavour to cause a Highlander to break his oath of fidelity, very faintly comprehended the national character, then existing in all its strength and all its weakness, —in its horror of petty crimes and its co-operation of great outrages, —in its small meannesses and lofty generous traits, —in its abhorrence of a broken vow or of treachery to a leader. The temptation offered was indeed considerable. Sir Ewan Dhu was to have a pension of three hundred a-year, to be perpetuated to his son, whom the Government were particularly anxious to entice back to Scotland. The old chieftain was also to be appointed Governor of Fort William. [249] But the emissaries of William the Third could not have chosen a worse period than that in which to treat with the brave and wary Cameron. The massacre of Glencoe was fresh in the remembrance of the people, and the stratagem, the fiendish snares which had been prepared to betray the unsuspecting Macdonalds to their destruction, were also recalled with the deep curses of a wronged and slaughtered people. The game of cards, the night before the massacre, between the villain

Campbell, and the two sons of Glencoe, —the proffered and accepted hospitality of the chieftain, whose hand was grasped in seeming friendliness by the man who had resolved to exterminate him and his family, were cherished recollections—cherished by the determined spirit of hate and revenge which contemplated future retribution.

Sir Ewan Dhu therefore rejected these dazzling offers; he neither recalled his son from France, nor accepted the command offered to him, but busied himself in schemes which eventually swayed the destinies of the Camerons.

Not many miles from Achnacarry, the seat of Lochiel, rose, on the border of Loch Oich, the castle of Alaster Dhu, or Dusk Alexander, of Glengarry. The territories of this chieftain were contiguous to those of Lochiel; and his character, which was of acknowledged valour, wisdom, and magnanimity, formed a still stronger bond of union than their relative position. Glengarry was the head of a very powerful clan, called Macdonnells, in contradistinction to the Macdonalds of the Isles, whose claim to superiority they always resisted; declaring, by the voice of their bards and family historians, that the house of Antrim, from whom the Macdonalds of the Isles were descended, owed its origin to the Macdonnells of Glengarry.

The clan Glengarry was now at its height of power under the heroic Alaster Dhu, its chieftain, whose immediate predecessor had risen to be a Lord of Session, at a time when that office brought no little power and influence to its possessors: he had gained both wealth and credit in his high seat; and, upon retiring, had visited Italy, had brought back a taste for architecture to his native country, and the castle of Invergarrie, part of the walls of which remain undemolished, rose as a memento of his architectural taste.

The Lord of Session had cherished sentiments of loyalty for the exiled family; these were transmitted to Alaster Dhu. The gallant Lochiel and the chief of Glengarry were therefore disposed to smother in their feelings of loyalty the feuds which too often raged between clans nearly approximate. They therefore formed a compact to promote, in every way, the interest of the royal exiles; and in this vain attempt at restoration which ensued, the fate of their clansmen was sealed. [250] That of the Camerons is yet to be told; a slight digression respecting their gallant allies may here be excused.

When the feudal system which subsisted between the Highland chieftains and their clansmen was dissolved, it became the plan of many of the landholders to rid themselves of their poor tenantry, and to substitute in their place labourers and farmers from the south of Scotland. The helpless population of the glens and hill-sides were thus sent to wander, poor and ignorant of anything but their own homes, and speaking no language but their mother tongue, and wholly unskilled in any practical wisdom. Some emigrated, but many were pressed into service on board the emigrant ships, although the commanders of those vessels could not, in some instances, prevail upon themselves to tear the Highlanders away from their wives and families.

To remedy this melancholy state of affairs, and to employ the banished mountaineers, it was proposed about the year 1794, to embody some of the sufferers, the Macdonnells of Glengarry in particular, into a Catholic corps, under their young chieftain, Alexander Macdonnell, and employ them in the service of the English Government. This scheme, after many difficulties, was accomplished. At first, it worked well for the relief of the destitute clan; but, in 1802, in spite of their acknowledged good conduct, the Glengarry regiment was disbanded.

The friend of the unfortunate, who had originally proposed the consolidation of the corps, was Dr. Macdonald, who had been afterwards appointed chaplain to the regiment. He now projected another scheme for the maintenance of the clan Glengarry; and, after some opposition, his plan was effected. It was to convey the whole of the Macdonnells, with their wives and families, to a district in Upper Canada, where the clan, at this moment, is permanently established. The place in which they live bears the name of their native glen, and the farms they possess are called by the loved appellations of their former tenements: and, when the American war tried the fidelity of the emigrants, the clan gave a proof of their loyalty by enrolling themselves into a corps, under the old name of the Glengarry Fencibles. [251]

In the battle of Killicrankie, Glengarry had led his forces to fight for James the Second; and after that engagement, in which Glengarry had had a brother killed, he had become very obnoxious to the Government, and had found it necessary to retire for some time, whilst his more favoured friend Lochiel tranquilly occupied his own house of Achnacarrie, a place wholly undefended. The retreat in which Glengarry hid himself was a small wooded island in Lochacaig; and in this seclusion a manoeuvre was planned, highly characteristic of the subtlety, and yet daring of the Highland chieftains who were engaged in it. It shows, also, the state of the national feeling towards the English Government, at a time when comparative quiet appeared to be established in the Highlands.

Attached to certain regiments which were then lying at Fort William, there were a number of young volunteers, men of good family, who had a soldier's pay, if they wished it, and were considered as pupils in the art of war, "at liberty to retire if they chose, and eligible, being often persons of family, to fill the vacancies which war or disease occasioned among the subalterns. "[252] This regiment was now about to occupy the garrisons, and on their way to the Tyendrum or Black Mount, the officers engaged in conversation, little dreading an assault in a country inhabited only by a few herdsmen, and considered by them as wholly subdued. But they were deceived in their sense of safety. Among the heath and bushes in a narrow pass, circumscribed, on the one side, by a steep mountain, and on the other by a small lake, which skirted the path, for road there was not, lay in ambush two hundred well-armed and light-footed Highlanders. The youths, or volunteers, were in the rear of the regiment; as they marched fearlessly through the deep solitude of this wild district, the Highlanders sprang forwards from their ambuscade; and before the young soldiers could recover their surprise or have recourse to their arms, eight or ten young men of family were seized on and hurried away. With these were mingled others, among these volunteers of less importance, who were carried away in the confusion by mistake. A few shots were fired by the soldiery, but without any effect, for the Highlanders had disappeared. This sudden attack excited the utmost consternation among the officers of the regiment, nor could they discover the object of this aggression; nor did they know either how to pursue the assailants, or in what terms to report to Government so ignominious a loss. They marched, therefore, silently to Dumbarton without attempting to pursue an enemy whose aim it might be to lure them into some fastness, there to encounter a foe too powerful, from the nature of the country, to be resisted. On arriving at Dumbarton the mystery was explained. There the commander of the corps found a letter, stating that "certain chiefs of clans had no objection to King William's ruling in England, considering that nation as at liberty to choose its own rulers; but that they never could, consistently with what they had sworn on their arms, take an oath to any other sovereign while the family of St. Germains remained in existence. They were, " the writers continued, "unwilling either to perjure themselves, or to hold their lands in daily fear, and subject to the petty instruments of power. They were willing to live peaceably under the present rule, but were resolved neither to violate the dictates of conscience, nor to have their possessions disturbed. In the meantime, to prevent encroachments upon their lands, and to prevent the necessity of rushing into hostilities with the Government, they had taken hostages to ensure their safety, and with these they would never part until Sir Ewan Dhu and Alaster Dhu had obtained assurances that they should never be disturbed for their principles whilst they lived peaceably on their estates. "

This declaration was accompanied by a powerful remonstrance upon the folly and danger of exasperating clans powerful from their union, and from the inaccessibility of the country which they inhabited. The tenderness of conscience, the fidelity to an exiled monarch, were made, the writers urged, a plea for every species of oppression and petty tyranny. The late massacre of Glencoe justified, they said, the measures of precaution they were taking; and, finally they threatened, should their petition be refused to take refuge in France, carrying with them their young hostages, there to proclaim the impolicy and injustice of the English Government. This address was dispatched, not to the Privy Council, but to the relations and friends of the young prisoners, who were interested in procuring a favourable reception for its negotiation; and the chiefs who subscribed to this address reasonably expected that the fear of their power, exaggerated in the sister kingdom, where a total ignorance of the manners and character of the Scottish mountaineers existed, would prevail to lend force to their arguments. This negotiation was never made public; it proved, however, effectual, as far as the comfort of some of the parties engaged in it were concerned.

By the influence of the rising party, who, espousing the interests of the Princess Anne, were gaining ground in the country during the decline of William, Sir Ewan Dhu and Glengarry, who were jointly considered as the promoters of this affair, remained unpunished for a manoeuvre on which public opinion in England was not inclined to pass a very severe judgment, after the recent massacre of Glencoe. [253] Some secret negotiations placed everything on a secure footing; and, during the reign of Queen Anne; the two chieftains lived in tranquillity, their mutual regard continuing undiminished during their lives, and becoming the subject, after their deaths, of the lays composed in their honour by their native bards.

During his latter days, Sir Ewan Dhu had the consolation of seeing his son happy in the choice of a wife. Beautiful and good, the young Quakeress soon established herself in the good opinions of all those who were acquainted with her; and there seems every reason to conclude that she inherited the virtues, without the peculiarities of her father, Robert Barclay of Urey. That eminent man was descended from a Norman family which traced its ancestry to Thomas de Berkley, whose descendants established themselves in Scotland. By his mother's side, Barclay was allied to the house of Huntley; and by his connection with the heiress of the mother's family, a considerable estate in Aberdeenshire was added to the honours of antiquity. Unhappily for the lovers of the old Norman appellations, the name of de Berkley was changed, in the fifteenth century, into that of Barclay. One of Robert Barclay's sons, who became a mercer in Cheapside, had the rare fortune of entertaining three successive monarchs when they visited the City on the Lord Mayor's Day, — George the First, George the Second, and George the Third; whose heart, as it is well known, was touched by the beauty of one of the fair descendants of Robert Barclay.

Previously to the marriage between Lochiel and the young Quakeress, the family into which he entered had been impoverished, and the estate of Mathers, from which the Barclays derived their name, sold to defray debt.

The career of Robert Barclay was singular. He was first converted to Popery during his residence in Paris, when he was fifteen; and he changed that faith for the simple persuasion of the Quakers when he had attained his nineteenth year. He adopted the tenets of the Friends at a period when it required much courage to adhere to a sect who were vilified and ridiculed, not only in England but in Scotland. It was to refute these attacks against the Quakers that Barclay wrote the book entitled, "Truth cleared of Calumnies. " His ability and sincerity have never been doubted; but some distrust of his reason may be forgiven, when we find the Quaker, a grave and happily married man, walking through the streets of Aberdeen, clothed in sackcloth and ashes, under the notion that he was commanded by the Lord to call the people unto repentance; he appealed to witnesses to prove the "agony of his spirit, " and how he "had besought the Lord with tears, that this cup might pass away from him. "

This singular act of humiliation was contrasted by frequent visits to the Court of Charles the Second, and to Elizabeth of Bohemia. To the house of Stuart, Barclay was ever fondly attached. His father had suffered in the civil wars; and the doctrines of non-resistance and passive obedience, avowed by the Quakers, were favourable to the Stuart dynasty. The last visit which Barclay paid to London was rendered memorable by the abdication of James the Second. As he was standing beside that monarch, near a window, the King looked out, and remarked that "the wind was fair for the Prince of Orange to come over. " "It is hard, " replied Barclay, "that no expedient can be found to satisfy the people. " James answered, that "he would do anything becoming a gentleman, except parting with liberty of conscience, which he would never do while he lived. " Barclay only survived that eventful period two years. His children, singular as it may seem, were all living fifty years after their father's death.

To the daughter of this inflexible and courageous man was Cameron of Lochiel united. During the first years of their marriage, even before the death of Sir Ewan Dhu, they lived peacefully in the home of their ancestors; and whilst Anne reigned, that happy tranquillity was undisturbed. The name of Anne was long cherished in the Highlands on account of the rare intervals of peace and plenty which her rule, and as it was thought, her pious prayers, afforded to a ravaged and oppressed country. Seven years' famine, during the reign of William, were charged upon the monarch's head: plenteous crops and peaceful abundance were ascribed to the merits of Queen Anne. [254] Meantime, the gentle and happy Lady of Lochiel won all hearts: she was distinguished, as tradition reports, for prudence, activity and affability. "One great defect, " adds Mrs. Grant, "she had, however, which was more felt as such in the Highlands than it would have been in any other place. She did not, as a certain resolute countrywoman of hers was advised to do, 'bring forth men-children only; ' on the contrary, daughters in succession, a thing scarce pardonable in one who was looked up to and valued in a great measure as being the supposed mother of a future chief. In old times women could only exist while they were defended by the warriour and supported by the hunter. When this dire necessity in some measure ceas'd, the mode of thinking to which it gave rise continued. And after the period of youth and beauty were past, woman was only consider'd as having given birth to man. John

Locheil's mind was above this illiberal prejudice: he loudly welcomed his daughters and caress'd their mother on their appearrance as much as if every one of them had been a young hero in embryo. His friends and neighbours us'd on these occassions to ask in a sneering manner, "What has the lady got? " To which he invariably answered, "A lady indeed: " this answer had a more pointed significance there than with us. For in the Highlands no one is call'd a lady but a person named to the proprietors of an estate. All others, however rich or high-born, are only *gentlewomen*. How the prediction intentionally included in the chief's answer was fulfill'd, will hereafter appear.

"Besides the family title, every Highland chieftain has a patronymic deriv'd from the most eminent of their ancestors, probably the founder of the family, and certainly the first who confer'd distinction on it. Thus Argyle is the son of Colin, Breadalbane the son of Archibald, &c. ; and the chief of the Camerons was always stil'd son of Donald Dhu, Black Donald, whatever his name or complexion may be, as well as the appellation deriv'd from it, because it would appear hereditary in the family, and at length it became a tradition or prophesy among the clan that a fair Lochiel should never prosper. "

At length, after the birth of twelve daughters, a son and heir made his appearance. But the satisfaction of the clans was dashed by hearing that the ill-starred little laird was fair, like his sisters. The prophecy that a fair Lochiel should never prosper, was recalled with dismay; and, unhappily, the fears of superstition were too mournfully realized by fact. The young Cameron was named Donald: his birth was followed by the appearance of two other boys, —Archibald, afterwards the ill-fated Dr. Cameron, and John, who was called Fassefern, from an estate. "The proud prediction of their father, " continues Mrs. Grant, "was soon amply fulfilled with regard to the daughters of this extraordinary family. " "Their history, " she adds, "unites the extravagance of romance with the sober reality of truth. "

The twelve daughters of Lochiel were admirably educated, and the fame of their modest virtues soon extended through the Highlands. The great point in matrimonial alliances in those rude regions was to obtain a wife well born, and well allied; and little fortune was ever expected with the daughter of a chief. Ancestry was the great point with a Highlander, for he believed that defects of mind, as well as of person, were hereditary. All, therefore, sought the daughters of Lochiel, as coming of an untainted race. The elder ones were married early, and seemed, as Mrs. Grant expresses it, by the solicitude to obtain them, as ever to increase, like the Sibyl's leaves, in value, as they lessened in number. Of the daughters, one, the youngest and the fairest, was actually married to Cameron of Glendinning, in the twelfth year of her age. She became a widow, and afterwards married Maclean of Kingasleet, so that she was successively the wife of two heads of houses. Another, Jean Cameron, who was the least comely of her family, but possessed of a commanding figure and powerful understanding, was married to Clunie, the Chief of the Clan Macpherson. She is said to have been celebrated in the pathetic poem, entitled "Lochaber no More, " the poet, who laments his departure from Lochaber, and his farewell to his Jean, having been an officer in one of the regiments stationed at Fort William.

By the marriage of his twelve daughters with the heads of houses, the political importance of Lochiel was considerably enhanced, and a confederacy, containing many noted families who were bound together by opinion and kindred, formed a strong opposition to the reigning Government. The sons-in-law of Lochiel were the following chiefs: Cameron of Dungallan, Barclay of Urie, Grant of Glenmoriston, Macpherson of Clunie, Campbell of Barcaldine, Campbell of Auchalader, Campbell of Auchlyne, Maclean of Lochbuy, Macgregor of Bohowdie, Wright of Loss, Maclean of Ardgour, and Cameron of Glendinning. All the daughters became the mothers of families; "and these numerous descendants, still, " observes Mrs. Grant, "cherish the bonds of affinity, now so widely diffused, and still boast their descent from these female worthies."[255]

Among most of the influential chieftains who espoused the daughters of Lochiel, was the celebrated Macpherson of Clunie, who afterwards took a very important part in the Rebellions of 1715 and 1745. The career of Clunie affords a melancholy, but rare, instance of indecision, if not of double dealing, in the Jacobites. Before the battle of Culloden, anxious to retrieve his affairs and to ensure his safety, he took the oaths to the English Government, and was appointed to a company in Lord Loudon's Highlanders. His clan, nevertheless, were eager to join Charles Edward, and urged him to lead them to his standard. Clunie hesitated between the obligation to his oath, and his secret devotion to the Stuarts. His defection irritated the British Government: he became one of those whose life was forfeited to the laws. After the battle of Culloden he secreted himself, and lived for nine years in a cave, at a short distance from the site of his own house, which had been burned by the King's troops. The cave was in front of a woody precipice, the trees, &c., completely concealing the entrance. It was dug out by his own people, who worked at night, or when time had slackened the rigour of the search. Upwards of one hundred persons knew of this retreat, and one thousand pounds were offered as a reward to any who would discover it. Eighty men were stationed there to intimidate the tenantry into a disclosure, but it was all in vain; none could be found so base as to betray their chief. [256]

For two years Sir Hector Monro in vain remained in Badenoch, for the purpose of discovering Clunie's retreat. The Macphersons remained true to their chieftain. At times he emerged from his dark recess, to mingle for awhile in the hours of night with his friends, when he was protected by the vigilance and affection of his clansmen, unwearied in their work of duty. At last, broken-spirited, and despairing of that mercy which was accorded by the English Government to so few of the insurgents, Clunie escaped to France, and there died, ten years after the fatal events of 1745. [257] The estate of this unfortunate chieftain was restored to his family, who claim to be the ancient representatives of the clan Chattan; with what justice it would be dangerous to declare, since no risk could be more rashly encountered than that which is incurred in discussing Highland prerogative.

Surrounded by his powerful relatives and fair daughters, Lochiel hailed with no very sanguine spirit the coming troubles which quickly followed the accession of the house of Hanover. Already was the Jacobite association busily at work in the south of Scotland; and it was impossible, from the temper of the populace in both nations, not to augur, in a short time, some serious popular outbreak. In the minds of the Highland chieftains a hatred of English dominion, and a desire of independence, constituted even a more potent source of adherence of the Stuarts than any personal feeling towards that line. Most of these chiefs languished to see a king of their own nation reign over them. To such a ruler they would, as they considered, be viewed not as a secondary object. Their interests had been neglected in the Treaty of Darien, —a settlement which had inspired the landholders of the Low Country with aversion to William.

Expectations had also been raised, tending to the belief that Anne, secretly well affected to her brother, had made such provisions in her will as would ensure the descent of the Crown in the direct line; and nothing could exceed the disgust and amazement of the Highlanders when they beheld a foreigner seated on a throne, from which, they well knew, it would be impossible to dispossess him. "To restore, " as Mrs. Grant observes, "their ancient race of monarchs to the separate Crown of Scotland, was their fondest wish. This visionary project was never adopted by the Jacobites at large, who were too well informed to suppose it either practicable or eligible. But it serv'd as an engine to excite the zeal of bards and sennachies, who were still numerous in the Highlands, and in whose poetry strong traces of this airy project may still be found. "

Soon after the accession of George the First, certain of the Highland chieftains dispatched a letter to the Earl of Mar, desiring that nobleman to assure the Government of their loyalty and submission. Among the names subscribed are those of Lochiel, of his friend Glengarry, and of Clunie. The address is said to have been a stratagem of Mar's to gain time, and to give him an opportunity of ripening his schemes. [258] But it appears more probable that there was, at first, a spirit of moderation and a desire for peace in the chieftains, until they were afterwards stimulated by the intrigues of the disappointed and baffled Earl of Mar. Lochiel, as well as many others, had little to gain, but much to lose, in any change of dynasty or convulsion in the state. Prosperous, beloved, secure, his fidelity to that which he believed to be the right cause was honourable to the highest degree to his character. That he was not sanguine in his hopes, is more than probable. Before he went to the battle of Sherriff Muir, he arranged his affairs so as to be prepared for the worst result that might befal his family. The frequent occurrence of feuds and civil wars in Scotland had taught the higher classes the use of stratagem and manoeuvre in these domestic disturbances. It was not unusual for a son and a father often to affect to take opposite sides, in order that the estate, happen what might, should be preserved to the family; and this was considered as consulting the general good of the clan. Lochiel, although he did not pursue this plan, yet left his affairs so arranged that, in the most fatal results of the Rebellion of 1715, his estate might be protected. His sons-in-law, powerful and devoted to the same cause, were well qualified to aid and to protect those members of the family who were entrusted to their friendly guidance. John Cameron was still styled "Cameron the younger, of Lochiel, " for the renowned Sir Ewan Dhu was living when Mar summoned the chieftains to the hunting-field of Braemar. The aged chieftain had, at this time, attained his eighty-seventh year; it had been his glory, in early life, to defend a pass near Braemar against Cromwell's troops, until the royal army had retired; and, in fact, to be the instrument of saving Glencairn's troops, keeping himself clear of those cabals which at that time fatally harassed the disorganized Royalists. It was now his fate to send forth, under the guidance of his son, his gallant Camerons, to the number of eight hundred, to espouse the cause of the Stuarts. [259] No jealousies disturbed the confidence reposed on the one side, nor alienated affection on the other. The affection of the Highlanders for their children was one of the softened features in the national character. It was usually repaid with a decree of reverence, of filial piety, which, however other qualities may have declined and died away in the Highland character, have remained, like verdant plants amid autumnal decay. The appalling spectacle of a parent forsaken, or even neglected, by a child, is a sight never known in the Highlands: nor is the sense of duty lessened by absence from the mountains where first the sentiment was felt. The Highland soldier, far from his country, is accompanied by this holy love, this inexhaustible stimulus to exertion, which induces him to save with what may be unjustly called a niggard hand his earnings, to support, in their old age, those who have given him birth. "I have been, " says General Stewart, "a frequent witness of these offerings of filial bounty, and the channel through which they were communicated; and I have generally found that a threat of informing their parents of misconduct, has operated as a sufficient check on young soldiers, who always received the intimation with a sort of horror. "[260]

Blessed, doubtless, with the approval of his father, Sir Ewan Dhu, Lochiel quitted his home. He left a wife whom he loved, a parent whom he reverenced, and whose span of life could not be long extended; he left a numerous and prosperous family, upon a sense of duty, a principle of loyalty, an adherence, so fixed and so sure among the Highlanders, to his engagements. The name of Cameron does not appear among the chieftains who were assembled at Braemar; but it appears probable that he attended the Earl of Mar's summons, since he was cited, by the authority of an act passed on the thirtieth of August, to appear at Edinburgh, as well as a number of other disaffected chieftains and noblemen, to give bail for his allegiance to the Government. The summons was not answered by a single individual, and the preparations for the fatal insurrection continued in unabated activity.

The details of the hopeless struggle contain no especial mention of John Cameron of Lochiel; but, from manuscript sources, we learn that, after the battle of Sherriff Muir, he continued with the Jacobite army, conducted by General Gordon, to whom James Stuart had entrusted the command of that remnant of his gallant and deserted adherents. The Jacobite army having marched to Aberdeen, were there informed by General Gordon of the flight of the Chevalier, of that of Lord Mar, and of the other principal leaders. A letter was then read to them from James, declaring that the disappointments which he had met with, especially from abroad, had obliged him to leave the country. He thanked his subjects for their services, and desired them to advise with General Gordon, and to consult their own safety, either by keeping in a body, or separating, and encouraged them to hear from him again in a very short time. A singular scene ensued. General Gordon and the chief officers of the army, are said to have pretended surprise at this disclosure, although they were previously in the secret; but the indignation of the soldiers was extreme.

"We are basely betrayed, " they cried out; "we are all undone; we have neither King nor General left! "

Shortly after this crisis, the Jacobite army dispersed; two hundred of them, amongst whom were many chieftains, went towards Peterhead, intending to embark, in vessels which they knew were waiting for them, for France; but the main body of the army marched westward, to Strathspey and Strath-dore to the Hills of Badenoch, where they separated. The foot-soldiers dispersed into the mountains, near Lochy, and the horse went to Lochaber, agreeing to reassemble, such was their undaunted fidelity and courage, on receiving notice from the Chevalier. [261] But such a summons never came, to arouse those brave men from the repose of their glens and fortresses.

Lochiel had entrusted the guidance of his clan to his son, afterwards well known by the name of "gentle Lochiel, " and the faithful promoter of Charles Edward's ill-starred enterprise. Persuaded that the safety and honour of his house were safe in the hands of this promising young man, who had been purposely kept in ignorance of the projected rising, and had taken no part in it, Lochiel resolved to consult his own safety, and to follow his royal master to France. After wandering for some time near Braemar, and in Badenoch, he escaped by means of one of the French frigates which were cruising near the coast of Scotland. [262]

In 1719 Sir Ewan Dhu expired, having witnessed the rise and fall of that attempt to restore the Stuarts, which was only succeeded by a more desperate and melancholy undertaking. He lived to see his son an exile, but he had the consolation of reflecting that the honour of his clan, the great desideratum with a chieftain, was yet unstained either by cowardice or disloyalty.

The Camerons do not appear to have had any participation in the abortive attempt in 1718 to revive the Stuart claim. Considered by the English Government as a proscribed rebel, and deemed of too much importance to be forgiven, Lochiel passed henceforth most of his days in the melancholy court of St. Germains, where he soon perceived how little faith there was to be placed in the energy and determination of James Stuart. At times his weary exile was relieved by secret visits to his own home at Achnacarry, where he found his son, dutiful and amiable, holding his possessions as in trust for his father. Lochiel was enabled by the power and alliance of his sons-in-law to remain in safety, as long as he pleased, during these visits; yet he professed to renounce Scotland until a change of Government should facilitate his return as a chieftain to his clansmen. In every district he found kindred ready to protect him, and he derived much importance from the influence he possessed through his children. His sons-in-law were mostly the heads of clans, and they all looked up to Lochiel with affectionate reverence. Had Lochiel been a remorseless partisan of James, instead of a true lover of his country, he might easily have stimulated his kindred, and set into motion the whole of that powerful connection of which he was the centre. But he perceived too plainly the risk of such a proceeding, and wisely declined involving the peaceful and the prosperous in the dangers of another contest. His moderate sentiments were confirmed by the early wisdom of his son, —one of those bright patterns of human excellence, gifted with every charm which attends a noble and gallant chieftain.

During the early part of the Rebellion of 1745, John of Lochiel remained in France; but, when the battles of Falkirk and of Preston Pans raised the hopes of his party, he came over to Scotland, and landed on the coasts of Lochaber, a short time before the fatal blow to the Stuart cause was given at Culloden. After taking a last look at his house, and visiting, with what feelings can well be conceived, the scenes of his childhood, the haunts of his ancestry, —the house of Achnacarry, which was soon, as he well might conjecture, to be the object of vengeance to a foe more ruthless and brutal than ever party spirit had infuriated in this country before, —Lochiel, embarking in the vessel which had brought him to Scotland, elate with hope, returned to France. His exile was cheered by the friendship of the Duke of Berwick, but his heart seems ever to have been in Scotland. A few years afterwards he came over again privately to Edinburgh, and there his eventful life was closed. [263] His estates were included, after the year 1745, in the numerous forfeitures which followed the Rebellion; but they were eventually restored, and they have remained in possession of the family. Intrepid and amiable as John of Lochiel appears to have been, and perilous as was his career, his character bears no comparison in interest with that of one who was one of the brightest ornaments of his party—his gallant unfortunate son.

Donald Cameron of Lochiel, had long exercised the authority of a chieftain, before the Rebellion of 1745 entailed upon him a participation in occupations still more arduous. He had, in short, arrived at middle age when he was called upon to support the claims of Charles Edward.

To the virtues and intentions of this chieftain, even his enemies have borne tribute. He was accomplished, refined, and courteous; yet brave, firm, and daring. The warlike tribes around him, unaccustomed to such a combination of qualities, idolized the gallant and the good Lochiel. His father, reposing on his honour and prudence, relied with security upon his son's management of the family estates, and this confidence was never disturbed by presumption on the one hand, nor by suspicion on the other.

Donald Cameron had imbibed the principles of his father; and there is little doubt but that, during the furtive visits of John Lochiel to Scotland, a tacit understanding had been formed between them to support the "good old cause, " as they termed it, whenever circumstances should permit. But Donald Cameron, although "he loved his King well, loved his country better; " nor could he be persuaded to endanger the peace of that country by a rash enterprise, which could never, as he justly thought, prosper without foreign aid, and the hearty co-operation of the English Jacobites. His own clansmen were, he well knew, prepared for the contest, come when it might; for the conversation of the small gentry and of the retainers consisted, to borrow a description from a contemporary writer, entirely of disquisitions upon "martiall atchievements, deer huntings, and even valuing themselves upon their wicked expeditions and incursions upon their innocent low-country neighbours. They have gott, " adds the same author, [264] "a notion and inviollable maxim handed down to them from their forefathers, that they, being the only ancient Scotsmen, that whole nation belongs to them in property, and look on all the low-country-men as a mixture of Danes, Saxons, Normans, and English, who have by violence robbed them of the best part of their country, while they themselves are penned up in the most mountainous and barren parts thereof to starve; therefore think it no injustice to commit dayly depredations upon them, making thereby conscience to interrupt their illegal possession (as they call it) in case it should prescribe into a right. "[265]

It would not have been difficult to have blown such combustible materials into a flame; but Donald Cameron adopted a different policy, and endeavoured to allay the angry passions of the tribe over which he ruled: nevertheless, his own conduct was perfectly consistent with his principles; and such was the notion entertained of his integrity and moderation, that though he never took the oaths to the reigning family, he was indulged in that tenderness of conscience and permitted to remain in peace, even though residing in the immediate neighbourhood of a great military station. [266]

Donald Cameron had indeed a more valuable stake in the country than houses or lands. He was married in the year 1723 to the daughter of Sir James Campbell of Auchinbreck, a lady of whom it is high praise to say, that she was worthy of being the companion of such a man.

Thus situated, the nominal holder of an estate which, though long maintained in the family, is said never to have exceeded in value five hundred pounds a-year, and less prejudiced against the English and the ruling powers than his predecessors, Donald Cameron felt, it is asserted, little desire to promote a second invasion of the country by the Chevalier. The slightest intimation of his father's wish to revive that cause would have been sufficient to set the whole family confederacy into motion; but the wisdom of the younger Lochiel had been ripened by the cautious and critical part which he had had to perform in life; and that prudent disposition, enforced by his father's circumspection, prevented any precipitate measures.

Of the favour and confidence of the Chevalier, Donald Cameron was well assured. In 1729, the following letter was addressed to him, under the name of Mr. Johnstone, by James. [267]

"I am glad of this occasion to let you know how well plessed I am to hear of the care you take to follow your father's and uncle's example in their loyalty to me; and I doubt not of your endeavours to maintain the true spirit in the clan. Allan is now with me, and I am always glad to have some of my brave Highlanders about me, whom I value as they deserve. You will deliver the enclosed to its address, and doubt not of my particular regard for you, which I am persuaded you will always deserve.

(Signed) "JAMES R. "

"April 11, 1727. "

In addition to these instructions, Donald Cameron received a letter from his uncle, Allan Cameron, (in 1729,) who attended the Chevalier during his residence at Albano; from which it appears that a full commission had been sent to Lochiel to treat with "such of the King's friends in Scotland, " as he thought were safe to be trusted concerning his affairs. It was also intimated that James had conceived a high opinion of the good sense and prudence of Lochiel, from his letters; and encouragement was given to any future exertions. The uncle then instructed his nephew how to answer the King's letter in the following explicit manner. These directions are tolerably minute: [268]

"I think it proper you should write to the King by the first post after you receive his letter. I need not advise you what to say in answer to such a gracious letter from your King, only let it not be very long. Declare your duty and readiness to execute his Majesty's commands on all occasions, and your sense of the honour he has been pleased to do you in giving you such a commission. I am not to chuse words for you, because I am sure you can express yourself in a dutiful and discreet manner without any help. You are to write, Sir, on a large margin, and to end, Your most faithful and obedient subject and servant; and to address to the King and no more; which inclose to me sealed. I pray send me a copy of it on a paper inclosed, with any other thing that you do not think fit or needful the King should see in your letter to me, because I will shew your answer to this, wherein you may say that you will be mindful of all I wrote to you, and what else you think fit. "

To these instructions assurances were added, that the elder Lochiel, who had, it seems, been in necessitous circumstances after his attainder, and during his exile, should be relieved at the Chevalier's expense; "so that, " adds the uncle, "your mind may be pretty easy upon that point. " Donald had, it appears, expressed some discontent at the comparative comfort in which some of the exiled Jacobites lived, and the poverty of his father's circumstances, which he had observed when in Paris a few years previous to this correspondence. Allan Cameron further advised his nephew to keep on good terms with Glengarry and all other neighbours; to let "byganes, be byganes, " as long as such neighbours continue firm to the "King's interests; " to avoid private animosities, and yet to keep a watch over their fidelity to the cause. "As to Lovat, " adds the uncle, "be on your guard, but not so as to lose him; on the contrary, you may say that the King trusts a great deal to the resolution he has taken to serve him, and expects he will continue in that resolution. But, dear nephew, you know very well that he must give true and real proof of his sincerity by performance, before he can be entirely reckoned on, after the part he has acted. This I say to yourself, and therefore you must deal with him very dexterously; and I must leave it to your own judgment what lengths to go with him, since you know he has always been a man whose chief view was his own interest. It is true, he wishes our family well; and I doubt not he would wish the King restored, which is his interest, if he has the grace to have a hand in it, after what he has done. So, upon the whole, I know not what advice to give you, as to letting him know that the King wrote you such a letter as you have; but in general, you are to make the best of him you can, but still be on your guard; for it is not good to put too much in his power before the time of executing a good design. The King knows very well how useful he can be if sincere, which I have represented as fully as was necessary.

"This letter is of such bulk, that I have inclosed the King's letter under cover with another letter addressed for your father, as I will not take leave of you till next post. I add only, that I am entirely yours,

(Signed) "A. CAMERON. "

Eight years afterwards (in 1736), when inquiries were made by the Chevalier concerning the temper of the people, and the state of the clans, it was stated that the most leading men among the clans were Cameron of Lochiel and Sir Alexander Macdonald. The Cameronians were, it was stated, well armed, and regularly regimented among themselves, but "so giddy and inconstant" that they could not be depended on; only that they were strongly enraged against the Government. "The leading men among the loyalists were reported much diminished; nor was it easy, from the necessity of concealing their sentiments, since the last rising, to make any estimate of the amount of those who would enter into any second scheme. "[269] Considering Cameron of Lochiel as thus empowered to give information of the first movements of James, the Jacobites in the Highlands were in continual communication with Cameron; yet, perhaps considering that those who engaged in the last insurrection, being nearly superannuated, would rather wish well to the cause than engage again, he still kept the fervent spirits of that political party whom he thus regarded in an equable state, —ready to act, yet willing to wait for a favourable occasion. In 1740 Donald Cameron signed, nevertheless, the association of seven carried by Drummond of Bochaldy to Rome; but when the Court of France, after the disaster at Dunkirk, withdrew its aid, he was one of those who sent over Murray to dissuade Charles from coming to Scotland, unless accompanied by a body of foreign troops: —so true were his professions of fidelity, and so finely was that fidelity tempered with prudence. Holding these opinions, which were amply verified by the result of the Rebellion of 1745, when Donald Cameron received a letter from Prince Charles, written at Borodale, and desiring to see him immediately, it was in sorrow and perplexity that he received the summons. He sent his brother, the unfortunate Dr. Archibald Cameron, to urge the Prince to return, and to assure him that he should not join in the undertaking. But the Prince persisted in the resolution he had formed of persevering in his attempt, and gave to Dr. Cameron the same reply that he had already given to others, and then, addressing himself to Macdonald of Scothouse, who had gone to the coast to pay his respects to the Prince, he asked him if he could go to Lochiel and endeavour to persuade him to do his duty. Young Scothouse replied, he would comply with the Prince's wishes, and immediately set out for Achnacarry. Such a message from such a quarter could not be resisted, and Lochiel prepared to accompany young Scothouse to Borodale. Lochiel's reluctance to assent was not, however, overcome: his mind misgave him. He knew well the state of his country, and he took this first step with an ominous foreboding of the issue. He left his home, determined not to take arms. On his way to Borodale he called at the house of his brother, John Cameron of Fassefern, who came out and inquired what had brought him from home at that early hour? Lochiel replied that the Prince had arrived from France, and had sent to see him. Fassefern inquired what troops the Prince had brought? what money? what arms? Lochiel answered that the Prince had brought neither money, nor arms, nor troops, and that he was therefore resolved not to be concerned in any attempt, and to dissuade Charles from an insurrection. Fassefern approved of his brother's decision, but recommended him not to proceed to Borodale, but to communicate his resolution by letter. "No, " rejoined Lochiel; "it is my duty to go to the Prince, and unfold to him my reasons, which admit of no reply. " "Brother, " returned Fassefern, "I know you better than you know yourself; if the Prince once sets his eyes upon you, he will make you do whatever he pleases. "[270]

Lochiel, nevertheless, proceeded to Borodale.

The gallant chief found the Prince surrounded by those who, like himself, had consented, unwillingly, to join in the ill-starred enterprise. The personal courage of Charles Edward has been doubted; but his determination and fearlessness at this critical moment, afford an ample contradiction of the charge. Whilst on board the ship which brought him to Scotland, it was represented to him that he must keep himself very retired, as the garrison at Inverlochie was not far off, and as the Campbells in the neighbourhood would be ready to take him. "I have no fear about that at all, " was his reply. "If I could get six stout trusty fellows to join me, " he said, on another occasion, "I would rather skulk about the mountains of Scotland than return to France. "[271]

The Prince was in this temper of mind when Lochiel reached him. Upon his arrival at Borodale, the Prince and he immediately retired to a long and private conference.

The conversation began, upon the part of Charles, by complaints of the treatment which he had received from the Ministers of France, "who had long, " he said, "amused him with vain hopes, and deceived him with promises: " "their coldness in his cause, " he added, "but ill agreed with the confidence which he had in his own claims, and with the enthusiasm which the loyalty of his father's brave and faithful subjects had inspired in him. " Lochiel acknowledged the engagements of the chiefs, but remarked that they were not binding, since his Highness had come without the stipulated aid; and, therefore, since there was not the least prospect of success, he advised the Prince to return to France, and reserve himself and his faithful friends to some more favourable opportunity. [272]

This counsel was extremely distasteful to Charles Edward; already had the young and gallant Prince declared to one of the Macdonalds, who had urged the same opinion, that he did not choose to owe the restoration of his father's throne to foreigners, but to his own friends, to whom he was now come to put it in their power to have the glory of that event. [273] He therefore refused to follow Lochiel's advice, asserting that there could not be a more favourable moment than the present, when all the British troops were abroad, and kept at bay by Marshal Saxe. In Scotland, he added, there were only a few regiments, newly raised, and unused to service. These could never stand before the brave Highlanders; and the first advantage gained would encourage his father's friends to declare themselves, and would ensure foreign aid. He only wanted "the Highlanders to begin the war. "

"Lochiel, " to use the words of Mr. Home, "still resisted, entreating Charles to be more temperate, and consent to remain concealed where he was, till he (Lochiel) and his other friends should meet together and concert what was best to be done. " Charles, whose mind was wound up to the utmost pitch of impatience, paid no regard to this proposal, but answered, that he was determined to put all to the hazard. "In a few days, " said he, "with the few friends that I have, I will erect the royal standard, and proclaim to the people of Britain that Charles Stuart is come over to claim the crown of his ancestors, to win it, or to perish in the attempt: Lochiel, " continued he, "who my father has often told me was our firmest friend, may stay at home, and learn from the newspapers the fate of his Prince; and so shall every man over whom nature or fortune hath given me any power. " Such was the singular conversation on the result of which depended peace or war; for it is a point agreed among the Highlanders, that if Lochiel had persisted in his refusal to take arms, the other chiefs would not have joined the standard without him, and the spark of rebellion must have instantly expired. [274]

To the details of this interview are added others, which somewhat reflect upon the disinterestedness of Lochiel. They rest, however, upon hearsay evidence; and, since conversations repeated rarely bear exactly their original signification, some caution must be given before they are credited: yet, even if true, one can scarcely condemn a man who is forced into an enterprise from which he shrinks, screening himself from all the consequences of defeat, and striving to preserve an inheritance which he might justly regard as a trust, rather than a property. It must also be remembered that Donald Cameron was at this time only nominally the proprietor of the patrimonial estates. The following is the extract from Bishop Forbes's diary, from which the information is supplied: —

"Leith, Thursday, April 9, 1752.

"Alexander Macdonnell, the younger, of Glengary, did me the honour to dine with me. In the course of conversation, I told young Glengary, that I had oftener than once, heard the Viscountess Dowager of Strathallan tell, that Lochiel, junior, had refused to raise a man, or to make any appearance, till the Prince should give him security for the full value of his estate, in the event of the attempt proving abortive. To this young Glengary answered, that it was fact, and that the Prince himself (after returning from France) had frankly told him as much, assigning this as the weighty reason why he (the Prince) had shown so much zeal in providing young Lochiel (preferably to all others) in a regiment. 'For, ' said the Prince, 'I must do the best I can, in my present circumstances, to keep my word to Lochiel. ' Young Glengary told me, moreover, that Lochiel, junior, (the above bargain with the Prince notwithstanding,) insisted upon another condition before he would join in the attempt, which was, that Glengary, senior, should give it under his hand to raise his clan and join the Prince. Accordingly Glengary, senior, when applied to upon the subject, did actually give it under his hand, that his clan should rise under his own second son as colonel, and Mac Donell, of Lochgary, as lieutenant-colonel. Then, indeed, young Lochiel was gratified in all his demands, and did instantly raise his clan.

"Glengary, junior, likewise assured me that Cluny Mac Pherson, junior, made the same agreement with the Prince, before he would join the attempt with his followers, as young Lochiel had done, viz. to have security from the Prince for the full value of his estate, lest the expedition should prove unsuccessful; which the Prince accordingly consented unto, and gave security to said Cluny Mac Pherson, junior, for the full value of his estate. Young Glengary declared that he had this from the young Cluny Mac Pherson's own mouth, as a weighty reason why he, Cluny, would not part with the money which the Prince had committed to his care and keeping. "

Lochiel, after these arrangements with the Prince, returned to Achnacarry, in order to prepare for the undertaking. A deep sadness pervaded his deportment when he began thus to fulfil his promise to the Prince; but having once embarked in the enterprise, he exerted himself with as much zeal and perseverance as if he had engaged in it with the full approbation of his judgment. We cannot wonder at his dejection, for his assent was the assent of all the clans. It was a point agreed among the Highlanders, that had Lochiel not proceeded to take arms, the other chiefs would not have joined the standard without him; and the "spark of rebellion, " thus writes Mr. Home, "must instantly have expired. " "Upon this, " says an eye-witness of the Rebellion, "depended the whole undertaking; for had Lochiel stood out, the Prince must either have returned to France on board the same frigate that brought him to Scotland, or remained privately in the Highlands, waiting for a landing of foreign troops. The event has shown that he would have waited for a long time. "[275]

From henceforth the career of Lochiel was one of activity and of exertions which it must have been almost melancholy to witness in one whose heart was sorrowing and foreboding. He arranged his papers and affairs as a man does before setting out on a journey from which he was not to return, [276] and he summoned his followers to give aid to a cause which as Mrs. Grant remarks, "a vain waste of blood adorned without strengthening. "[277] He sent messengers throughout Lochaber and the adjacent countries in which the Camerons lived, requiring his chieftains to prepare and to accompany their chief to Glenfinnin. Before, however, the day appointed had arrived, a party of the Camerons and the Macdonalds of Keppoch had begun the war by attacking Captain John Scott, at High Bridge, eight miles from Fort William. The chief glory of this short but important action is due to Macdonald of Keppoch; the affair was over when Lochiel with a troop of Camerons arrived, took charge of the prisoners, and carried them to his house at Achnacarry.

On the nineteenth of August (old style), Lochiel, followed by seven hundred men, marched to Glenfinnin, where Charles was anxiously awaiting his approach. When the Prince landed from one of the lakes in the glen, Lochiel was not to be seen; and the adventurer, entering one of the hovels, waited there two hours, until the sound of the bagpipes announced the approach of the Camerons. These brave men who were thus marching to their destiny advanced in two lines of three men deep, whilst between the lines were the prisoners taken at High Bridge, unarmed, trophies of the first victory of the Jacobites. The Camerons were reputed to be as active and strong and as well skilled in the use of arms as any of the clans of Scotland, and as little addicted to pilfering as any Highlanders at that time could be; for Lochiel had taken infinite pains to make them honest, and had administered justice among them with no little severity. "He thought, " says a writer of the time, "his authority sufficient to keep his clan in subjection, and never troubled his head whether they obeyed him out of love or from fear. "[278] Lochiel had not been able to prevail upon any of his brothers-in-law to accompany him, although they wished well to the undertaking, and, in some instances, afterwards joined it. One member of his family made, however, a conspicuous figure in the vale of Glenfinnin.

This was the celebrated Jenny Cameron, daughter of Cameron of Glendessery, and a kinswoman of Lochiel. She is reported to have been a widow, and upwards of forty, according to one account, —to another, of fifty years of age. Her father, whose estate did not exceed in value one hundred and fifty pounds a year, had endeavoured to improve it by dealing in cattle, a business frequently followed even by men of good family in the Highlands. He had been some time dead, and the estate had devolved upon his grandson, a youth of weak intellect, to whom Miss Cameron acted as curatrix or guardian. The young man, although then of age, left all matters of business entirely to his aunt; and she came, therefore, to the standard of Prince Charles, as the representative of her nephew.

Her appearance, if we are to accredit contemporary statements, must have been extremely singular. Having collected a troop of two hundred and fifty men, she marched at the head of it to the camp at Glenfinnin. She was dressed in a sea-green riding-habit, with a scarlet lappet, laced with gold; her hair was tied behind in loose curls, and surmounted with a velvet cap, and a scarlet feather. She rode a bay gelding, with green furniture, richly trimmed with gold; in her hand she carried a naked sword instead of a riding-whip. Her countenance is described as being agreeable, and her figure handsome; [279] her eyes were fine, and her hair as black as jet. In conversation she was full of intelligence and vivacity. [280] The Prince, it is said, rode out of the lines to receive her, and to welcome the addition to his army, and conducted her to a tent with much ceremony. It was reported that Mrs. Cameron continued in the camp as the commander of her troop, and accompanied the Prince into England. But this account is contradicted by Bishop Forbes. "She was so far, " he says, "from accompanying the Prince's army, that she went off with the rest of the spectators as soon as the army marched; neither did she ever follow the camp, nor was ever with the Prince but in public, [281] when he had his Court in Edinburgh. "[282]

The Prince remained at Glenfinnin two days, and was observed to be in high spirits. Here he was presented by Major Macdonell with the first good horse that he had mounted in Scotland. Charles Edward then marched his little army to Lochiel, which is about five miles from Glenfinnin, resting first at Fassefern, the seat of Lochiel's brother, and then proceeded to a village called Moidh, belonging to Lochiel.

From this time the fate of Lochiel was inevitably bound up with that of the Prince. At the siege of Edinburgh he distinguished himself at the head of his Camerons in the following manner: —When the deputies who were appointed by the town council to request a further delay from Charles set out in a hackney coach for Gray's Mill to prevail upon Lord George Murray to second their application, as the Netherbow Port was opened to let out their coach, the Camerons, headed by Lochiel, rushed in and took possession of the city. The brave chief afterwards obtained from Prince Charles the guard of the city, as he was more acquainted with Edinburgh than the rest of the Highland chiefs; and his discipline was so exact that the city guns, persons, and effects were as secure under his care as in the time of peace. There was indeed some pilfering in the country, but not more than was to be expected in the neighbourhood of an army of undisciplined Highlanders.

Lochiel remained in Edinburgh while the Prince continued there, and witnessed the brief splendour of the young Chevalier's Court: it is thus described by an eye-witness: [283]—"The Prince's Court at Holyrood soon became very brilliant. There were every day, from morning till night, a vast affluence of well-dressed people. Besides the gentlemen that had joined or come upon business, or to pay their court, there were a great number of ladies and gentlemen that came either out of affection or curiosity, besides the desire of seeing the Prince. There had not been a Court in Scotland for a long time, and people came from all quarters to see so many novelties. One would have thought the King was already restored, and in peaceable possession of all the dominions of his ancestors, and that the Prince had only made a trip to Scotland to show himself to the people and receive their homage. Such was the splendour of the Court, and such the satisfaction that appeared in everybody's countenance. "

At the battle of Falkirk, Lochiel was slightly wounded, as well as his brother Archibald. [284] Throughout that engagement, as well as during the whole of the unhappy contest of 1745-6, Lochiel distinguished himself by his clemency, gallantry, and good faith. An incident which happened after the battle of Falkirk, shows the respect paid to the head of the clan.

While Charles Edward was standing at an open window at his house in Falkirk, reading a list of prisoners just presented by Lord Kilmarnock, a soldier in the uniform of one of King George's regiments made his appearance in the street below. He was armed with a musket and bayonet, and wore a black cockade in his hat, as it appeared, by way of defiance. Upon perceiving this, Charles directed the attention of Lord Kilmarnock, who was standing near him, to the soldier. Lord Kilmarnock ran down stairs immediately, went up to the soldier, struck the hat off his head, and set his foot on the black cockade. At that instant a Highlander came running across the street, and laid hands on Lord Kilmarnock, and pushed him back. Lord Kilmarnock pulled out a pistol and presented it at the Highlander's head: the Highlander drew out his dirk and pointed it at Lord Kilmarnock's heart. After remaining in this position a few seconds they were separated: the man with the dirk took up the hat and put it on the head of the soldier, who was marched off in triumph by the Highlanders.

This little scene was explained to some of the bystanders thus: The man in the King's uniform was a Cameron, who, after the defeat of the Government army, had joined his clan. He was received with joy by the Camerons, who permitted him to wear his uniform until others could be procured. The Highlander who pointed the dirk at Lord Kilmarnock's breast, was the soldier's brother; the crowd who surrounded him were his kinsmen of the clan. No one, it was their opinion, "could take that cockade out of the soldier's cap, except Lochiel himself. "[285] Lochiel accompanied the Prince in his disastrous expedition to Derby.

At the end of February 1746, he was sent with General Stapleton to besiege Fort William. He left that enterprise when summoned by

Charles Edward to assemble around his standard on the field of Culloden. On the eventful fourteenth of April, the day before the battle, Lochiel joined the Prince's army: that night, the Highlanders, who never pitched a tent, lay among the furze and trees of Culloden Wood, whilst their young leader slept beneath the roof of Culloden House.

The following extract from the Duke of Cumberland's orderly-book shows how closely that able general and detestable individual had studied the habits of those whom it was his lot to conquer; and mark also his contempt for the "Lowlanders and arrant scum" who sometimes made up the lines behind the Highlanders. [286]

"Edinburgh, 12 Jan. 1745-6. Sunday Parole, Derby.

"Field-officer for the day: to-morrow Major Willson. The manner of the Highlander's way of fighting, which there is nothing so easy to resist, if officers and men are not prepossessed with the lyes and accounts which are told of them. They commonly form their front rank of what they call their best men, or true Highlanders, the number of which being allways but few, when they form in battallions they commonly form four deep, and these Highlanders form the front of the four, the rest being Lowlanders and arrant scum; when these battallions come within a large musket-shott, or three-score yards, this front rank gives their fire and immediately throw down their firelocks and come down in a cluster with their swords and targets, making a noise and endeavouring to pearce the body, or battallions before them. Becoming twelve or fourteen deep by the time they come up to the people, they attack. The sure way to demolish them is at three deep to fire by ranks diagonally to the centre where they come, the rear rank first, and even that rank not to fire till they are within ten or twelve paces; but if the fire is given at a distance you probably will be broke, for you never get time to load a second cartridge; and if you give way, you may give your foot for dead, for they being without a firelock, or any load, no man with his arms, accoutrements, &c. can escape them, and they give no quarters; but if you will but observe the above directions, the are the most despicable enemy that are. "

On the following day when the army, being drawn up on Drumossie Moor, waited in vain till mid-day for the approach of the enemy, Charles addressed his generals and chiefs, and proposed to attack the Duke of Cumberland's camp at Nairn that evening.

His proposal was, unfortunately for his brave followers, not seconded by the powerful voice of Lord George Murray. Lochiel, who was not a man given to much elocution, recommended delay, and urged that the army would be at least fifteen hundred stronger on the following day. The return of the army to Culloden, fatigued and famished, between five and six o'clock on the following morning, was the result of that ill-advised attempt. At eight o'clock the alarm was given at Culloden House by one of the clan Cameron, that the Duke's army was in full march towards them.

When the army was formed into two lines, Lochiel's regiment was placed on the left, next to the Athole Brigade. The Camerons, with the Maclaclans and Macleans, the Mackintoshes, the Stuarts, attacked sword in hand. Most of the chiefs who commanded these five regiments were killed, and Cameron of Lochiel, advancing at the head of his regiment, was so near Burrel's regiment[287] that he had fired his pistol, and was drawing his sword when he fell wounded with grape-shot in both ankles. His two brothers, afterwards more unfortunate even than himself, were on each side of him; they raised him up, and bore him off the field in their arms. The Camerons, at the field of Culloden, sustained the greatness of their fame; nor have the imputations which were cast upon other clans, perhaps had a just foundation of truth. No reliance can be placed upon the opinions of the English press at the time. [288]

The blood of Cameron of Lochiel was sought, as Mrs. Grant expresses it, with the "most venomous perseverance. " His own country, to which he was at first removed, affording him no shelter, [289] he sheltered himself in the Braes of Bannoch. He suffered long from his wounds, until in June, his friend Clunie Macpherson brought from Edinburgh a physician, Sir Stewart Threipland, who gave him the benefit of his aid. Meantime the spirit of Lochiel remained undaunted; and he who had entered into the insurrection unwillingly, was almost the last to give up the cause. A resolution was taken on the eighth of May by the chieftains to raise each a body of men, for the service of the Prince; and the rendezvous was appointed at Achnacarry on the fifteenth instant. We find a letter addressed by Lochiel on May the twenty-fifth to the chiefs, accounting for his not having met them according to promise, by the risk of a surprise, and recommending them to keep quiet until a promised succour from France. The letter speaks the language of hope; but whether that was the real feeling of the writer, or only intended to keep up exertion, cannot be ascertained. In the postscript

Lochiel states his regret that many had given up their arms without his knowledge. "I cannot, " he adds, "take upon me to direct in this particular, but to give my opinion, and let every one judge for himself. "

During May, Lochiel continued at Loch Arkeg, preparing for a summer campaign, and corresponding with Clunie Macpherson and with the treacherous Murray of Broughton on the subject. He was, at this time, in want of food and money. "I have scarcely a sufficiency of meal, " he writes, "to serve myself and the gentlemen who are with me for four days, and can get none to purchase in this country. "[290] After the breaking up of the scheme of fresh cooperations in May, and when Lochaber was occupied by the Government troops, Lochiel became anxious to retire to Badenoch. This district is one of the wildest parts of the Highlands; though destitute of wood, it afforded shelter in its rocky dens and in the sides of its rugged hills. Not only did Lochiel desire repose and safety, but he longed to be beyond the reach of those heartrending accounts which were ever brought to him of the sufferings of his people, and of the dwellers in Lochaber. The severities and cruelties of the military, licensed by the Duke of Cumberland to every atrocity, to use the simple language of Mr. Forbes, "bore very hard upon him. " One day[291] when accounts were brought to Lochiel, in Badenoch, that the poor people in Lochaber had been so pillaged and harassed that they had really no necessaries to keep in their lives, Lochiel took out his purse and gave all the money he could well spare to be distributed among such in Lochaber. "And, " said a friend who was with him, "I remember nothing better than that Sir Stewart Threipland at that time took out his purse and gave five guineas, expressing himself in these words: "I am sure that I have not so much for myself; but then, if I be spared I know where to get more, whereas these poor people know not where to get the smallest assistance! ""

Meantime the news reached Lochiel of the total destruction of his house at Achnacarrie. Previously to the demolition of the house, the family had buried or concealed many things in the earth. The English soldiers, encamping round the smoking ruins, are said, on tradition, to have actually boiled their kettles at the foot of each of a fine avenue of plane-trees. The avenue remains, and fissures can still be traced running up the stem of each tree. Not a memorial of the House of Achnacarrie remained. For this, and other acts of wanton barbarity, the pretext was that the Camerons, as well as other tribes, had promised to surrender arms at a certain time, but had broken their word. "His Royal Highness, the Duke of Cumberland, " to borrow from a contemporary writer, "began with the rebels in a gentle, paternal way, with soft admonitions, with a promise of protection to all the common people that would bring in their arms, and submit to mercy. " Since, however, some equivocated, and others broke their word, the Duke was obliged to lay "the rod on more heavy. " Fire and sword were therefore carried through the country of the Camerons; the cattle were driven away; even the cotter's hut escaped not: the homes of the poor were laid in ashes: their sheep and pigs slaughtered: and the wretched inmates of the huts, flying to the mountains, were found there, some expiring, some actually dead of hunger. The houses of the clergy were crowded with the homeless and starving: whole districts were depopulated: the Sabbath was outraged by acts of destruction, which wounded, in the nicest point, the feelings of the religious mountaineer; and the goods of the rebels were publicly auctioned, without any warrant of a civil court. During all these proceedings, the "jovial Duke, " as he was called, was making merry at Fort Augustus in a manner which, if possible, casts more odium on his memory even than his atrocious and unpunished cruelties. [292]

Achnacarrie was razed to the ground. A modern structure, suitable in splendour to the truly noble family who possess it, has arisen in its place; but no erection can restore the house of Sir Ewan Dhu, and the home of his "gentle" grandson, Donald Cameron. As the plunderers ransacked the house, they found a picture of Lochiel, and one which was accounted a good likeness. This was given to the soldiers, who were dispatched over Corryarie in search of the wounded and unfortunate original. On the top of that mountain the military encountered Macpherson of Urie, who, being of a fair and pleasing aspect, was mistaken by them for Lochiel.

"Urie, " writes Mrs. Grant, who had the story from himself, "was a Jacobite, and had been *out*, as the phrase was then. The soldiers seized him, and assured him he was a d——d rebel, and that his title was Lochiel. He, in turn, assured them that he was neither d——d, nor a rebel, nor by any means Lochiel. When he understood, however, that they were in search of Lochiel, and going in the very direction where he lay concealed, he gave them reason finally to suppose he was the person they sought. They returned to Fort Augustus where the Duke of Cumberland then lay, in great triumph with their prisoners; Urie, as he expected, from the indulgence of some who were about the Duke, was very soon set at liberty. "

This temporary captivity of Urie had, however, the effect of allowing Lochiel time to contrive means of escape from the country. There was one, however, dear to him as his own life, whose continuance in Scotland ensured that of Lochiel. This was Prince Charles, who evinced for Lochiel a regard, and displayed a degree of confidence in his fidelity, which were amply merited by the tried affection of the chieftain. For nearly three months Lochiel remained ignorant of the fate of Charles, until the joyful tidings were brought of his being safe at Loch-Arkeg. Lochiel was at Ben Aulder, a hill of great circumference in Badenoch, when he received this intelligence from one of his tenants named Macpherson, who was sent by Cameron of Clunes to find out Lochiel and Clunie, and to inform them that their young master was safe.

Upon the return of Macpherson to Cameron of Clunes, the Prince, being informed where Lochiel was, sent Lochgarry and Dr. Archibald Cameron with a message to them. Since it was impossible that Lochiel could go to the Prince on account of his wounds, it was agreed between Lochiel and these friends, that Charles should take refuge near Achnacarrie, as the safest place for him to pass some time; and Dr. Cameron and Lochgarry returned to Charles to impart the details of this arrangement. The attachment of Charles to Lochiel was shown in a very forcible manner: when he was informed that the chief was safe and recovering, he expressed the greatest satisfaction, and fervently returned thanks to God. The ejaculation of praise and thanksgiving was reiterated three or four times.

Charles now crossed Loch Arkeg, and took up his abode in a fir-wood on the west side of the lake, to await the arrival of Clunie, who had promised to meet him there. The impatience of the Prince to behold his friends Clunie and Lochiel was so great, that he set out for Badenoch before Clunie could arrive.

Lochiel had, during the months of June and July, remained on Ben Aulder, under which name is comprehended a great chase belonging to Clunie. His dwelling was a miserable shieling at Mellamir, which contained him and his friend Macpherson of Breackachie, also his principal servant, Allan Cameron, and two servants of Clunie. Here Clunie and Lochiel, who were cousins-german, were chiefly supplied with provisions by Macpherson of Breackachie, who was married to a sister of Clunie. The secret of their retreat was known to many persons; but the fidelity of the Highlanders was such, that though the Earl of Loudon had a military post not many miles from

Ben Aulder, he had not the slightest knowledge of the place of Lochiel's concealment. The same high principle which guarded Prince Charles in his wanderings, and resisted the temptation of a large reward, protected Lochiel in his retirement.

In this retreat he was found by the Prince, who had missed Clunie, and had gradually made his way through Badenoch to the Braes of Bannoch, accompanied by five persons. When Lochiel from his hut beheld a party approaching, all armed, he concluded that a troop of militia were coming to seize him. Lame as he was, it was in vain to think of retreating: he held a short conference with his friends, and then resolved to receive the supposed assailants with a general discharge of fire-arms. He had twelve firelocks and some small pistols in the botine or hut; these were all made ready, the pieces levelled, and planted; and Lochiel and his friends trusted to getting the better of the searchers, whose number did not exceed their own. Thus Charles Edward, after the unparalleled dangers of his recent wanderings, ran a risk of being killed by one of his most devoted adherents! "But, " observes Clunie, in relating this circumstance, "the auspicious hand of God, and his providence, so apparent at all times in the preservation of his Royal Highness, prevented those within from firing at the Prince and his four attendants, for they came at last so near that they were known by those within. "[293]

It was, indeed, no difficult matter to discern in the person of Charles Edward the handsome and princely youth who had presided over the Court at Holyrood. He had discarded the old black kilt, philibeg, and waistcoat which he had worn at Loch Arkeg, for a coarse, brown, short coat: a new article of dress, such as a pair of shoes and a new shirt, had lately replenished his wardrobe. He had a long red beard, and wore a pistol and dirk by his side, carrying always a gun in his hand. Yet "the young Italian, " as the Whigs delighted to call him, had braved the rigours of his fate, and thriven beneath the severities of the Scottish climate. His spirits were good; his frame, originally slender, had become robust: he had fared in the rudest manner, and had acquired the faculty of sleeping soundly, even with the dread of a surprise ever before him.

Lochiel, on the other hand, was lame, and had suffered long from his close quarters, and from anxiety and sorrow. Tradition has brought down to us the accounts of the chief's personal beauty. Though fair, he was not effeminate; his countenance was regular and expressive. But those attributes which completed the romance of Lochiel's character must have been almost obliterated during these months of trial, infirm health, and uncured wounds. His spirit was not yet subdued. Eventually that noble heart was broken by all that it had endured, but, at that epoch of his eventful life, it still throbbed with hope.

When Lochiel perceived that it was Charles Edward who approached, he made the best of his way, though lame, to receive his Prince. "The joy at this meeting, " writes Clunie, "is much easier to be conceived than described. " Lochiel attempted to kneel. "Oh no, my dear Lochiel! " cried the Prince; "we do not know who may be looking from the top of yonder hills; and if they see any such motions, they will conclude that I am here. " Lochiel then shewed him into his habitation, and gave him the best welcome that he could: the Prince, followed by his retinue, among whom were the two outlaws, or "broken men, " who had succoured him, and whom he had retained in his service, entered the hut. [294] A repast, almost amounting to a feast in the eyes of these fugitives, was prepared for them, having been brought by young Breackachie. It consisted of a plentiful supply of mutton; an anker of whiskey, containing twenty Scots' pints; some good beef sausages, made the year before; with plenty of butter and cheese, besides a well-cured ham. The Prince pledged his friends in a hearty dram, and frequently (perhaps, as the event showed, too frequently) called for the same inspiring toast again. When some minced collops were dressed with butter, in a large saucepan always carried about with them, by Clunie and Lochiel, Charles Edward, partaking heartily of that incomparable dish, exclaimed, "Now, gentlemen, I live like a prince. " "Have you, " he said to Lochiel, "always lived so well here? " "Yes, sir, " replied the chief; "for three months, since I have been here with my cousin Clunie, he has provided me so well, that I have had plenty of such as you see. I thank Heaven your Highness has been spared to take a part! "

On the arrival of Clunie two days afterwards, the royal fugitive and his friend Lochiel removed from Mellamur, and went two miles further into Ben Aulder, until they reached a shiel called Uiskchiboa, where the hut was peculiarly wretched and smoky; "yet his Royal Highness, " as Clunie related, "put up with everything. " Here they remained for two or three nights, and then went to a habitation still two miles further into Ben Aulder, for no less remote retreat was thought secure. This retreat was prepared by Clunie, and obtained the name of the Cage. "It was, " as he himself relates, "a great curiosity, and can scarcely be described to perfection. " It is best to give the account of the edifice which he had himself constructed, in Macpherson's own words. "It was situated in the face of a very rough, high, and rocky mountain, called Lettemilichk, still a part of Ben Aulder, full of great stones and crevices, and some scattered wood interspersed. The habitation called the Cage, in the face of that mountain, was within a small but thick wood. There were first some rows of trees laid down, in order to level a floor for the habitation; and, as the place was steep, this raised the lower side to an equal height with the other; and these trees, in the way of joists or planks, were levelled with earth or gravel. There were betwixt the trees, growing naturally on their own roots, some stakes fixed in the earth, which, with the trees, were interwoven with ropes, made of heath or birch-twigs, up to the top of the Cage, it being of a round or rather oval shape, and the whole thatched and covered over with bog. This whole fabric hung, as it were, by a large tree, which reclined from the one end, all along the roof to the other, and which gave it the name of the Cage; and by chance there happened to be two stones, at a small distance from one another, in the side next the precipice, resembling the pillars of a chimney, where the fire was placed. The smoke had its vent out here, all along the face of the rock, which was so much of the same colour that one could discover no difference in the clearest day. The Cage was no larger than to contain six or seven persons, four of whom were frequently employed playing at cards, one idle looking on, one baking, and another fixing bread and cooking. "[295]

Charles and Lochiel remained six or seven days in this seclusion, which was one of several to which Clunie was in the habit of retiring, never even informing his wife or his most attached friends whither he was going. But the deliverance of the Prince and Lochiel was now at hand. Several small vessels had arrived from France, and touched on the west coast, expressly to carry away the Prince, but not being able to find him out, they had returned. By the fidelity of the Highlanders and the connection between every member of the different clans, the Prince had been able to keep up a continual communication with persons on the coast, without discovery. This was managed by some of his adherents skulking near the shore; and though they knew not where Charles was, yet they conveyed the intelligence to others, who imparted it to persons in the interior, who again told it to those who were acquainted with the obscure place of his retreat. At last two French vessels, l'Heureux and la Princesse de Conti, departed under the command of Colonel Warren, from St.

Malo, and arrived at Lochnarmagh early in September. This event was communicated to Cameron of Clunes, who, on the other hand, learned where the Prince was from a poor woman. A messenger was immediately dispatched to the Cage, and he reached that place on the thirteenth of September. Charles Edward and Lochiel now prepared to bid Scotland a final adieu. Notices were sent round by the Prince to different friends who might choose to avail themselves of this opportunity of escape; and it was intimated to them that they might join him if they were inclined.

The place of embarkation was Borodale, whence Charles had first summoned Lochiel to support his cause. The party travelled only by night, and were six days on their road. They were joined by Glengary, John Roy Stewart, Dr. Cameron, and a number of other adherents. On the twentieth of September they left Lochnarmagh, and had a fair passage to the coast of France. The Prince had intended to sail direct for Nantes, but he altered his course in order to escape Admiral Lestoch's squadron; and after being chased by two men-of-war, he landed at Morlaix, in Lower Bretagne, in a thick fog, on the twenty-ninth of September.

Lochiel was accompanied in his flight to France by his wife, the faithful and affectionate associate of his exile. His eldest son was left in the charge of his brother Cameron, of Fassefern. In Paris Lochiel found his father, who was then eighty years of age; and to this aged chief the Prince paid the well-merited compliment of placing him in the same carriage with himself and Lord Lewis Gordon, when he first went to the Court of Louis the Fifteenth in state. The Prince was followed on that occasion by a number of his friends, both in coaches and on horseback. Lord Ogilvy, Lord Elcho, and the Prince's secretary Kelly, preceded the royal carriage: the younger Lochiel and several gentlemen followed on horseback. Amid this noble train of brave men, the Prince appeared pre-eminent in the splendour of his dress. A coat of rose-coloured velvet, lined with silver tissue, presented a singular contrast to the brown short coat in which some of his adherents had formerly seen him. His waistcoat was of gold brocade with a spangled fringe, set out in scollops, and the white cockade in his hat was studded with diamonds. The order of St. Andrew and the George on his breast were adorned with the same jewels: "he glittered, " as an eye-witness observed, "all over like the star which they tell you appeared at his nativity. " But all this display, and the feigned kindness of his reception, were but the prelude to a heartless abandonment of his cause on the part of Louis the Fifteenth.

Lochiel was, eventually, provided for by the French Monarch. He was made Colonel of a French regiment, and having a peculiar faculty of attaching others to him, he soon became beloved by those under his command. The Prince showed him affectionate respect; and, blessed in the society of his wife, and in a daughter whom he called Donalda, Lochiel might have passed the rest of his days in tranquil submission to the course of events: but his heart yearned for Scotland; he could not give up the hopes of another expedition, which he desired to undertake with any force that could be collected. Cherishing this scheme, the coldness of the Court of France, and the rashness of the Prince, gave great sorrow to his harassed mind. Soon after his arrival in Paris he opened a correspondence with the Chevalier St. George, and represented to him that the misfortunes which had befallen the cause were not irretrievable, and that if ten regiments only could be landed in Scotland before the depopulating system adopted by the English Government had taken effect, an insurrection might again be raised with good grounds for the hope of success.

Still hoping thus to return to his country, and again to take arms in her service, as he deemed it, it was long before Lochiel consented to accept the command of the French regiment, "intending still, " as he said, "to share the fate of his people. " "I told his Royal Highness, " he wrote to the Chevalier St. George, "that Lord Ogilvy or others might incline to make a figure in France, but my ambition was to save the crown and serve my country, or perish with it. His Royal Highness said, he was doing all he could, but persisted in his resolution to procure me a regiment. If it is obtained, I shall accept it out of respect to the Prince; but I hope your Majesty will approve of the resolution I have taken to share in the fate of the people I have undone, and, if they must be sacrificed, to fall along with them. This is the only way I can free myself from the reproach of their blood, and show the disinterested zeal with which I have lived, and shall dye.

"Your Majesty's most humble, most obedient, and most faithful servant. "[296]

When Prince Charles, disheartened at the growing indifference of the French Court to his interests, contemplated leaving Paris, Lochiel objected to a proposal which seemed to imply an abandonment of the cause which he had pledged himself to support. His representations to the Prince were ineffectual, for a stronger influence had arisen to baffle the endeavours of Charles's friends; and he was under the sway of one who was, not inaptly, termed "his Delilah. " He left Paris and arrived at Avignon, to which place Lochiel addressed to him a letter full of the most cogent reasons why he should not leave Paris. From his arguments it appears that the English Jacobites had expressed their willingness to rise, had the Prince either supplied them with arms or brought them troops to support them.

"For Heaven's sake, sir, " wrote Lochiel, [297] "be pleased to consider these circumstances with the attention that their importance deserves; and that your honour, your essential interest, the preservation of the royal cause, and the bleeding state of your suffering friends, require of you. Let me beg of your Royal Highness, in the most humble and earnest manner, to reflect that your reputation must suffer in the opinion of all mankind, if there should be room to suppose that you had slighted or neglected any possible means of retrieving your affairs. "

These remonstrances were at last so far effectual, that Charles returned to Paris, and was only again removed from that capital by force.

The spirit of Lochiel was meantime broken by the mournful tidings which reached him of the death of friends on the scaffold, the cruelties enacted in Scotland, and, more than all, of the Act which took effect in August 1747, disarming the Highlanders and restraining the use of the Highland garb. By this statute it was made penal to wear the national costume: a first offence was punished with six months' imprisonment; a second, with transportation for seven years. Such were the efforts made to break the union of a fiery but faithful people, and such the attempt to produce a complete revolution in the national habits!

Many were the projects which amused the exiled Jacobites into hopes that ended in bitter disappointment, and many the fleeting visions of a restoration of the Stuarts. During one of these brief chimeras, Lochiel and Clunie visited Charles at a retreat on the Upper Rhine, whither he had retired after the perfidious imprisonment at the Castle of Vincennes. They found the Prince sunk in the lassitude which succeeds a long course of exciting events, and of smothered but not subdued misery. The visit yielded to neither party satisfaction. Charles was deaf to the remonstrances of Lochiel, and Lochiel beheld his Prince wholly devoted to Miss Walkinshaw and her daughter, afterwards Countess of Albany, and completely under the influence of his mistress, who was regarded by Lochiel and Clunie as a spy of Hanover.

Lochiel left the Prince, and they never met again. The health of the chief began to decline; his malady was a mental one, and admitted of no cure but a return to those vassals who had been so faithful and so much attached to him, and to friends with whose misfortunes he seems to have blamed himself. Of the affection of the clansmen he received frequent proofs. "The estates of Lochiel, " says Mrs. Grant, "were forfeited like others, and paid a moderate rate to the Crown, such as they had formerly given to their chief. The domain formerly occupied by the Laird was taken on his behoof by his brother. The tenants brought each a horse, cow, colt, or heifer, as a free-will offering, till this ample grazing-farm was as well stocked as formerly. Not content with this, they sent a yearly tribute of affection to their beloved chief, independent of the rents they paid to the commissioners for the forfeited estates. Lochiel's lady and her daughters once or twice made a sorrowful pilgrimage among their friends and tenants. These last received them with a tenderness and respect which seemed augmented by the adversity into which they were plunged. "

At last the suffering spirit was released. Lochiel is conjectured to have died about the year 1760, and is generally thought to have sunk under the pressure of hopeless sorrow, or, to use the words of one who spoke from tradition, "of a broken heart. " His daughter Donalda, who was about fourteen at the time of his death, had attached herself so fondly to her father, that after his decease she pined away, and never recovered. She died soon after her father, and the mother did not long survive her daughter. Never, perhaps, did a brave and unfortunate man sink to rest more honoured by society at large, more admired and respected by his friends, more revered by his vassals, than the gentle Lochiel. The beauty of his character showed itself also in the close ties of domestic life: and in some of these, more particularly as a brother, his warm and constant affections were destined to be severely wounded. He felt deeply the banishment of his brother Cameron of Fassefern; and still more severely the cruel fate of another brother, Dr. Archibald Cameron.

The fate of that young man, who attended Charles Edward in most of his wanderings, presents, indeed, one of the saddest episodes of this melancholy period. Dr. Cameron, after sharing the dangers which the Prince ran, and following him to France, returned to Scotland in 1749. Charles Edward had left a large sum of money in the charge of Macpherson of Clunie, upon leaving Scotland; and Dr. Cameron was privy to the concealment of the money. He visited Clunie, and obtained from him six thousand louis-d'ors, for which, however, Clunie took Dr. Cameron's receipt. In 1753, Dr. Cameron made another visit, which is conjectured to have had a similar object. The money was concealed near Loch Arkeg, to the amount of twenty-two thousand louis-d'ors. Some degree of obscurity rests upon this transaction, which undoubtedly throws a degree of discredit on the memory of Dr. Cameron. Among the Stuart papers there is a letter from Mr. Ludovick Cameron to Prince Charles, alluding to the "misfortune" of his nephew, Dr. Cameron, in taking away a good round sum of his Highness's money, and clearing himself from the imputation. This proves that there was no commission, as it has been suggested, [298] to Dr. Cameron, but that the transaction was regarded in a disgraceful light, even by the relative of the unfortunate young man.

A severe retribution awaited the offender, who intended, it is said, to enter into a mercantile concern at Glasgow with the money thus procured. He was taken prisoner in the house of Stewart of Glenbuckie, by a party of soldiers from the garrison at Inversnaid. He was carried to London, arraigned upon the Act of Attainder in 1745, in which his name was included, and sentenced to the death of a traitor. His wife, who then resided at Lisle, hurried to London to proffer fruitless petitions for mercy. Whatever may have been Dr. Cameron's errors, his death was worthy of the name he bore, and he sustained his fate with calmness and resignation. Seven children were left to deplore his loss. The Chevalier St. George, kindly passing over his fault, wrote of him in these terms. "I am a stranger to the motives which carried poor Archibald Cameron into Scotland; but whatever they may have been, his fate gives me the more concern, as I own I could not bring myself to believe that the English Government would carry their rigour so far. " The French Government settled a pension of one thousand five hundred livres upon Mrs. Cameron, and an annual allowance of two hundred livres to each of her sons, who were in their service. The unfortunate Dr. Cameron was buried in the Savoy in London. The family of the man who betrayed him is said, in the Highlands, to have been visited with a severe retribution, having, ever since, had one of its members an idiot. Such is the notion of retributive justice in the Highlands.

The death of this brother, and still more the stain upon the honour of Dr. Cameron, must have added greatly to the burden of sorrow which fell so heavily upon Lochiel. His son was, however, spared for some years, and was cherished by the Scots as the representative of their ancient chiefs. He was, it is true, what they called a "landless laird, " yet the clansmen paid him all the honours due to the eldest son of Lochiel. He received a good education, and was prevented by his friends from taking any part in the various schemes set on foot at certain intervals for the return of Charles. He married at an early age. Government was at that time engaged in levying men for the American war, and found it convenient to use the influence of the clans for that purpose; Lochiel was offered a company in General Fraser's regiment, the seventy-first, provided he could raise it among his clan. Poor and broken as they were, the clansmen, true to their bond of fidelity, mustered around their landless laird; and Lochiel marched at the head of his company to Glasgow, in order to embark for America.

It happened that whilst here, he was taken ill of the measles, a disorder which prevented his marching. It was therefore arranged that the first lieutenant should take his place. When, on the point of marching to Greenock in order to embark, the clansmen discovered this, they laid down their arms, declaring that they had not engaged with King George, but with Lochiel; and they refused to move. The chief hearing of this dilemma, ill as he was, arose, dressed himself, and went down to his people. He harangued them, and represented that unless they went on board, their conduct would be imputed to disaffection, and might injure, if not ruin his interests. The men immediately took up their arms, huzzaed their chief, and began to march. The result is melancholy. Enfeebled by this effort, Lochiel again took to his bed; the day on which he had made this fatal exertion was a raw November morning. He never recovered from that exposure, but died in a few days afterwards.

Most of the company of Camerons perished in the contest which ensued. Thrice during the American war was General Fraser's regiment renewed. [299] Such was the devotion of this gallant race of men to their chief; and such were the services which those whose fathers had fought at Culloden, devoted to the cause of the English Monarch.

Late in the eighteenth century, the estates of Lochiel were restored to the grandson of Lochiel; and the descendants of that race, in which so much honour, such disinterested exertion, such kindness and heroism existed, are again the Lords of Achnacarry.

FOOTNOTES:

[247] I am indebted to a MS. account of Cameron of Lochiel for the most interesting facts in the following memoir. It was communicated to me by R. Chambers, Esq., and was written by Mrs. Grant of Laggan. In her letters unpublished, she declares the source of her information to have been some papers in the possession of a Scotch clergyman, "which, " says Mrs. Grant, "it appears he did not give to John Home, who would scarcely have asked the favour, keeping very shy of his old brethren. "

[248] Brown's History of the Highlands, part ii. p. 141.

[249] Mrs. Grant's MS.

[250] Mrs. Grant's MS.

[251] Brown's Highlands.

[252] Mrs. Grant's MS.

[253] "The credit of this feat, " writes Mrs. Grant, "rests merely on the country tradition: and the silence concerning it, in the publications and records of those times, is accounted for, first, by the shame which the commanders of the party felt at being thus surprised and outwitted by an inferior number of those whom they had been accustomed to style barbarians and to treat as such. "—*MS.*

[254] Mrs. Grant's MS.

[255] Mrs. Grant's MS.

[256] Sketches of the Highlands, vol. i. pp. 60, 61.

[257] Brown's Highlands.

[258] Reay, p. 88.

[259] See Culloden Papers.

[260] Stewart's Sketches, vol. i. p. 86.

[261] Reay, p. 271.

[262] Mrs. Grant's MS.

[263] Mrs. Grant's MS.

[264] Conjectured to be Lord Lovat.

[265] Appendix to the Memoirs of Sir Ewan Cameron of Lochiel, p. 177.

[266] Mrs. Grant's MS.

[267] Appendix to Home's History of the Rebellion, No. II.

[268] See Appendix, No. II.

[269] Home. Appendix. From the papers of Cameron of Fassefern, Lochiel's nephew.

[270] In the year 1781, Fassefern repeated this conversation to Mr. Home. History of the Rebellion, p. 7.

[271] Forbes, p. 19.

[272] Home, p. 5.

[273] Forbes, p. 19.

[274] Home, p. 6.

[275] Maxwell of Kirkconnel's Narrative, p. 23.

[276] The beautiful poem of Campbell, entitled "Lochiel, " is founded on this circumstance.

[277] Mrs. Grant's MS.

[278] Life of Jenny Cameron. London. Printed for C. Whitefield, in White Friars, 1746.

[279] Life of Jenny Cameron.

[280] Forbes, p. 23.

[281] The poem entitled "Jeanie Cameron's Lament, " is, with other inedited Jacobite songs, likely soon to be given to the world, arranged to true Scottish airs, and published in parts. These songs are collected by a member of one of the most ancient Jacobite families. The accomplished young lady who has engaged in this undertaking is Miss Charlotte Maxwell, the sister of Sir William Maxwell, Bart., of Menteith, Wigtonshire, and a descendant of the Earl of Nithisdale. The ballad of Sherriff Muir, is among the first of the interesting collection.

[282] Forbes, p. 23.

[283] Maxwell of Kirkconnel, p. 45.

[284] Maxwell, p. 105.

[285] Home, p. 164.

[286] Dated, Edinburgh, 12th Jan. 1745-6. This extract, for which I am indebted to Mr. Macdonald, who possesses the orderly-book, was considered an extremely curious passage by Sir Walter Scott.

[287] Burrell's regiment was so broken, that not two men were left standing. Home, Appendix.

[288] In a letter among the papers of Mr. Murray of Abercairney, the imputations upon the Highlanders are strongly and ably refuted. For obvious reasons I have not given the extract, nor gone more closely into a subject which belongs to the province of history.

[289] See Mrs. Grant's MS.

[290] Home, Appendix, p. 373.

[291] See note 2 in Chambers's History of the Rebellion, p. 121.

[292] See History of the Rebellion, taken from the Scots' Magazine, p. 353.

[293] Cluny Macpherson's Narrative. Home, Appendix, p. 365.

[294] Of one of these there is an interesting anecdote in the Tales of a Grandfather, vol. iii. p. 295, note.

[295] Home's History of the Rebellion, Appendix, p. 146.

[296] Brown's History of the Highlands, Part II. App. CVII. from the Stuart Papers.

[297] Brown's History of the Highlands. No. LXX.

[298] Chambers, p. 145.

[299] Mrs. Grant's MS.

END OF THE FIRST VOLUME.

Printed in the United Kingdom
by Lightning Source UK Ltd.
134525UK00003B/74/P